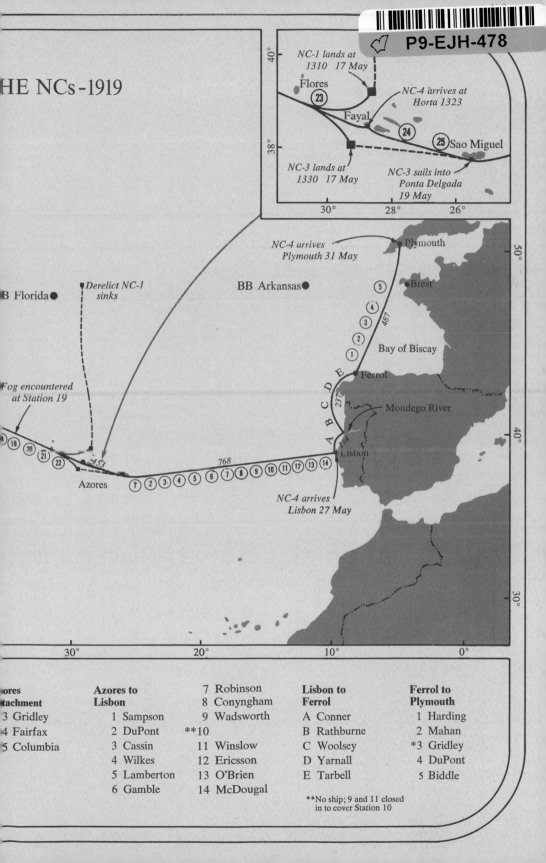

HE NCs - 1919

NC-1 lands at
1310 17 May

Flores
㉓

NC-4 arrives at
Horta 1323

Fayal

㉔

㉕ Sao Miguel

NC-3 lands at
1330 17 May

NC-3 sails into
Ponta Delgada
19 May

NC-4 arrives
Plymouth 31 May

Plymouth

B Florida●

Derelict NC-1
sinks

BB Arkansas●

⑤

●Brest

④

③

487

②

①

Bay of Biscay

E

Ferrol●

D

Fog encountered
at Station 19

C

237

Mondego River

⑲ ⑳

B

㉑ ㉒

A

153

154

Azores

Lisbon●

768

① ② ③ ④ ⑤ ⑥ ⑦ ⑧ ⑨ ⑩ ⑪ ⑫ ⑬ ⑭

NC-4 arrives
Lisbon 27 May

ores tachment	Azores to Lisbon		Lisbon to Ferrol	Ferrol to Plymouth
3 Gridley	1 Sampson	7 Robinson	A Conner	1 Harding
4 Fairfax	2 DuPont	8 Conyngham	B Rathburne	2 Mahan
5 Columbia	3 Cassin	9 Wadsworth	C Woolsey	*3 Gridley
	4 Wilkes	**10	D Yarnall	4 DuPont
	5 Lamberton	11 Winslow	E Tarbell	5 Biddle
	6 Gamble	12 Ericsson		
		13 O'Brien		
		14 McDougal		

**No ship; 9 and 11 closed
in to cover Station 10

FIRST ACROSS!

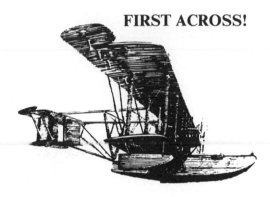

FIRST ACROSS!

The U.S. Navy's Transatlantic Flight of 1919

by Richard K. Smith

Naval Institute Press
Annapolis, Maryland

Library of Congress Catalog Card Number: 72-85396
ISBN: 0-87021-184-6

Printed in the United States of America

for
Loretta Cunningham Smith
my mother

Aviation History Unit

Foreword

The landing of our seaplane *NC-4* in England is the realization of an epoch-making event which has long been the serious desire of the Navy.

It will rank with the laying of the Atlantic cable and other events which have marked a distinct and significant advance in the history of the mastery of the elements by man.

From this achievement it is hoped we shall learn lessons of value and when we shall have learned them they will be used to perfect the conquest of the air and promote the utilization of aircraft for the comfort, convenience and advancement of Mankind.

Josephus Daniels
Secretary of the Navy

Washington, D.C.
1 June 1919

Contents

Appendixes

Transatlantic Flight of 1919

With a wingspan only four feet shorter than that of a modern Boeing 707, the NC-1 was a giant in 1918. There was nothing else like her in the United States. The huge flying boat is shown here in her original trimotor configuration, with a man in the gunner's cockpit atop the upper wing; the pilot and copilot sat in a cockpit in the after part of the center engine nacelle.

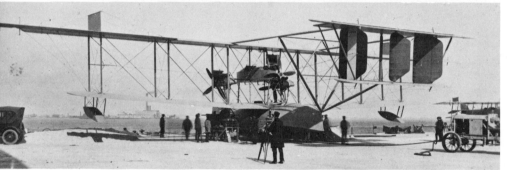

Keenly interested in the projected transatlantic flight of the NCs, Assistant Secretary of the Navy Franklin D. Roosevelt (top) went up for a nine-minute flight in the NC-2T in April 1919. Behind the hatless secretary, Commander H. C. Richardson is seen removing his flight helmet. Above, the NC-2 in her original trimotor configuration, her center engine a pusher; the two pilots sat in tandem in the center engine nacelle. Later, she was converted to a four-engine, twin-tandem configuration (below), known as the NC-2T.

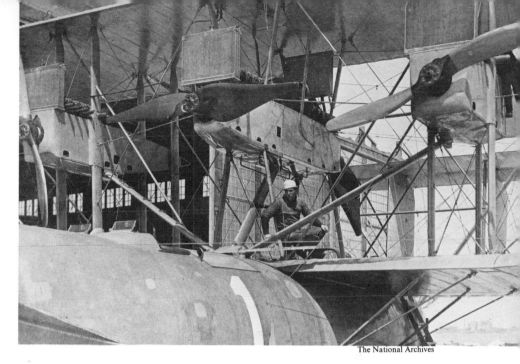

The NC-1 *modified to a four-engine airplane, the engines equipped with the original Olmstead propellers, which were efficient but tended to crack. They were replaced with standard Navy props of oak before the transatlantic flight. Richard E. Byrd (below), a fledgling aviator in 1919 whose name later became synonymous with aerial exploration of the Arctic and Antarctic, leans over the NC-3's drift indicator to examine the flares used for night landings. Chief Machinist's Mate Edward H. Howard (bottom) lost his opportunity to make the flight when his hand was amputated by the NC-1's after propeller.*

The NC-3 leaves Rockaway Air Station 8 May 1919, en route to Newfoundland. Lieutenant Commander Emory Coil waves a casual goodbye from the control car of the C-5 (below) as the airship takes off from the Naval Air Station, Montauk, Long Island. The C-5, shown moored on the shore of Quidi Vidi Lake, Newfoundland, was scheduled to make a nonstop flight to Ireland, but was lost when strong winds wrenched her free of her mooring cables and carried her out to sea.

Aviation History Unit

Steam supplied by the base ship Aroostook *keeps the NC-3's engine oil warm while moored in the cold waters of Trepassey Harbour, Newfoundland. Bellinger, Towers, and Richardson (above) watch Willis R. Gregg of the U.S. Weather Bureau and Navy aerologist Lieutenant Roswell Barratt track a pilot balloon with a theodolite during the NCs' six-day weather watch, an essential preliminary to the overseas flight. Albert C. Read (below), commanding officer and navigator of the NC-4, relaxes before takeoff for the Azores.*

The National Archives

The National Archives

Patrick N. L. Bellinger, commanding officer of the NC-1, gets a send-off from Captain Tomb of the Aroostook. Richardson looks on, while Towers heads for the gangway and his NC-3. After 15 hours and 13 minutes of flying time, the NC-4 rides at her mooring in Horta, the Azores, the first leg of the ocean flight accomplished. Below, the big flying boat being moored inside the breakwater at Ponta Delgada.

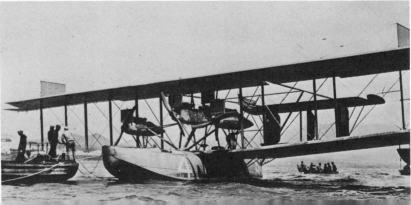

Captain Wortman of the Melville (back to camera) talks to the crew of the NC-4 at Ponta Delgada: Stone, Rhoads, Hinton, Rodd, Breese, and Read. With the destroyer Harding standing by, the battered NC 3 heads for the protection of the harbor at Ponta Delgada after her 1,240-mile flight and subsequent dramatic 53-hour sea voyage of 205 miles. Her weary crew (below)—Moore, Lavender, McCulloch, Richardson, and Towers—immediately after arrival. At bottom, the NC-4 in the Tagus Estuary, Lisbon, 28 May 1919. Machinist's mates work on the engines and a rigger lounges against the tailframe, while Herbert Rodd walks aft to check his trusty radio.

Stone and Read are evidently reminding Hinton that the ribbon of his Portuguese decoration is to be worn below his naval aviator's wings. Below, the NC crews line up on the Barbican for a formal welcome to Plymouth, England, by the Mayor, resplendent in cocked hat and flowing robe. (Opposite page) Harry Hawker, the Australian aviator who tried for the transatlantic prize but had to ditch at sea and was given up for lost for seven days, finally meets A. C. Read at the Hendon air display. In July 1919, the wives of the NC fliers awaited the return of their husbands to New York: Mrs. Breese and daughter, Mrs. Towers, Mrs. Bellinger, Mrs. Read, Mrs. Montfort (whose husband was not on the flight), Mrs. Hinton, Mrs. Talbott (whose husband was not on the flight), and Mrs. Richardson with daughter. Later, the fliers posed in Washington, D.C. Front row: Read, Secretary of Navy Josephus Daniels, Towers, Assistant Secretary of Navy Franklin D. Roosevelt, and Bellinger. Second row: Rodd, Sadenwater, Barrin, Richardson, and McCulloch. Third row: Breese and Lavender (almost obscured). Last row: Rhoads, Christensen, Stone, Hinton.

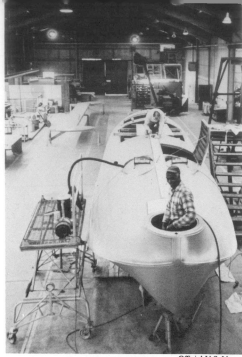

The NC-4, after extensive restoration by the Smithsonian's Air and Space Museum, is put on exhibit on the Mall, Washington, D.C., for her fiftieth anniversary, May 1969. Above, left, reassembling a rudder and, right, the nearly refurbished hull.

FIRST ACROSS!

To whatever height we may
carry human knowledge, I hope
we shall never forget those
energetic and enterprising
men who met the difficulty
in its rudest shape.

—Sydney Smith
  Lectures on Moral Philosophy (1804)

John T. McCutcheon Cartoon
The Chicago Daily Tribune, May 1914

Atlantic Air Barrier
1840-1919

In the spring of 1919 the attention of the world was divided between the poisoned political atmosphere that enveloped the eighteenth-century splendor of the palace at Versailles, and a wholly new form of suspense that was building up on the bleak, rockbound shores of Newfoundland. At Versailles a corps of exhausted old men were muddling through the last rites for a nineteenth century that had lived too long, and acting as fumbling wet nurses to a turbulent twentieth century so recently born of the World War. In Newfoundland there were two dozen young men, their supporting groups and five machines, all anxious to be the first to demonstrate that the science of aeronautics was capable of creating a new link between the New World and the Old.

The ocean which these aviators essayed to cross was, and remains, the most malignant body of water in the world. It is over the North Atlantic where the warm air masses convoying the Gulf Stream to Europe clash with the Polar air masses pressing down from the Arctic in the world's oldest battle of the Atlantic. This ancient struggle sways back and forth across 3,000 miles of icy seas and bits of desperate terrain scattered between Cape Chidley and North Cape, south to a line between Cape Race and Finisterre. Nature's battle of the Atlantic creates a vast and wild no man's land where men have always trespassed at their peril. Men had nevertheless learned how to make their way across its waters, slipping beneath the timeless struggle overhead . . . and they had transformed the North Atlantic into the most heavily traveled and lucrative seaway in the world.

The aviators of 1919 envisioned the North Atlantic some day becoming an equally great airway. But whereas the Atlantic provided a highway for seacraft, it posed a formidable barrier to aircraft. The most obvious barrier that had to be hurdled between Newfoundland and Ireland was the 1,800 miles of water, and only a few less miles by way of the midatlantic Azores, from where Europe was but a nominal distance. The airplane of 1919 did well to plod across the sky at 90 miles per hour, which meant a flight of from 16 to 20 hours over these transatlantic tracks. In 1919 there were few aircraft in the world that could lift enought fuel for so long a flight; thus overloaded their performance was marginal, and there was always a question if the aero engines of the day would endure so many hours of constant operation at almost full power.

The most formidable aspect of the Atlantic air barrier was the air itself—that vast, three-dimensional theater of combat where the air masses struggled for hegemony over the ocean's skies. The airmen had to make their way through this terrible and often terrifying battleground in frail machines of spruce and linen that were held together by carriage bolts, wood screws, wire, and glue, and the only charts they had to guide them through the conflict were almost worse than useless. The proverbial "fog of war" that overhung this primitive battle of the Atlantic was often literal and it held rain, sleet, frightening icing conditions, miles upon miles of zero visibility, and mountainous walls of clouds whose damp envelopes enclosed turbulent worlds that could throw an airplane completely out of control and even tear the machine to pieces.

Nor could there be any respite in the passage; the belligerent air masses recognized no "neutral rights" on their battlefield. Forced landings might be made; but once down, it was likely that the wind and sea would conspire to keep even the best seaplanes on the surface, and see to their ultimate destruction. This was the Atlantic air barrier that the aviators of 1919 sought to penetrate, and with the limitations of their aircraft the barrier would have to be *penetrated;* it could not be overflown at high altitudes.

Sky blazers though they were, the aviators of 1919 were not the first to think of flying the Atlantic; nor were they the first to attempt the passage. Incredible as it may seem, by 1919 the dream of transatlantic flight was almost a hundred years old. In 1936, after making a remarkable balloon flight from England to Germany, the great British balloonist Charles Green proposed to fly the Atlantic in a balloon; but he was unable to raise the funds for the huge aerostat that would have been necessary. In 1843 John Wise, the greatest of America's nineteenth-century balloonists, proposed to take advantage of the prevailing west wind for a transatlantic flight to Europe—and then on around the world! Wise petitioned Congress for assistance, asking $15,000; but he may as well have been asking for billions to launch a rocket to the moon.[1]

It required a daring imagination to conceive a transatlantic flight in the 1840s and substantial funds for the conception's execution. Without the latter, however, just a bit of the former might suffice, if only for a moment. This was demonstrated by *The New York Sun* of 13 April 1844, which announced:

The great problem is at length solved! The air, as well as the earth and the ocean, has been subdued by science, and will become a common and convenient highway for mankind. *The Atlantic has been actually crossed in a Balloon!*

The British balloonists Monck Mason and Robert Holland (former associates of Charles Green), and six other persons had quietly taken off from Penstruthal, Wales, on 6 April in the balloon *Victoria,* and seventy-five hours later landed on Sullivan's Island near Charleston, South Carolina! The *Sun* included a detailed diary that was maintained during the flight, and the newspaper concluded:

This is unquestionably the most stupendous, the most interesting, and the most important undertaking ever accomplished or even attempted by man. What magnificent events may ensue, it would be useless now to think of determining.

And indeed it would have been, if true. However, this transatlantic crossing was not made by the flight of a balloon but by a flight of the imagination of one of the *Sun*'s more creative correspondents, a sometime poet and mystery writer named Edgar Allan Poe. The event has come to be known as Poe's "great balloon hoax."[2]

From the 1840s to the end of the century not a decade passed without balloonists making serious proposals to fly the Atlantic. Among their numbers were Richard Clayton, Thaddeus S. C. Lowe, John La-Mountain, Washington Donaldson, Samuel King, and John Wise again and again.[3]

These nineteenth-century aeronauts may have been visionaries; but they definitely were not madmen. Using the prevailing west wind, as they all proposed, any one of them just might have achieved a successful flight from North America to Europe. John Wise, the most scientifically inclined of the balloonists, was convinced that if he could ascend high enough he would find a great river of air that would sweep him across the ocean to Europe. His primitive knowledge of the upper air had given him a blurred glimpse of those powerful stratospheric winds that have come to be known as "jet streams."

By the end of the nineteenth century no one had succeeded in flying the Atlantic except Jules Verne's fabulous Robur in his great VTOL aircraft named the *Albatross,* as related in Verne's *Clipper of the*

5

Clouds (1886). Verne's book was not only written as entertainment, but as a polemic against the balloon which could not be steered nor flown against the wind; according to Verne, the future of aerial navigation belonged to a heavier-than-air "flying machine." However, even as he wrote, the *ballon dirigible* (steerable balloon), better known as the "dirigible" and more correctly as an airship, was being perfected in France. By the late 1890s, the relatively cheap internal combustion engine had become available for propulsion, and a wave of airship building seemed to sweep the world of aeronautics.

Thus early on Saturday morning, 15 October 1910, Walter Wellman, a crew of five, and a black kitten took off from Atlantic City, New Jersey, in the airship *America* with Europe as their destination.

For size the *America* had no peers in the world except the German Zeppelins. The *America* was rendered airborne aerostatically by 345,000 cubic feet of hydrogen gas inside her 228-foot-long hull, which provided a gross lift of 23,000 pounds; she was propelled by two 80 horsepower gasoline engines, each geared to turn two propellers on outriggers. The *America* was rendered airborne financially by *The New York Times,* the *Chicago Record-Herald,* and *The Daily Telegraph* of London, which had bought the exclusive rights to Wellman's story. The story was lively and short.

Seventy-two hours and 1,008 miles out of Atlantic City, after great difficulties with the weather, their engines and control systems, the *America* came down at sea alongside the Royal Mail Line's steamer *Trent* and her crew abandoned ship. Relieved of the weight of her crew, the *America* sprang back into the air and disappeared over the Atlantic. All hands, including the kitten, were landed ashore in New York a few days later. Wellman said that he would try it again, but his financial backers had their fill of transatlantic aeronautics, and this was his first and last attempt.[4]

When Wellman and his crew of the *America* were being fished from the sea, the airplane had been on the scene of aeronautics for seven years. Frail and flimsy as it was, the airplane was scoring some impressive records. In 1909 Louis Bleriot startled the world by flying across the English Channel, which was the airplane's first significant over-water flight. A year later Glenn H. Curtiss flew from Albany to New York City; but even over those 150 miles he had to land twice en route. In 1911 Calbraith Rodgers made the first coast-to-coast flight, from New York to Long Beach, California. His flying time was 82 hours, but his primitive airplane required 68 landings en route for maintenance and repairs, and his elapsed time was 59 *days.*

There is a substantial difference between the 21 miles of the

English Channel and the 1,800 miles of the Atlantic air barrier. Flying the Atlantic, no one could expect to make the more than five dozen landings en route, as did Calbraith Rodgers. Thus on 1 April 1913, when the London *Daily Mail* announced that it was offering a prize of £ 10,000 (about $50,000 at that day's rate of exchange) to the first person to fly the Atlantic, the announcement was received with surprise, incredulity, and finally with derision. It was noted that the date on which the prize was offered was All Fools' Day, and other British newspapers responded by offering similar prizes for the first flight to the Moon, Mars and Venus.

The terms of the *Daily Mail* prize were not unrealistic; in 1913 they did not insist on a nonstop flight. The essential conditions were that only one aircraft could be used, all intermediate landings had to be made on the sea, and the aircraft could be towed if necessary. A pilot could land at sea and board a ship to eat or sleep; but he had to resume his flight from the same point where he alighted. The starting and finishing points could be anywhere in Newfoundland or the British Isles; but the total elapsed time of the flight could not exceed 72 consecutive hours.[5]

Most of the world doubted the possibility of transatlantic flight by a "flying machine"; but the American aviation journal *Aero and Hydro* observed that "the feat can be accomplished by the use of machines available, the success of the venture being more a matter of careful preparation and execution than the discovery of new phases of aviation."[6] A dozen aviators of the North Atlantic community agreed. In France, Roland Garros, Mark Pourpe, and Brindejonc des Moulnais, who were all experienced long-distance fliers, announced that they would compete for the prize. In Italy, Enea Bossi set about to design a new flying boat for what was becoming a transatlantic air race, while in England Gustav Hamel, a celebrated long-distance aviator, commissioned Martin & Handasyde, Ltd., to build him a special, long-range monoplane for the flight. Anxious to join Hamel as copilot and navigator was Captain Mark Kerr of the Royal Navy. Another British airman and aircraft builder named Frederick Handley Page also set about the design of a transatlantic airplane.

In the United States the pioneer flying boat designer Glenn Curtiss was the favorite contender for the prize; but Antony Janus of the Benoist Company announced his intention to compete, and Benoist had a reputation for building good airplanes. From Germany there were rumors that Count Ferdinand von Zeppelin, famous as an airship builder, had a brilliant protegé named Claudius Dornier who was designing an all-metal flying boat for the flight. And there was speculation

7

about developments in Russia, where a young man named Igor Sikorsky had just flown his *Grand,* a huge four-engine biplane, and was finishing work on his even more phenomenal *Illya Mourmetz.* Surely these giant Russian aircraft would be capable of flying the Atlantic.

Only Hamel and Curtiss became serious challengers for the prize. In the spring of 1914 Hamel sent W. deB. Whittaker to Newfoundland to find a suitable airfield; but on 23 May Hamel disappeared during a flight over the English Channel and that was the end of his effort. Martin & Handasyde were not out of the running, however; five years later, with their name contracted to Martinsyde, they had another transatlantic airplane ready to fly from Newfoundland. And the names of Mark Kerr and Handley Page would be heard again in 1919.

The Curtiss project proved to be the most ambitious. This was owed to the generous financial support of the department store magnate Rodman Wanamaker. Inspired by the forthcoming centennial of the Peace of Ghent of 1815, which would mark one hundred years of peace between the United States and Great Britain, Wanamaker thought that a transatlantic flight would be a dramatic hands-across-the-sea gesture toward Anglo-American goodwill.[7]

On 22 June 1914 the Curtiss-Wanamaker flying boat stood completed on its slipway at the Curtiss factory on Lake Keuka near Hammondsport, New York. Miss Katherine Masson, who drew straws with three other girls for the honor of christening the plane, solemnly read a poem composed for the occasion by Dr. Albert F. Zahm:

> Majestic courser of the sea and air,
>> Within this ample hold
>> Two navigators bold,
> The Atlantic main abridging, are to bear
>> Glad greeting from the New World
>> to the Old,
> Peace herald of the century,
>> *America,* I christen thee.[8]

Miss Masson picked up a bottle of Great Western champagne and slammed it against the *America's* bows, but the bottle simply bounced off the flying boat's cedar hull. Three more blows only served to break the wires around the bottle. This was an omen of the airplane's obstinate characteristics. Finally a hammer was brought to bear on the problem, the bottle disappeared in an explosion of frothy wine, and the "majestic courser of the sea and air" slid down the ways into Lake Keuka. The next day the *America* made her maiden flight.

The pilots of the *America* were expected to be 30-year-old Lieutenant John Cyril Porte, formerly of the Royal Navy, and 28-year-old Lieutenant John H. Towers of the U.S. Navy. Porte had been invalided out of the Royal Navy with tuberculosis in 1911; but instead of accepting a quiet life to slow death, he took up flying and became a significant figure in British flying boat development. John Towers had been taught how to fly by Glenn Curtiss himself, at Hammondsport during 1911, and he was the U.S. Navy's Naval Aviator No. 3. In 1914 Towers was fresh from naval aviation's first combat operations during the American naval demonstration and amphibious landings at Vera Cruz, Mexico.

Porte and Towers would have made an ideal team for Wanamaker's Anglo-American goodwill flight. But Towers had the Navy's permission to participate in the flight only if he believed that it had a good chance of success. Towers came to have serious doubts about the *America*'s transatlantic capability, but he remained on hand as the Navy's observer and Curtiss's adviser during the flying boat's testing.

As the *America*'s trials continued into the summer it became unpleasantly clear that she was not going to get off the water with the fuel load necessary for a direct flight between Newfoundland and Ireland, and the route was changed to Spain via the Azores. This was a small concession. The *America*'s two Curtiss OX engines, of a nominal 100 horsepower each, were still not equal to breaking the water's suction on her hull with a full fuel load. The hull was altered, its planing surface widened, but to little effect. A third engine was added; it served to get the aircraft off the water, but in flight it increased fuel consumption to such an extent that even the Azores might be beyond reach. By this time Towers had been joined at Hammondsport by Lieutenant Patrick N. L. Bellinger, another pioneer naval aviator, and the Navy's Aviator No. 8. Neither Towers nor Bellinger believed that the *America* could successfully challenge the Atlantic air barrier.

Curtiss and Porte also had their doubts, but they were confident that the *America* had a marginal transatlantic capability. By the end of July the *America*'s hull had been completely redesigned and rebuilt, and the construction of an unnamed sister ship was being rushed as a just-in-case spare. A base was being prepared near St. John's, Newfoundland, and John Lansing Callan, a Curtiss pilot and later Naval Aviator No. 1442, was sent to the Azores to arrange for base facilities in the islands.[9]

Meanwhile, on 28 June 1914, the Archduke Francis Ferdinand was assassinated at Sarajevo, and within thirty-nine days most of Europe was locked in the bloody conflict of World War I.

Within a few days of the outbreak of war in Europe, John Porte was aboard the Cunard linear *Lusitania*, hurrying home to England where he was accepted back into the Royal Navy. John Towers was also en route to Europe, but on board the battleship *California;* in London he joined the staff of the American Naval Attaché. And some months later the *America* also crossed the Atlantic, not by air, but in a cargo hold of the *Mauritania.*

In England, Porte had convinced Captain Murray Sueter, director of the Admiralty's Air Department, that the Curtiss flying boat provided an excellent prototype for a patrol bomber to be used against U-boats and Zeppelins, and Sueter promptly concluded a contract with Curtiss for the *America* and her unnamed sister ship. In the hands of the Royal Naval Air Service they became the prototypes for the very successful wartime series of Porte-Felixstowe flying boats.

During the years 1914–18, would-be transatlantic fliers could only dream, scheme and fantasize. They might wonder at the exploits of the sagacious Robur and his *Albatross,* or scoff at the ease with which H. G. Wells sent a great fleet of Zeppelins across the Atlantic, towing airplanes behind them, to lay waste to the cities of the United States in his *War in the Air* of 1911. And they could speculate over the prophecy contained in Rudyard Kipling's *With the Night Mail* of 1908, in which great fleets of airships carried thousands of passengers annually back and forth between Europe and North America while express mails dashed across the ocean in special airplanes. But real transatlantic flight efforts were suspended for the duration of the war.

Although the World War frustrated the transatlantic projects of 1914, it was the war that made successful transoceanic flight a foregone conclusion by the time the war ended in 1918. The requirements of war snatched aviation out of the hands of its pioneers, the lonely scientists and inventors, the tinkerers, dilletantes and sportsmen, and it transformed a disorganized spectrum of *ad hoc* developments into a rationalized industry. In 1914 aviation was the pampered property of some few hundreds of imaginative and daring individuals; the war drafted aviation and its small corps of pioneers to the service of the state. Thousands of persons were put at aviation's disposal as engineers, managers, craftsmen, mechanics and operators; and when these talents were not available, millions of francs, marks, pounds, rubles and dollars were spent to train men to these hitherto romantic pursuits. Farsighted practical men who had been adjudged eccentric visionaries by their contemporaries prior to 1914, suddenly had the resources of nations thrust upon them and were told to produce. The billions of national treasure expended upon aviation during World War I squeezed out of four years a technological progress and an industrial base that otherwise would have been realized only over a decade or more.

In 1913, Igor Sikorsky's *Grand,* with its 92-foot wingspan, four

100-horsepower engines, and a gross weight of 9,000 pounds was considered a phenomenon. And indeed it was. By 1918, however, aircraft of similar dimensions, and with much greater performance and reliability, were commonplace among the Allies and the Central Powers. Of equal and of perhaps greater import, was the tremendous improvement in the power and reliability of aircraft engines that was realized during the war. In 1914, a 100-horse-power engine was the ultimate; it weighed about 4.5 pounds per horsepower, and its life between overhauls was about 10 or 15 hours. By 1918 aero engines were moving beyond the 400 mark in horsepower, they weighed only some 2.7 pounds per horsepower, and their span between major overhauls was almost 100 hours. As Major General W. Sefton Brancker of the Royal Air Force told Americans in the summer of 1918, "the war has been the making of aviation."[10]

By the summer of 1918, the great German offensive in the West had been broken, but no one imagined that the end of the war was only a few months away. So when the *Daily Mail* suddenly renewed its transatlantic prize during July, it came as a great surprise.[11] A month later the world of aeronautics was even more startled and perplexed by an article in the American *Flying* magazine, the journal of the Aero Club of America, which announced that the Atlantic had been clandestinely flown only a few weeks before.

On the morning of 28 July an American flying boat had taken off from Harbour Grace, Newfoundland, and 24 hours and 10 minutes later alighted at Dingle Bay, Ireland. The *Flying* article included a detailed narrative of the flight, photographs taken from the airplane, the navigator's log, and a reproduction of a chart that showed the projected line of flight and the track actually flown.

It was 1844, *The New York Sun,* and Edgar Allan Poe all over again. The *Flying* story was a hoax, but not for the sake of sensationalism; its purpose was to focus attention on the prospect of transatlantic flight. And that it did, indeed.[12]

Initially, the *Flying* story received widespread acceptance. Among those fooled was the U.S. Naval Institute's *Proceedings,* which duly reported the "event" in its "Professional Notes"—only to correct it in the next issue.[13] In any case, the subject of transatlantic flight was stimulated. The Armistice came on 11 November 1918, and by that time a transatlantic flight was the most talked-about and most glamorous goal of postwar aviation.

The early spring of 1919 saw several feverish efforts on both sides of the ocean that were preparing to challenge the Atlantic air barrier. In England, the Air Ministry announced plans to send one of its big rigid airships across; a Handley Page *V/1500* four-engine bomber, and the five-engine Porte/Felixstowe "Fury" flying boat would also attempt the flight. In the realm of private efforts, all aimed at the *Daily Mail* prize, Frederick Handley Page was preparing a modified version of one of his *V-1500* bombers; Vickers was considering a stripped-down modification of its *Vimy* twin-engine bomber; Boulton-Paul, C. R. Fairey, and Alliance announced entries, while Short Brothers had a civil conversion of their "Shirl" torpedo plane being readied for takeoff. Sopwith and Martinsyde had their airplanes shipped to Newfoundland well in advance of their competitors and by mid-April both were ready to fly.

There were vague rumors of French preparations and from Italy it was believed that Caproni would surely enter one of his giant triplanes in the race, especially since it was known that dring the war Caproni had personally urged the creation of a transatlantic aerial courier service between Washington and Europe.[14] But no aircraft were forthcoming from these sources. Russia was being wracked by a terrible civil war and was completely out of the running. Indeed, in the spring of 1919 Igor Sikorsky was a refugee walking the streets of New York, looking for someone who wanted to hire an airplane designer. Germany was not wanting for capable aircraft. She had her great Zeppelin airships, Gotha bombers and the phenomenal Staaken, A.E.G.-Aviatik, and Siemens-Schuckert *Riesenflugzeug* types, all of them huge multi-engine bombers. And there were the Dornier flying boats. However, the strict terms of the Armistice had German aviation absolutely grounded. In any case, in February 1919 the rules of the *Daily Mail* competition were revised to exclude aviators and aircraft of the former Central Powers.[15]

In the United States, the birthplace of practical aviation, aircraft design had kept pace with that in Europe, but development and production had lagged far behind until the catalyst of war was applied after 6 April 1917. However, eighteen months provided only time enough to get everything in the pipeline, and by that time the war had ended. In the spring of 1919 there were very few aircraft in the United States that had a transatlantic capability.

During the war, the Army had undertaken production of the British twin-engine Handley Page 0/400 bomber in the United States, and by mid-1918 the first aircraft were beginning to roll off the lines at the Standard Aircraft Corporation in Elizabeth, New Jersey. These bombers were to be crated and shipped to Europe for assembly on the Western Front. The Army briefly listened to a scheme for flying them to Europe via the Azores; but the Handley Page was a landplane, and there were no airfields in Newfoundland, the Azores, or Portugal capable of handling them.[16] This was aside from problems of modifying the aircraft with extra tankage, logistics support, training navigators, and extending the training of pilots for over-water flying, weather forecasting, and coping with all the other hazards of the Atlantic air barrier.

In Bayonne, New Jersey, a Swedish aviator named Hugo Sundstedt was preparing an airplane for the transatlantic competition. Sundstedt was an aviator of some renown, and his aircraft, named *Sunrise*, was a clean-looking, twin-float biplane powered by two Hall-Scott engines. The *Sunrise* had a completely enclosed cabin for the comfort of her crew, which was a genuine novelty in 1919. The airplane was designed and built by the Wittemann-Lewis Company of Newark, which enjoyed an excellent reputation in the industry, and there seemed not a reason in the world why Sundstedt should not make it across the Atlantic successfully. [17]

A few Americans announced their intentions of entering the *Daily Mail* competition. For the most part these were publicity gestures; none had an aircraft ready to go. Nor did the U.S. Army's Air Service, which in early 1919 still had a wise policy of "don't go near the water"— or at least over it to any great extent. The Army was still content to leave transoceanic flying to the Navy.

The United States' transatlantic effort proved to be a national venture, and the Navy and naval aviation was its instrument. The Navy had a large aircraft that was specifically designed to penetrate the Atlantic air barrier. This was the NC flying boat, and in 1919 four of them were being readied for the flight.

With the exception of the British Air Ministry's projected flights, all of the British fliers were competing for the *Daily Mail's* lucrative prize. As a government organization, the U.S. Navy refused to consider itself or any of its personnel eligible in this competition.

There was nevertheless a prize in the transatlantic air race of 1919 that transcended all of the money in the world—and that was the immortal honor of being *first!*

It was this honor that the Navy won for the United States, and the instrument of its transatlantic triumph was the NC flying boat.

The NC flying boat was not conceived in terms of an air race nor even in terms of national prestige; it was created to meet a special requirement of war. The man who conceived the NC boat was not a dashing aviator, nor one of the widely known pioneers of American aeronautics, much less a young aeronautical engineer; he was a 55-year-old flag officer whose career and brilliant reputation had been built from the keel up around steel ships.

The NC flying boat was conceived on a summer day in 1917 when Admiral David W. Taylor reflected on the needs of the hour and decided that a transatlantic aircraft was a wartime requirement.

"OVER THE TOP"

The *New York Tribune,* August 1918
(This remarkable cartoon, published several months before the World War I Armistice, suggests the possibility of delivering bombing aeroplanes to the Allies by flying them across the Atlantic.)

Admiral Taylor Creates a Requirement

World War I was almost thirty-seven months old by August 1917, but only four months had passed since the arrogance of Kaiser Wilhelm's unrestricted submarine warfare had finally provoked the United States into declaring war on Germany. Washington, D. C., had long since become charged with urgency as the nation rushed to expand its tiny Army, to re-equip its Navy for antisubmarine warfare, and to create combat air forces for the Army and Navy.

In the magnificent Victorian pile of gingerbread masonry on the corner of Pennsylvania Avenue and Seventeenth Street, which in 1917 still housed most of the already burgeoning departments of State, War, and Navy, Rear Admiral David W. Taylor, chief of the Bureau of Construction and Repair, was wrestling with the needs of the hour.[1] On this twenty-fifth day of August he was thinking out a memorandum that contained the seed of the NC flying boat.

Fifty-five years old in 1917, Admiral Taylor had been a witness to and an active participant in the most dramatic period of development in the history of the United States Navy. When he entered the Naval Academy in 1881 the Navy was a curious collection of old wooden hulls topped by sails, and a few superannuated ironclads left over from the Civil War. When he graduated at the head of his class in 1885 the Navy's first steel ships of the controversial "White Squadron" were just beginning to come off the shipways.

By the 1880s the United States Navy had slipped far behind the modern marine engineering and naval architectural practices of Europe, and Taylor was ordered to England for postgraduate work at the Royal Naval College in Greenwich. He graduated in 1888 with the highest record that any student—British or foreign—had attained at the college. After returning to the United States his career as a naval constructor had paced and kept a few steps ahead of the New Navy—the Navy that won the United States a Pacific empire in 1898, and the even newer

Navy that President Theodore Roosevelt sent around the world in 1907-09. When David W. Taylor became the Navy's Chief Constructor in 1914, he had long since become a world-renown figure as a result of his three books and many original technical papers on the power plants, hull forms, and speed of ships. Few officers knew the Navy as well as he—literally from the keel up. Taylor well knew that the creation of the New Navy had been the labor of hundreds of persons spread over decades; now there was the prodigal naval aviation, which had grown remarkably in only five years and in the hands of a few dozen officers.[2]

Admiral Taylor's own Aircraft Division was evidence of this growth. In 1913 it had consisted of one man: Lieutenant Commander Holden C. Richardson, who shuttled between one desk in the Washington Navy Yard's model basin and another tucked away in a corner of the Battleship Design office; and in 1913 aviation's annual appropriation of $10,000 trickled through the Bureau of Navigation. Three years later the appropriation jumped to a million dollars, Lieutenant Commander Jerome C. Hunsaker had relieved Richardson, and similar aviation desks were created in the office of the Chief of Naval Operations and in the Bureaus of Steam Engineering and Ordnance. In 1916, too, the Aircraft Division was able to hire its first draftsman, and then three more. After the declaration of war, the division's personnel proliferated at such a rate that they had to be moved to another building; and the end of its expansion was nowhere in sight.

Aviation moved fast, it was expensive and promised to become more so; Admiral Taylor had no illusions on this point. Only two weeks before, ground had been broken at Philadelphia for a multimillion dollar naval aircraft factory that was aimed at producing an H-16 flying boat every day. And the admiral had on his desk this day fresh data relating to a new 12-cylinder aircraft engine that had no practical existence ninety days before. It was designed by Jesse G. Vincent of the Packard Motor Company and E. J. Hall of Hall-Scott Motors during a 72-hour session in Washington's Willard Hotel. It was generally referred to as the "United States Motor," but Admiral Taylor had suggested that it be given the name by which the engine would become best known: "Liberty."[3] The engine had just completed a successful 50-hour test run, and it appeared to be exactly the type of engine needed to power a large multi-engine airplane the admiral had in mind for long-range, antisubmarine patrols.

By the summer of 1917 the German U-boat offensive was pushing Allied shipping losses toward a million tons per month. What the Navy needed was an airplane that could operate from the sea in most kinds of weather and stay airborne for about 16 hours. With such a patrol bomber, the U-boats could be harassed from the air almost on an around-the-clock basis. Of almost equal importance was that an airplane having such an extraordinary endurance would not have to use critically short shipping space for its transportation to the European war zone. An airplane did not weigh much, but its components were very bulky and demanded a prodigious amount of space in a freighter's cargo hold. The airplane Admiral Taylor had in mind would be capable of flying itself across the Atlantic. With this requirement in mind he put his thoughts down in a memorandum to commander Hunsaker:

The United States motor gives good promise of being a success, and if we can push ahead on the aeroplane end, it seems to me that the submarine menace could be abated, even if not destroyed from the air.

The ideal solution would be big flying boats or the equivalent, that would be able to keep the sea (not air) in any weather, and also be able to fly across the Atlantic to avoid difficulties of delivery, etc.

Please think it over very carefully, particularly as to the method of procedure to develop something as close to the ideal as possible.[4]

Hunsaker informed his already overworked staff of the admiral's memo. It was a staggering proposal, but it was exactly this type of problem that the 31-year-old Naval Constructor's career had prepared him to handle. Hunsaker was not an aviator, but an aeronautical engineer; and from 1916 to when he resigned his commission in 1926, he was one of the principal architects of United States Naval Aviation. After graduating from the Naval Academy at the head of his class in 1908, he was sent to the Massachusetts Institute of Technology two years later. By 1912 he had a master's degree from M.I.T., a commission in the Navy's Construction Corps, and assignment to the Boston Navy Yard, which was conveniently near the engineering campus in Cambridge.

While at M.I.T., the new science of aeronautics had seized Hunsaker's attentions. The French were at the fore of aeronautical research at that time, and Hunsaker translated into English Gustav Eiffel's *Resistance of Air,* which came off the presses in 1913 and remained a basic text for many years. When the president of M.I.T. decided to establish an aeronautics curriculum in 1913, he asked the Navy for the loan of Hunsaker's services. This was granted, and after an extensive tour of Europe's research facilities, Hunsaker returned to Cambridge in 1914, where he organized a program of studies for a master's degree in aeronautical engineering. This was the first curriculum of its kind in the United States.

During the next two years Hunsaker taught at M.I.T. and obtained his doctor's degree. Among his students were Alexander Klemin, later head of the Guggenheim School of Aeronautics at New York University; Virginius E. Clark, who would give his name to a series of classic airfoils; Donald Douglas, producer of the great Douglass DC-transport series; Garland Fulton, who became the Navy's central engineering figure in its development of the rigid airship; LeRoy Gruman, who subsequently produced several generations of great Navy fighter planes; and Edward P. Warner, later Assistant Secretary of the Navy for Aeronautics and an outstanding statesman of American aviation. In 1916 the Navy recalled Hunsaker from Cambridge and he went to Washington, where he was put in charge of the Bureau of Construction and Repair's Aircraft Division.[5]

A few days after Admiral Taylor had dropped his Transatlantic Memorandum on Hunsaker, Lieutenant Commander George C. Westervelt arrived back in the bureau. Westervelt graduated from the Naval Academy with the class of 1901; he transferred to the Construction Corps in 1904 and was introduced to aviation while on duty in Seattle during 1915. A man named William E. Boeing was having difficulties in designing an aircraft and Westervelt collaborated with him in the design and construction of a single-engine, twin-float biplane of 2,800 pounds. The Boeing Aircraft Company regards this aircraft as its Model No. 1, but refers to it as the "B&W"—for Boeing & Westervelt. As a result of his Boeing experience, Westervelt was made inspector of naval aircraft at the Curtiss Aeroplane and Motor Company in Buffalo, until ordered overseas in the spring of 1917. In September he had just returned from Europe after a three-month tour and study of British, French, and Italian aircraft facilities as a member of the Bolling Mission.

A few days later Admiral Taylor called Hunsaker and Westervelt to his office to press his concept of a transatlantic flying boat. Westervelt was not enthusiastic. He told the admiral that in Europe he found a consensus among aeronautical engineers that airplanes of such great size and performance were on the far fringes of the state of the art. Hunsaker confirmed these estimates. The admiral listened patiently, then waved his hand to end the discussion and closed the meeting with a remark to the effect that he wanted to see some results.

In the passageway outside Admiral Taylor's office, the two officers looked at each other in wonder.

"What do we do now?" asked Hunsaker.

"I wish I knew," said Westervelt.[6]

Both of them well knew what had to be done. What had seemed a passing flight of speculation had just become a solid requirement; now it had to be turned into a flyable fact. Its prospects were not impossible, but in the light of existing technology the project seemed somewhat impracticable. Further discussions and studies, however, served to draw the prospects of a transatlantic airplane into the realm of practicability; and at this point a telegram was sent to Glenn H. Curtiss, asking him to come to Washington to get his estimates of the project.

Glenn Hammond Curtiss was one of the world's great pioneers of aviation; and in the United States he was one of the greatest. Like the Wright brothers, he was originally a bicycle manufacturer; but unlike the Wrights he was less a research man than a developer. Curtiss was a great *ad hoc* engineer whose genius was in his ability to improvise, synthesize, and simplify promising ideas and devices at hand, and to transform them into something immediately useful—and marketable. The Wrights' manufacturing ventures were short-lived. Curtiss, however, had a tough Yankee talent for business and quickly moved from bicycles to motorcycles, engines, and airplanes.

Glenn Curtiss's association with United States Naval Aviation dated from its beginnings. It was a Curtiss airplane that Eugene Ely flew off the improvised flight deck on the USS *Birmingham* on 14 November 1910 at Hampton Roads, Virginia. It was a Curtiss airplane that Ely used in his landing aboard and takeoff from the USS *Pennsylvania* on 18 January 1911 in San Francisco Bay. These were both historic "firsts." What is more, it was Glenn Curtiss himself who taught many of the pioneer naval aviators how to fly; first at Hammondsport, New York, and later at his camp on San Diego's North Island. These included Theodore G. Ellyson, John H. Towers, and Patrick N. L. Bellinger, Naval Aviators Nos. 1, 3 and 8, respectively.*

Until World War I Curtiss's business operations were conducted almost as a family affair. With the war in Europe came the success of his *America* flying boat in England, John Cyril Porte's development of it at Felixstowe, and the Admiralty's demands—and orders—for a "Large America" type. In order to expand to meet British production orders Curtiss struck a financial alliance with automotive interests in 1915, and the Curtiss Aeroplane and Motor Company was organized. A new factory tooled for intensive serial production was erected at Buffalo, and aircraft manufacturing at the old plant in Hammondsport soon trailed off to nothing. The Buffalo plant was the first of several new Curtiss manufacturing centers; it proved to be the beginning of a great aeronautical empire that flourished until 1950.

---

*Naval aviators have been assigned numbers since January 1918, when the Bureau of Navigation prepared a list of 282 names according to the date of qualification. Gold wings, engraved with the aviator's name and designation number on the back, were given to each new naval aviator until April 1924, when their issue was stopped.

When Curtiss arrived at the Navy Department on 9 September 1917, he was accompanied by William L. Gilmore and Henry C. Kleckler, his design and engineering associates from the original Hammondsport organization. In a general discussion with Admiral Taylor, it was decided that although the proposed airplane imposed on the state of the art, it was nevertheless a practicable proposition. The performance target was a Newfoundland-to-Ireland nonstop capability, with Portugal via the Azores as the absolute minimum.

Curtiss and his staff retired to Buffalo to return three days later with two proposals. One described a huge flying boat with five engines; the other a somewhat smaller trimotor; otherwise, their general configurations were approximately the same. Each was a biplane with a short hull, its tailgroup suspended on outriggers, an aspect which would be peculiar to the NC boats. It is suspected that this configuration was an extrapolation from the much smaller Curtiss BT-1 "Flying Lifeboat," a single-engine flying boat that Curtiss was currently testing for the Coast Guard.[7]

Admiral Taylor favored the larger design. But the 5-engine proposal had to be rejected because of the necessity of a hydraulic servo-system to control its rudders, elevators and ailerons, and the extensive time required simply to build one prototype of such complexity. In any case, the smaller design—which Curtiss called its TH-1—promised to have enough problems and some of these erupted immediately. Originally conceived as a biplane with a 140-foot wingspan having 3,370 square feet of wing area to support 20,000 pounds of airframe, as its details were developed on paper the weight of the aircraft quickly grew to 25,000 pounds.

The first and last factors in an airplane's design—be it a contemporary jetliner or a flying boat of 1919—are weight and lift. An aircraft's lift is quite finite; but its weight can be relatively infinite—in which case it never gets off the ground. The designer's struggle is to hold the weight of the aircraft's structure to a minimum without sacrificing strength, while at the same time achieving maximum lift.

The difference between the aircraft's weight when empty and the maximum weight at which it will fly is called disposable lift, which is the key to performance in a long-range aircraft. Disposable lift consists of crew, fuel and payload, which may be passengers, cargo, or a load of ordnance. These constituents are subject to "trade-offs": a long-range flight calls for a maximum fuel load, and to carry the fuel, payload must be reduced or even eliminated. On a short flight fuel can be reduced and the payload increased. But the all-inclusive "magic" figure is that of disposable lift, and it was this figure that was foremost in the minds of the engineers in Washington and Buffalo who worked and reworked the calculations for a transatlantic flying boat. For them the heart of this figure centered around 4,800 pounds—the weight of 800 gallons of gasoline.

While the TH-1's weight moved up and down on paper, Lieutenant Commander Holden C. "Dick" Richardson was recalled to Washington from his duties at the Pensacola Air Station and was ordered to the Curtiss plant at Buffalo. Richardson was a Construction Corps officer, an aviator, and one of the outstanding engineering figures of early United States Naval Aviation and American seaplane hull design. Graduating from the Naval Academy in 1901, he spent two years at sea and then went to the Massachusetts Institute of Technology for postgraduate work prior to his appointment as a Naval Constructor. While at the Washington Navy Yard's model basin in 1912, he was attracted to the problems in the design of seaplane hulls and floats and the development of a catapult to launch seaplanes. In 1915 Richardson obtained orders to Pensacola. Then as now there was a tendency to believe that flying was a "young man's game"; but Richardson was 38 years old when he won his wings on 12 April 1916 and became the Navy's thirteenth aviator.

When the National Advisory Committee for Aeronautics was created in 1915, Richardson was appointed to it as the Navy's engineering member, and he coincidentally became the committee's first secretary. A few months later he became the Bureau of Construction and Repair's first Assistant Constructor for Aircraft. The tentative expansion of naval aviation in 1916 coincided with a rash of serious training accidents and a bitter controversy over the relative safety of airplanes with tractor engines as opposed to those with pusher engines. In the latter, the pilot sat in front of the engine; in a crash the flimsy airplane usually folded up and the heavy engine tore loose, and hurtled forward to crush the pilot. Richardson was sent to Pensacola to investigate this situation, and he remained there to look after the air station's other material problems until recalled to Washington in 1917 to assist with the NC design.

Richardson studied Curtiss's TH-1 data and judged the design almost hopelessly overweight relative to its prospective power plant. The Curtiss engineers were reluctant to accept his seemingly intuitive judgment until Hunsaker arrived in from Washington with a bundle of data from the National Physical Laboratory in England, which included the latest drag coefficients. The TH-1 design was immediately reexamined in the light of these new data, Richardson was proved correct, and the design was reduced to 19,000 pounds supported by 2,375 square feet of

21

wing with a 106-foot span. This proved to be a precipitate reduction, however, and by December its weight had grown to 21,350 pounds and its dimensions increased to those that would actually fly as the NCs. In the meantime, the Liberty engine, originally rated at 300 horsepower, promised 400 horsepower in a new higher compression model; this was a quantum increase that allowed the NC designers considerably greater prospective lift.

Initially, the Aircraft Division began its NC design work with Curtiss only as a consultant; but as general design studies evolved into detailed design work, Hunsaker saw that it was absorbing too much of his small staff's time. Thus on 24 November the bureau concluded a development contract with Curtiss for the "plans and designs for a 1,000 H.P. flying boat."

The contract covered Curtiss's direct expenses, plus an overhead of 100 percent, topped by a 15 percent profit. But it also specified that the finished design would become the property of the Navy Department, and this was not at all to Curtiss's liking. Curtiss wanted not only the cash but the credit too, and proprietorship over the design's future—in spite of the government's footing the cost. That the government should own a design developed at its expense was far from unreasonable; but as the American aircraft industry grew to adolescence during World War I there was an increasing outcry from the aircraft companies against this practice. This was a problem that did not begin to move toward its resolution until the late 1920s.

It was relative to this question of proprietorship that the NCs received their designation. Curtiss referred to the design as its TH-1. Westervelt wanted to credit the Navy and Admiral Taylor with its creation; he suggested that it be called the DWT-1. This suggestion never got beyond the Aircraft Division where everyone agreed that the strongest objections to it would come from D.W.T. himself. A compromise of sorts was struck with the initials *NC,* the *N* for Navy, *C* for Curtiss.

During December the design had progressed to such a promising degree that Admiral Taylor and Admiral Robert S. Griffin made a joint recommendation to Secretary of the Navy Josephus Daniels that the NC be put into limited production. Admiral Griffin was the Chief of the Bureau of Steam Engineering, which was in charge of the Navy's power plant development and procurement, including aircraft engines. Taylor and Griffin recommended procurement of four aircraft and estimated that the first should be ready to fly within three months. They described the NC project as "urgent" and recommended that it be "undertaken at once and pushed vigorously."

Daniels approved the recommendation, but with the qualification that "the construction of these seaplanes shall in no way interfere with the production of aircraft to meet the program already laid down." This was not unreasonable, but it had the unfortunate effect of seeming to drain the NC project of that sense of urgency that can generate pressure to get things done quickly. Admiral Taylor and Hunsaker realized this, much to their discomfort; it developed that the Curtiss Company found few difficulties in living with it.

The production contract, concluded on 8 January 1918, was not awarded to the Curtiss Aeroplane and Motor Company of Buffalo, but to the Curtiss Engineering Company of Garden City, Long Island. The Buffalo organization was concerned wholly with mass production. The Garden City subsidiary was created as a research and development facility where Glenn Curtiss and his old Hammondsport associates—few of whom had much liking for the repetitive mechanics of serial production—could pursue their individual projects. The Garden City plant was very small and the Navy had to spend several thousand dollars to make it large enough for the assembly of the NC boats on a two-at-a-time basis.

While the Garden City plant was being prepared, the design work went ahead at Buffalo. Then one Friday evening in late December 1917, Curtiss loaded its design staff, drawings and files aboard a special railroad coach that was attached to an express train bound for New York City. By Monday morning the NC work was being continued as usual at Garden City.

Because of the floor space problem at Garden City and a shortage of skilled aircraftsmen, it was decided to use Curtiss only as an assembly agent. The Navy contracted directly with other manufacturers for the production of the NCs' various components. This was a system the Navy had for long used in its construction of ships, had adopted in its own Naval Aircraft Factory, and found quite satisfactory.

The hull of the first flying boat, the *NC-1*, was built by Curtiss, so it would be immediately at hand for the first assembly. Lawley & Sons, boat builders of Boston, supplied the hulls of the *NC-2* and *NC-3;* while the Herreschoff Company, a well-known boat building concern of Bristol, Rhode Island, built the hull of the *NC-4.* Of all the NC components the boat hulls required the most labor, and the reason for spreading their manufacture among three contractors was with the expectation of having all four ready for assembly at approximately the same time. However, this proved to have shortcomings in quality control. The design weight of an NC hull, bare of internal fittings, was 2,400 pounds; but as built, the variations among the four were considerable. With its long

23

aircraft experience, Curtiss was the most conscientious in holding close to the specifications; but the boat builders, who had a natural inclination to "build strongest," were unaccustomed to the stringent weight restrictions in aircraft, which is illustrated by the results. However, it should be noted that with its second production, Lawley & Sons were beginning to come down the "learning curve":[8]

Hull	Builder	Weight	Over Weight	Percent
NC-1	Curtiss	2,583	183	7.6
NC-2	Lawley	2,787	387	16.1
NC-3	Lawley	2,700	300	12.5
NC-4	Herreschoff	2,825	425	17.7

The 242-pound differential between the hulls of the NC-1 and NC-4 may seem relatively inconsequential. Hunsaker's staff, however, did not read this figure as 242 pounds too much, but rather as 80 gallons of gasoline too little. At a speed of 75 miles per hour and a fuel consumption of 80 gallons per hour (86 proved to be about average for the NCs), this hull weight reduced the aircraft's range by 75 miles.

As the transatlantic flight turned out, this proved to be of small moment. But Hunsaker, Westervelt, Richardson, and their assistants were not clairvoyants, and did not dare to hazard such an assumption in 1918.

The wings, tailgroups, and struts of the NC boats were manufactured by the Locke Body Company, ordinarily a builder of automobile bodies, located in nearby Manhattan. The wingtip floats came from the Albany Boat Company of Watervliet, New York, and the tailbooms from the Pigeon-Fraser Hollow Spar Company of Boston, ordinarily a builder of sailing-ship masts. The Aluminum Corporation of America fabricated the aluminum fuel tanks, which were a genuine novelty in a day when most aircraft fuel tanks were brass or copper. The great variety of metal fittings required were fabricated by Unger Brothers & Company, ordinarily a jewelry manufacturer, and the Beaver Machine Company, both in Newark; and the Brewster Body Company of New York City. The Liberty engines were manufactured by the Ford and Packard motor companies in Detroit.

The overall supervision of design and construction was centered in Hunsaker's office in Washington, with most of the work handled by his executive officer, Lieutenant Commander Garland Fulton, and the day-to-day structural problems of the NCs were handled by Ensign C. J. McCarthy. Direct supervision of the NC construction was handled by Westervelt in the bureau's office at 411 Fifth Avenue in New York City.

Richardson kept an eye on assembly progress at Garden City and at the Rockaway Naval Air Station, while Ensign Theodore P. Wright shuttled among all three places as an inspector.

Power plant problems were handled from the Bureau of Steam Engineering in Washington, where Commander Arthur K. Atkins was in charge, while his assistant at Buffalo and later at Garden City and Rockaway was Lieutenant Commander Harold W. Scofield. It deserves appreciation that by 1918 the name of the Bureau of Steam Engineering had long since become an anachronism. It was a bureau cognizant of *all* types of power plants; and among other seemingly strange functions it was responsible for the Navy's radio development. And if the bureau structure seems inordinately clumsy, it should be understood that the Navy was still a rather small and personal organization in 1918, and in an emergency the bureaus' imperial structure, "channels," and organization charts were easily bypassed by the personalities involved. Naval aviation managed to transcend the whole imperial structure in 1921, when it received its own Bureau of Aeronautics, and established its own empire.

It has been customary since the 1930s to describe the transition of an airplane from its design stage into production in terms of a decision to "cut metal." In 1918, however, there was precious little metal in an airplane (aside from its engines and ordnance), to be cut. If there was a similar expression during World War I, it was to "saw wood"—or to "cut cloth."

Airplane manufacturing in 1918 had more in common with cabinetmaking, boatbuilding, sailmaking, and piano manufacture than it did with the aircraft industry of only fifteen years later. The airplane of 1918 probably contained no more metal in its structure than that in a symphony orchestra's brass horn (and indeed, most of it was brass); and an airplane's aluminum content was no more than that in a large kitchen saucepan. In 1918 aluminum was a fascinating light metal, but a soft and untrustworthy one. The process for alloying and rolling aluminum into tough duralumin alloys was still a trade secret of Germany, which had only begun to be understood by the Allies in 1916.

The basic constituents of the 1918 airplane were wood, linen, and wire, held together by nuts and bolts, woodscrews, glue and paint. During World War I the timberlands of the United States and Canada, and the flax fields of Ireland, Belgium, and Russia held more "strategic" aircraft materials than all the aluminum buried away in bauxite-rich Dutch Guiana.

The 44.75-foot-long hull of the NC boats had five two-ply mahogany transverse bulkheads spaced along a keel of Sitka spruce, and these

25

main members were joined together by stringers of ash. Each bulkhead had a port and starboard watertight door to allow communication among the hull's six compartments. These doors were just barely large enough for an average-sized man to squirm through; it is doubtful if the barrel-shaped H. C. Richardson made many passages through the NCs' hulls.

The nose compartment was occupied by the aircraft commander and navigator; No. 2 compartment had cockpits for the two pilots*; Nos. 3 and 4 each enclosed four 200-gallon fuel tanks; No. 5 accommodated one 200-gallon fuel tank, the radio set, radio operator, and an engineer and mechanic; while the No. 5 compartment in the tail housed a radio direction-finding apparatus. The planking along the hull's V-bottom was of two-ply Spanish cedar that varied in total thickness from 5/16 to 7/16 of an inch; and the two plys were glued together with a layer of batiste—a fine cotton muslin—between them. The lower sides of the hull were two-ply mahogany 1/4-inch thick, while the curved upper deck was one course of 3/32-inch white cedar covered by cotton duck fabric glued to its planking.

The 126-foot wings, their spars and ribs and those of the tail-group were made of spruce. The structural design of the wing ribs was adopted from Handley Page's developments in England and the airfoil used was the R.A.F. (Royal Aircraft Factory) No. 6. Each rib was 12 feet long, but weighed only 26 ounces. The struts that joined and reinforced the upper and lower wings were hollow boxes of 1/4-inch spruce planking, four inches square in cross-section. The square shape made for a very poor flying surface, so the struts were enclosed in streamline-shaped shroudings of micarta. Even the wires that braced the wings were enclosed in long, routed-out streamlined shroudings of wood. About 6,000 square feet of cotton fabric was required to cover the framework of one flying boat's wings and tailgroup. The surfaces of the tailgroup alone were greater than the wing area of most single-engine airplanes of 1918.

It would be nice to say that work on the NCs was prosecuted with vigor and production proceeded apace. But there were problems. During World War I the New York metropolitan area was the center of the American aircraft industry. Skilled labor was in short supply, the Garden City factory was a newcomer to the area, and Curtiss had to compete in the labor market with L.W.F. Engineering at College Point,

---

*This describes the final transatlantic configuration of the NC flying boats; the NC-1 prototype and the NC-2 were originally somewhat different.

Sperry in Brooklyn, and Gallaudet in East Greenwich; while in nearby New Jersey there was Witteman-Lewis in Newark, Standard Aircraft at Elizabeth, and Aeromarine in Keyport. Aside from such economic factors over which no one had control, Curtiss resented the Navy's close supervision of work on the NCs and seemed inclined to sulk and dawdle. The Curtiss staff at Garden City was comprised mostly of research and development personalities who had little talent for and no interest in the vagaries of management, much less with humdrum production. And by the summer of 1918 production was obviously dragging.

Admiral Taylor had estimated that if the work was pushed, the first airplane could be flying three months after "sawing wood." But because the project was not given an urgent priority the contract allowed Curtiss six months in which to produce the first article, and this was without guarantees. Six months came and went and the *NC-1* seemed to be yet another six months from sliding down the marine railway at the Rockaway air station. Admiral Taylor had long since become impatient; and on 9 July he wrote Glenn Curtiss:

> I have been disappointed, from month to month, when I inquire about the progress of the *NC-1* construction, and it has been suggested to me that, while your company appears to go ahead with this work in good faith, they have at no time shown anything like the zeal which they display in rushing to completion designs which have been originated entirely by themselves.
>
> Such a state of affairs may be to some extent unavoidable, as it is only human nature for an individual to take the greatest interest in that which he has originated. However, the experience so far with the *NC-1* has been so disappointing to me that I shall seriously consider the advisability of developing an experimental and designing organization inside the Navy, and discontinuing such work with your company. You can easily appreciate that the Navy cannot afford to run the risk of having its development work not under control and not conspicuously successful.
>
> In the particular matter of the *NC-1,* I wish you would make it your personal business to impress upon the members of your organization that this is the most important single piece of work which has been intrusted to them, and I am expecting you to stand behind this work and bring it to a successful conclusion.[9]

Admiral Taylor thus not only delivered a not very subtle scolding but also raised a bogeyman to frighten Curtiss. This was the threat of creating a complete aircraft design staff in the bureau. The Navy had for long designed its own ships and built many of them in its own shipyards. In 1917 the Naval Aircraft Factory had been established to produce existing designs, and N.A.F. had proved itself to be a very capable organization.[10] The Navy could also make itself almost wholly independent of private industry in terms of design work. If it did, this would leave slim pickings to private enterprise in general—perhaps to Curtiss in particular—after the war had ended and aircraft procurement was drastically reduced.

Glenn Curtiss had been read the Gospel and he immediately saw the Light. There was an immediate tightening up of affairs at Garden City, and by the first week of September the *NC-1* stood fully assembled.

The bringing together of the *NC-1's* components was not a simple matter, nor was it without some amusing aspects. The Locke Body Company that fabricated the wings and tailgroups was located at 453 East Fifty-sixth Street, in the heart of New York City. The transportation of these large assemblies through the busy streets of Manhattan Island, across Brooklyn Bridge, and into the hinterland of Long Island promised to be awkward at best, so the movement was made in the dead of night. Motor trucks of any great size did not exist in 1919 and the only wagons capable of handling the large NC wing panels happened to be those of a company that specialized in hauling theatrical scenery. It was a bizarre procession that made its way through Manhattan's streets during the August nights of 1918: a naval officer in an automobile waving a red lantern to warn away oncoming traffic, followed by a caravan of horse-drawn wagons carrying the NC wing sections and tail assemblies, all hung with red lanterns. An officer in another automobile brought up the rear, with a red lantern in hand to ward off traffic astern. This was an operation that had to be repeated for the components of the *NC-2, NC-3,* and *NC-4.* And it had to be repeated twice with each aircraft: once from New York City to the Curtiss plant for preliminary assembly, and again from Garden City to the Naval Air Station at Rockaway.

The preliminary assembly of the *NC-1* at Garden City was simply to determine how the several components from so many diverse sources finally mated. There proved to be a few square pegs for round holes, but none of any great consequence. Within a few days the *NC-1* was again reduced to her several parts and from 11 to 22 September a procession of horses and wagons moved her components over the 21 miles of country roads to Rockaway where she would be reassembled for flight. In its own rustic way, this was an operation comparable to the movement of the 200-ton, 8-engine Hughes *Hercules* flying boat from Culver City to Long Beach, California, a quarter of a century later.

The U.S. Naval Air Station at Rockaway Beach, New York, was built shortly after the United States entered the war on 94 acres of land leased from the city of New York that was—and is yet—the site of Jacob Riis Park. The station faced Jamaica Bay and had a hangar for servicing HS-2 flying boats, another for housing blimps, and, during

28

1918, a 110 × 165-foot hangar was erected to house two NC boats. A second NC hangar was authorized, but its funds were lost in the "peace hysteria" and frantic demobilization that occurred after the Armistice. This created a housing problem for two of the four NC boats, but it was assumed that no more than two at a time would need hangar service; the others could either be held at anchor in the bay or hauled up on the parking apron ashore.[11]

Within a week of the arrival of her components at the air station, the *NC-1* stood assembled in Rockaway's hangar. After being duly weighed, and her empty weight determined as 12,956 pounds, fuel and oil were pumped aboard and her engines were tested. She was ready to fly.

On Friday, 4 October 1918, the formidable silhouette of the *NC-1* was towed from the cool shadows of her hangar into a bright noonday sun. Even a half-century later the NC flying boat ranks as a large airplane. Its 126-foot wingspan is 18 feet *greater* than that of a Boeing 727 jetliner and is only four feet shorter than the wingspan of a Boeing 707. In 1918, however, the *NC-1* was a GIANT! There was nothing else like her in the United States and she had few peers in Europe.

At a distance the NC boat was a handsome airplane. The aerodynamically and hydrodynamically clean and graceful lines of its hull clung purposefully to the massive wings that nested its engines, while its formidable tailgroup almost seemed to "fly" by itself at the end of its tailbooms. On closer inspection, however, the eye becomes snagged by a forest of struts, the busy webs of interplane wiring, the odd-looking "skid fins" near the tips of the upper wing, and the unclean corners of the engine nacelles with their ugly radiators grasping for the slipstream. These were all hallmarks of the pre-1930 airplane.

On this day in 1918 Donald Douglas was designing bombers for Glenn Martin that were every bit as square-cornered and cluttered as the *NC-1;* Boeing's airplanes were also a tangle of struts, wires, and drag-producing protuberances; and those airplanes associated with the name of Lockheed (which was still spelled "Loughhead" in 1919), were no better. The only men who had a reasonably clear vision of the modern airframe's future at this date were Hugo Junkers, Claudius Dornier, and Adolf Rohrbach of Germany, who were already building all-metal airplanes with internally braced cantilever wings. Such was the state of the art on the eve of the 1920s.

All this was unknown, of course, to the men at Rockaway; for them a performance this day was more important than appearances. Their anticipation was great as Richardson hefted his 243 pounds up the curved ladder over the *NC-1*'s hull, climbed aboard and made his way aft to the ladder that went up to the pilots' cockpit. The original NC design had the pilot and copilot located in a cockpit in the after part of the center engine nacelle. After Richardson, Lieutenant David Mc-Culloch climbed aboard and took the copilot's seat; then Navy Machinist Philo Danly and the Curtiss engineers Van Sicklen and George Robinson climbed aboard. Danly hand-cranked the center engine to a start, then Richardson pulled the toggles on the Bijur electric starters on the outboard engines. Soon all 36 pistons were driving back and forth, splashing their cranks and connecting rods through their oil baths 1,350 times per minute.

At a signal from Richardson the beach crew slacked off the wires of the carriage that lowered the flying boat down the 15-degree incline of the marine railway into the waters of Jamaica Bay. At 1423 the *NC-1* was afloat.

Richardson taxied out onto the glassy surface and made several speed runs up and down the bay, to get the feel of the airplane and to create waves to assist takeoff. It can be very difficult to get a seaplane into the air off of smooth water, especially if the wind is light. However well designed and carefully vented a seaplane hull may be, it will tend to plane forever on a smooth surface; waves create an irregular surface which serve to break the water's suction on the hull.

At the end of one speed run, Richardson swung the *NC-1* around into the light west wind and the spectators ashore caught a new urgent sound from her engines. The *NC-1*'s bow wave rose higher, the spray flying into the air aft of her wings increased in height, width, and whiteness, her frothy wake narrowed to a silver thread—and vanished. The great flying boat's shadow was chasing after it across the water. The *NC-1* was airborne.

A great cheer went up among the Navy and Curtiss people who crowded the shoreline. But the *NC-1*'s "flight" climbed no higher than 50 feet, and within 30 seconds her hull was again planing the surface of the bay. On this first day Richardson wanted only to determine her water-handling and takeoff characteristics. If she promised good flying characteristics he would take her up—but he found her to be tail-heavy. He was satisfied that the *NC-1* would fly well, but she would fly even better after this deficiency was corrected. This "flight" was the first of six similar ones this day, with a total of four minutes and 40 seconds "flying" time.

By 1514 the *NC-1* was high and dry on her beaching gear and Richardson and his crew were receiving the congratulations of all on shore. But this was only a beginning. On this day the *NC-1* had only 120 gallons (720 pounds) of fuel on board and her gross takeoff weight was

30

16,930 pounds. It remained to be seen how gracefully she would behave at her design takeoff weight of 22,000 pounds.

Between her first flight and the end of 1918 the *NC-1* made 36 flights, logging 28 hours in the air. The longest flight was from 7 to 9 November to Washington, D.C., Hampton Roads, Virginia, and back to Rockaway. This flight was also the *NC-1*'s public debut.

The flight to Washington was not without its trials. The day was cold, the crankcase oil thick, and the engines were started only after much coaxing and cursing. The center engine behaved badly until its carburetor was cleaned. Then it was discovered that the tides had covered the marine railway with sand, and two hours were required to get it shoveled clear. By 1045 the *NC-1* was finally in the water with Richardson and McCulloch at her controls, a crew of seven on board, 691 gallons of fuel, and with a gross weight of 20,277 pounds. After a 40-second takeoff run Richardson jerked her off the water, climbed her gradually to 1,000 feet, and pointed her nose down the coast of New Jersey.

Asbury Park was passed at 1112 and Point Pleasant was in sight when a leak was discovered in the center engine's radiator. The engine was secured and the machinists climbed up around the nacelle to attempt in-flight repairs. It was futile.

The *NC-1* could fly on two engines, but Richardson planned to shortcut across the Maryland peninsula to Chesapeake Bay and follow the bay up to the Potomac and Washington. In 1918 and for some years thereafter, the operation of a flying boat over land was considered an unnecessary hazard; if another engine failed during the short overland leg it would mean a disastrous forced landing for the *NC-1*. As they approached Barnegat Inlet, Richardson decided to land at sea for repairs.

At 1125 Richardson neatly eased the *NC-1* down among the ten-foot ocean swells. The leak was soon repaired; but then there occurred one of those maddening complications that makes a ten-minute job run to an hour. The leak was fixed, but all of the radiator's water had drained away. Sea water would do for an emergency coolant, and in the *NC-1*'s circumstances the supply of sea water was infinite—but there was no bucket available to haul the stuff aboard. A hand bilge pump was rigged over the side; it lifted the water into an empty ammunition box that happened to be on board. Then (with language appropriate to the occasion) the pump had to be shifted to take a suction from the ammo box and discharge to the radiator. These labors were none too pleasant. With the *NC-1* heaving up and down from trough to crest of the deep swells, several of her crew became frightfully seasick.

31

After a long, uncomfortable hour the radiator was finally filled, the engine started, and Richardson looked to the takeoff. With prevailing sea conditions its prospects held a good possibility of unpleasantness, especially as there was no wind. But after a 60-second takeoff run across the swells he put her in the air. Five hours later the *NC-1* was a technological celebrity bobbing at anchor in the calm waters off the Anacostia Naval Air Station.

A month earlier or a few weeks later the *NC-1*'s arrival at Anacostia would have been a sensational event. But during the first week of November 1918 the newspapers were filled with the exciting news of the rapid collapse of the Central Powers and the imminent end of the World War. Armistices had already been concluded with Bulgaria, Turkey and Austria; Germany was being swept by a revolution. On 9 November the hated Kaiser Wilhelm had abdicated and a German Republic was proclaimed. In this tumult of events so long awaited, the arrival of the *NC-1* was hardly noticed.

The Washington *Evening Star* found a small space on one of its inside pages of 9 November to mention the flying boat's arrival; it reported that "the largest seaplane in the United States, the U.S.S. Nancy I, flew over Washington yesterday."[12] This twisting of the *NC-1*'s designation into a proper name is probably owed to a misunderstanding over the telephone. In any case, it did not go unnoticed and it caught the popular fancy. Among many persons in 1919, and thereafter—jaded journalists in particular—the NCs came to be called the "Nancy boats."

After an overnight stop at Anacostia the *NC-1* flew to Hampton Roads, and the next day returned to Rockaway in four hours and 23 minutes. By 1745 that Saturday evening she was back in her hangar, where she was soon swarming with machinists who were removing her sparkplugs, cleaning her carburetors, and wiping down her engines, while a gang of riggers walked her wings and horizontal stabilizers to check the tension of their wire bracings. On the following Monday morning the *NC-1*'s log reads:

No work done.
Machine not out of hangar.

Small wonder.

The date was 11 November. Germany had accepted an armistice—and this was *the* Armistice. THE WAR WAS OVER!

During 1914–18, aviation had a rapid rough-and-tumble growth from childhood to adolescence under the cloak of wartime security and censorship. With the end of the war the wraps came off. Aviation immediately began to develop a new, dynamic, and glamorous aura as its thousands of young men sought to publicly demonstrate the peaceful utility that mechanical flight promised to civilization. These young men would make 1919 aviation's great year of demonstration. There were many who were impatient, and only a few weeks after the Armistice the demonstration was already under way.

While the *NC-1's* testing continued at Rockaway, a converted Handley Page *V/1500* bomber took off from Cricklewood, England, for a flight over London—with 41 persons on board. This was a world's record for passenger-carrying.[13]

The men at Rockaway could not let this go unchallenged, and on 26 November, 46 men were crammed into the *NC-1's* hull while Richardson and McCulloch manned the controls. The boat's gross weight was 23,578 pounds, the wind was slack, and the most they could get her three Liberty engines to do was to jerk her through two short jumps off the water.

The next day the *NC-1's* fuel was reduced to 91 gallons and 48 men were carefully packed aboard, each stepping on a scale to be weighed before boarding the aircraft. With the two pilots they made a nice round figure of 50 persons. McCulloch got the *NC-1* off the water at a weight of 22,028 pounds for a flight of about 1,000 yards at an altitude of 50 feet, and a world's record for lifting persons was claimed.

When the *NC-1* was hauled ashore and the passengers duly counted again, it was discovered that instead of 48 there were 49. Determined to be on board for the flight, 2nd Class Machinist's Mate Harry D. Moulton had squeezed himself into the narrow passageway between the fuel tanks and the hull an hour and a half before takeoff. He could not see anything; the most he got out of the flight was the feeling of the machine in motion, and being able to say he was on board. However, more than a half century later only the names of the two pilots and Harry Moulton stand out in the record; the other 48 men are no more than a blurred 6,963 pounds.[14]

This 50—or 51—man flight was a stunt as executed. But the *NC-1* was capable of an extended flight at the same weight. As if to prove it, a week later she took off at 22,141 pounds for a nonstop return flight to Montauk at the eastern tip of Long Island.

By the end of 1918 the *NC-1* had proved most of the capabilities expected of her. Indeed, she even managed to exceed her design takeoff weight of 22,000 pounds. In view of the fact that no one concerned with her design and construction had even been remotely associated with such an ambitious exploitation of the state of the art, the NC flying boat was a remarkable achievement in design, engineering, and production.

33

Within thirteen months and ten days, Admiral Taylor's requirement was transformed from a three-paragraph memorandum to an 11-ton flying boat that met most of its design specifications.

The *NC-1* nevertheless had problems. Her fuel consumption data was incomplete, but it was enough to indicate that she would not be able to fly the Atlantic with a safe margin of fuel. However, thus far she had been flying with early model Liberty engines that had a compression ratio of 5:1 and produced only 330 horsepower. A later model with a compression ratio of 5.4:1 that produced 400 horsepower had just become available, and with a special modification of their carburetors that the Bureau of Steam Engineering was working out it was expected that they could get the *NC-1* into the air with 24,000 pounds. Beyond this, new calculations by Ensign C. J. McCarthy showed that by adding a fourth engine an NC boat's gross takeoff weight could be increased to 28,000 pounds. A fourth engine would weigh 820 pounds, or 1,315 pounds with all its accessories, and it would require more fuel; but McCarthy calculated that the additional power more than compensated for the new weights.

The Armistice, however, threw the NC program out of gear for several weeks. After 11 November 1918, the great war machine had to be stopped and put in reverse. Plans had to be made for the liquidation of naval bases and air stations in France and England; and with the sudden clamor to "bring the boys home!" schedules had to be prepared for shipping to move the U.S. Army back across the Atlantic to the United States. It was April 1917 all over again, but worse, because as the work increased, so did the discharge of Reserve officers and men, which left fewer and fewer personnel to do more and more. In this hectic atmosphere it was easy to temporarily shelve action on some of the answers to the NCs' problems.

Meanwhile, in Room 3409 of the new Main Navy Building on Washington's Constitution Avenue, there was an officer who had for long had his eye on the Atlantic's air routes, the *NC-1*'s progress, and the development of her sister ships. Even before the Armistice was signed he had proposed that the NCs be prepared for an operation that would be an epoch-making event.

A Great Naval Achievement

The remarkable flying boat shown in the photograph above is one of the epoch making achievements of naval aviation. It is the largest flying boat in the world—a craft capable of flying with eleven (11) tons. This same naval plane recently flew with fifty Navy men and pilot aboard.

Developed and built at The Curtiss Engineering Corporation, Garden City, by Naval Constructors working in collaboration with Glenn H. Curtiss and his engineers, it stands today as a proved product of unquestioned superiority, entirely American in its conception, evolution, manufacture and performance.

CURTISS AEROPLANE & MOTOR CORPORATION
32 Vanderbilt Avenue   New York City, New York
Factories: Buffalo and Hammondsport

Curtiss Engineering Corporation, Garden City, L. I., N. Y.

A Curtiss Corporation advertisement for 1919

John Towers' Epoch-Making Event

By the end of October 1918 the *NC-1* had made eighteen flights, had demonstrated her ability to meet most of her design requirements, and preparations were under way at Rockaway for her flight to Washington. Few persons in the Navy Department had been studying the *NC-1*'s promise more closely than Commander John Towers in the Chief of Naval Operations' Aviation Section. Towers had seen enough to feel sure of the airplane's capabilities and had heard enough from officers in the Bureau of Construction and Repair to be convinced of her potential. On 31 October, a week before the *NC-1* flew to Washington, Towers proposed to the Chief of Naval Operations that the Navy immediately organize a determined effort to fly across the Atlantic before the summer of 1919.

The essence of Towers' memorandum was that the United States should be the first to fly an aircraft across the Atlantic. He pointed apprehensively at Sundstedt's preparations in Newark. The Swede's airplane, named *Sunrise,* was not yet completed; but Witteman-Lewis had a reputation for building good aircraft and Towers believed that Sundstedt had a good chance of success. There were no other civil aircraft available that could make the transatlantic flight, the Army's Air Service had none; the Navy was the United States' only instrument for being first to fly the Atlantic. And Towers felt that the Navy had an obligation to history to dramatize the recent resurgence of American aviation:

> The prestige gained in aviation by the United States in early stages of aviation, and now being regained, should be held, and the first flight across the Atlantic will go down in history as an epoch-making event.[1]

The war was still in progress, but Towers did not believe that transatlantic preparations for the NC boats would interfere with operations against Germany. In any case, the Navy had a different transatlantic aviation project in its planning stages, and Towers believed that an early flight by the NCs would assist this other project, which was the ferrying of F-5L flying boats to Europe by air. Towers pointed out that he was the Navy's senior aviator,[2] had been adviser to the Curtiss-Wanamaker transatlantic project of 1914, and had for long studied the problems associated with transatlantic flight. In conclusion he requested that he be given command of the transatlantic operation if it was approved.

Towers' proposal was novel only in its immediacy, its emphasis upon national honor, and his stress upon preparing *now* for the spring of 1919. Admiral Taylor had conceived the NC boat as a transatlantic aircraft, and Hunsaker and his staff, working with Curtiss, had designed the airplane accordingly. What is more, in the summer of 1918 there had been some considerable agitation for transatlantic flight operations. For the most part this was owed to William H. Workman, the American representative of Handley Page, who insisted upon the urgency of flying the American-built Handley Page 0/400 twin engine bombers directly to Europe, transatlantic via Newfoundland and the Azores.[3] Workman was assisted in his publicity campaign by the Aero Club of America. Forty pilots at the Army airfield at Mineola, Long Island, responded to Workman's incantations by volunteering to fly the bombers across, and they petitioned their commanding officer to be selected for duty in the proposed transatlantic ferry operation.[4] The War Department, however, knew more about the logistical support of aircraft than Workman and Handley Page; it refused to be bulldozed by a noisy publicity campaign and the Army continued with its plans to move the bombers to Europe by sea.[5]

Aside from the required transatlantic range of the NC boats, during July 1918 the Navy began studying a modification of the twin-engine F-5L flying boat for the purpose of flying them directly to Europe, via the Azores, in the summer of 1919. The F-5L was an American version of the British Porte-Felixstowe F.5 boat, and the first of them were beginning to come off the production lines of the Naval Aircraft Factory in the summer of 1918. The F-5L's transatlantic modifications would include extra fuel tankage and a new geared-down Liberty engine that was under development. As rumors of these plans began to trickle out of the Navy Department, a half-dozen or more naval aviators responded by requesting assignment to the prospective transatlantic ferry operations.

In September the Chief of Naval Operations directed Admiral Sims' headquarters in London to make a survey of European servicing facilities, especially in the Azores Islands, for the transatlantic F-5Ls.

The Navy was already in the Azores; the First Marine Aeronautic Company had been flying antisubmarine patrols out of their base at Ponta Delgada since January 1918. But the Navy was also interested in the harbor of Horta on the island of Fayal, which was closer to Newfoundland. For a base to jump off from in North America, Lieutenant Richard E. Byrd, commanding officer of the U.S. Naval Air Station at Halifax, Nova Scotia, was ordered to survey the east coast of Newfoundland for a suitable harbor. Three months later the Armistice made these preparations superfluous—except as they might be applied to a postwar transatlantic flight of the type conceived by John Towers.[6]

Thus when Towers dictated his October NC flight memorandum, considerable transatlantic spadework had already been started—and Towers had a hand in most of it. Towers' immediate concern was that the F-5L flying boats would not be ready for almost a year, whereas Sundstedt would be ready to fly in the spring. Meanwhile, the NC-1 was immediately available, with sister ships in prospect, and they provided the means of putting the United States across the ocean first.

What makes John Towers' October memorandum significant is that it focused attention upon transatlantic flight as something more than a wartime expedient in moving aircraft from one side of the ocean to the other; and it is noteworthy that Towers underscored the historical moment. Most significant, however, is that Towers' memorandum initiated a series of decisions that created the Navy's transatlantic flight organization of 1919.

A board consisting of Captain John T. Tompkins, Towers, and Lieutenant Commander Godfrey deC. Chevalier was appointed to study the transatlantic project. Meanwhile, the Armistice and all its subsequent confusion intervened, and the board's terse seven-page report was not made until 1 February 1919. The board studied four routes: via the sub-Arctic islands of Greenland and Iceland; to Ireland, nonstop from Newfoundland; the proposed F-5L ferry route to Portugal via Newfoundland and the Azores; and even a route that went down the coast of South America to cross the Atlantic between the bulge of Brazil and French West Africa. The route via the Azores was recommended. The board's report concluded that the flight should be made, preparations begun as soon as possible, and they should be aimed at a takeoff date of 1 May.

On 4 February, Secretary of the Navy Josephus Daniels gave the transatlantic flight his approval, assigned it an "AA" priority, and John Towers found himself in charge of the Chief of Naval Operations' newly created "Transatlantic Section."

Because of the uncertainties involved in the project, and not wanting to be harassed by the newspaper press, the Navy Department sought to keep its transatlantic plans a secret until the flight was almost ready to go. But a routine listing of personnel transfers mentioned that Towers was being assigned new duties relative to preparations for a transatlantic flight. A bored reporter who could find nothing else to read chanced upon this notice—and the word was out.

When interviewed by the press, Secretary Daniels admitted preparations for the flight. A reporter asked him if the Navy expected to beat the British in making the first flight across the Atlantic. It was still a great day of spread-eagle Americanism and Daniels felt no need of mumbling mealy-mouthed apologies. He retorted: "We hope to beat the world!"[7]

In 1919 there was less of a problem in the Navy beating the world, than there was of the world of aeronautics—the Navy included— beating the malignant environment of the North Atlantic.

During the three months between Towers' October memorandum and the board's report, much detailed spadework was done. The prime considerations of a transoceanic flight (in 1919 and probably forever after) are: (1) range of the aircraft, including a margin of fuel in case of extraordinary headwinds, bad terminal weather, or both; (2) adequate weather intelligence; (3) a means of navigation; (4) communications; and (5) facilities for survival and rescue if forced down at sea. That the Azores were within the prospective range of the NC boats there was no question by the end of 1918; and until April it was hoped that this might be stretched to permit a nonstop flight from Newfoundland to Ireland. Considerably less was known, however, about aerological conditions over the North Atlantic—except that they were usually bad. Much of Towers' time between February and May was spent in creating an organization to report, study, and forecast the ocean's prospective weather.

In 1919 there were no ocean station vessels CHARLIE, DELTA, and ECHO straddling a thousand miles of the North Atlantic's fortieth meridian, much less the six other weather ships that have been reporting that ocean's wretched weather since 1949. In 1919 the North Atlantic's weather was just as good and just as miserable as it would be fifty years later; but the tools that men had for its study were still primitive and their knowledge of it was substantially less.

When Towers' aerological officer, Lieutenant (j.g.) Roswell F. Barratt, went to the U.S. Weather Bureau for assistance, the science of aerology enjoyed use of the meteorograph, an instrument package for recording atmospheric conditions, which was lifted into the upper air by a kite, a captive balloon, or a free balloon. The balloon-carried meteorograph was of no use, however, unless its instruments were recovered, which was possible over land but unlikely over the sea.* Beyond the meteorograph, the only other instrument available was the pilot balloon, a large rubber balloon inflated with hydrogen, that was released and then observed through a theodolite to determine the wind's direction and speed.[8]

The synoptic weather maps of 1919 (such as they were) displayed only the familiar isobars, which showed crudely constructed "highs" and "lows." There was no "Arctic Air," nor "Maritime Polar Air," nor "Continental Air" with their respective "fronts." Indeed, there were no air masses at all, nor were there any "fronts." This terminology (familiar to children fifty years later), along with its system of air mass analysis, was unknown to the world of 1919. When Roswell Barratt was perplexing the U.S. Weather Bureau by his requests for information about the North Atlantic's weather, the great Norwegian meteorologist Jakob Bjierknes was only beginning to put the finishing touches to his epochal theory of air mass analysis. Bjierknes' theory would not be published until 1921; and it would take the world another ten years to assimilate it.[9]

The world's knowledge of the Atlantic's weather that Towers and Barratt were able to use was only a little better than it was in the days of Matthew Fontaine Maury who, in the first half of the nineteenth century, had charted the oceans' winds for the benefit of sailing ships. And these data were confined to surface conditions. Of the upper air there were only thousands upon thousands of cubic miles of ignorance.

Charles F. Marvin, chief of the Weather Bureau, turned over Barratt's problems to Willis R. Gregg of the aerological division, who began sifting and synthesizing ten years of weather data compiled between 1906 and 1915. These data were synoptic weather maps constructed from reports in ships' logs. Radio reports were very few. Only eighteen years had passed since Marconi sent his first signal across the Atlantic on 12 December 1901. Most merchant ships were not equipped with radio. The equipment was expensive, the service was even more expensive, and those ships that had radio were not inclined to squander money on weather reporting.

Even the data Gregg was able to assemble showed conditions only along established shipping lanes, and it was sketchy. Beyond these well-traveled tracks were great areas of the unknown. The only upper air data available was from the British steamer *Scotia*, which had made a

*The radiosonde, a small, inexpensive radio set that transmits the meteorograph's data from the sounding balloon, would not become available until the 1930s.

brief aerological survey offshore of Newfoundland in 1913, and the U.S. Coast Guard cutter *Seneca* during 1915. The *Scotia* had made nine kite flights with meteorgraphs, the *Seneca* had made ten, and none exceeded an altitude of 1,200 feet. This was pretty thin stuff.[10] By comparison, present-day ocean station vessels send off eight surface reports, four upper wind reports, and two upper air reports, *every twenty-four hours;* and within a few minutes their data are plotted by aerologists on all sides of the Atlantic basin. The transatlantic fliers of 1919—and those of the succeeding twenty years—had to chart a virtually unknown medium on more than one count.

If this information was dismaying to Barratt, he got no more comfort from Dr. Alexander McAdie of Harvard University's Blue Hill Observatory. McAdie had served as a Navy aerologist during the war and had but recently been released from active duty as a reserve officer. Towers had requested that he return to temporary duty to assist the NC flight; but McAdie was reluctant. However, Franklin D. Roosevelt, who was not only Assistant Secretary of the Navy but a close acquaintance of McAdie, convinced the meteorologist that he should. McAdie had no better data than Gregg and their conclusions were the same. Statistical analyses showed what anyone might have guessed: the best time for a flight across the Atlantic was between May and September.

A vague weather picture was in hand, but for the flight a reporting and forecasting system had to be created. This would require the closest cooperation among the U.S. Weather Bureau and the meteorological organizations of Western Europe, England and Canada; a schedule of reporting had to be agreed upon and a system of communications arranged. In addition to reports from these shoreside facilities on the North Atlantic's rimland, there would be a network of Navy aerological ships at sea; their reports would be channeled to the Weather Bureau and to base ships with forecasters on board at Halifax, Newfoundland, the Azores, and Lisbon.

Weather information had been classified "secret" during the war, especially in England and Ireland. This was because Europe's weather is created on the North Atlantic and by imposing a "weather blackout" on Germany, the enemy was burdened with a measure of uncertainty in scheduling military operations. The creation of a weather reporting system to serve the needs of the Navy's NC flight fortuitously coincided with efforts to reestablish the prewar international exchange of weather data. By April a system was arranged for an exchange of four daily reports. Data from Europe, Scandanavia, and Iceland were routed to the British Meteorological Office and broadcast on its radio at Carnarvon; data from the United States, Canada, and the Navy's station ships were channeled into the U.S. Weather Bureau and broadcast on the Navy's powerful radio installation in Annapolis. The Admiralty's radio station at Mount Pearl, outside of St. John's, Newfoundland, was also tied into this network. At Mount Pearl there were two aerologists from the Royal Air Force who were assisting the fliers who were competing for the *Daily Mail* prize.[11] The North Atlantic's weather would not be subjected to such intensive surveillance again until World War II.

As compared to the flight's aerological problems, those related to navigation were relatively simple. Nevertheless, the adaptation of celestial navigation to the needs of aviation was in such a primitive state in 1919 that a year later Harry E. Wimperis could remark in the preface to his textbook on aerial navigation that "the remarkable transatlantic flights of 1919 have shown that the art of sea navigation can, with suitable modifications, be applied to the air."[12] Unlike aerology and knowledge of the upper air, the principles of navigation were almost 500 years old by 1919, had been much refined in the meantime, and were rather easily bent to the uses of aviation.

Towers assigned these preparations to Richard E. Byrd. In 1919 Byrd had been out of the Naval Academy only seven years, was a fledgling aviator, and a decade away from when his name would become synonomous with the aerial exploration of the Arctic and Antarctica. While learning to fly at Pensacola in the spring of 1918, Byrd and Lieutenant Walter Hinton had prepared great schemes for a transatlantic flight, and to make such a flight almost became an obsession with Byrd after he was told about the Navy's plans for ferrying F-5Ls transatlantic. Byrd soon became absorbed in the problems a transoceanic flight presented to navigation. A very serious problem here was that one of the navigator's basic instruments, the sextant, was ill-suited to use aboard aircraft and could be virtually useless.

In taking a sight through a sextant the horizon is necessary as a reference. This was no problem aboard a ship; it sailed almost on the same level as the horizon. An airplane, however, flies well above the horizon which, often as not, is lost to sight in clouds or haze. In any case, no one dared count on a clear day with sharp horizons in the gray world of the North Atlantic. An aerial sextant required an artifical horizon of a type that would be simple, rugged, and easily kept in sight while the airplane was in rough air. Byrd devised an artificial horizon by using a bubble in a calibrated glass tube filled with a yellow liquid. The invention was not unique. L. B. Booth of the Royal Aircraft Establishment had a similar instrument concurrently under development. The fact remains that the needs of the NC flight created one of the roots of the bubble sextant's invention and development—an instrument that

43

proved vital to transoceanic aerial navigation for almost the next twenty years.[13]

With the urgent authority of the NC project behind him, Byrd quickly had the assistance of the Naval Observatory in refining his bubble sextant and its manufacture for the transatlantic flight. As a precaution, the Navy canvassed instrument makers in the United States, England and Europe, but found nothing comparable to Byrd's. The British Air Ministry had Booth's bubble sextant under development, but it was not expected to be available for several months.

A similar effort was made in the procurement of a drift indicator. This is an instrument that shows the difference between an aircraft's heading and the actual track being flown. One designed by Elmer Sperry was found in the United States and two were procured in Europe. The latter were designed by the Italian aeronautical scientist Arturo Crocco. They were for use aboard airships and had to be modified to the needs of the NC boats by C. B. Truscott, a civilian engineer in the Chief of Naval Operations' Aviation Section.

Another problem was to work out a quick method of navigation that could be conducted with a minimum of gadgetry in a small, cramped space that was subject to sudden violent motions in three dimensions. The chartroom of a ship is ordinarily generous in its space for spreading out charts and working out problems; but the navigator's space in an NC flying boat was hardly as large as a telephone booth. Furthermore, with a ship moving at 14 knots navigation can be conducted in a leisurely fashion. If half an hour is spent in figuring out a position, the ship has traveled only seven miles in the meantime. But in an airplane such as the NCs, hurtling across the sky at about 100 miles per hour, time-consuming procedures could be dangerous. Byrd found an answer to these needs in a new short method of navigation devised by George H. Littlehales of the U.S. Hydrographic Office.[14]

With respect to communications, the Navy was in excellent condition. The United States Navy was at the fore of radio development, and its communications network was equal to any in the world. The installation of the NCs' radio equipment was assigned to Lieutenant Commander Robert A. Lavender, one of the Navy's pioneers in the development of aircraft radio and wartime head of the Bureau of Steam Engineering's Aircraft Radio Section.

When Lavender graduated from the Naval Academy in 1912 the Navy's experience with radio was barely eleven years old. In the Fleet, Lavender found himself attracted to the new medium of communications, and he subsequently became radio officer to several successive commands. While assigned to the old armored crusier *Seattle*, which was flagship of the Atlantic destroyer squadrons, he became acquainted with naval aviation's radio problems. Among the *Seattle's* many functions she also carried a handful of seaplanes. It may be thought that the aviators rushed to embrace radio as a tremendous aid to their operations. Nothing could be farther from the truth. They regarded radio as an overweight nuisance that degraded the flying characteristics of their underpowered airplanes. Lavender discovered that the pilots found any excuse was good enough to leave their radios on the ground. His early experiences with the growing pains of aircraft radio installations were always interesting, often exciting, but not usually his happiest.

In early 1917, Lavender was flying radio tests in an N-9 floatplane with Geoffrey deC. Chevalier as pilot when the airplane stalled at a low altitude and plunged into the harbor. The dazed Chevalier climbed out of the wreck with cuts and bruises, but Lavender had both his arms broken. Aboard the *Seattle* Lieutenant Kenneth Whiting saw the plane crash close aboard. He dashed down the gangway, commandeered the admiral's barge and charged off to the rescue. He lifted the helpless and hapless Lavender out of the wreckage just before it sank.

By the summer Lavender was out of the hospital and had his arms working again, and he was assigned to supervise the radio installations aboard the Goodyear, Goodrich, and Connecticut Aircraft B-type blimps that were being erected and flown at Wingfoot Lake, outside of Akron, Ohio. In the summer of 1918 he was sent to Europe for an inspection of British and French radio manufacturing and their field installations; then he was ordered to Pensacola. At Pensacola he was dismayed to discover few of the airplanes flying with their radio sets. Most of the radios were neatly stacked in a warehouse. It was the same old story: the aviators wanted to *fly;* they did not want to be bothered with twirling knobs on a heavy but fragile black box that never seemed to work when it was needed. In any case, learning how to send and receive on a radiotelegraph key was a bore. With the support of his bureau chief, Lavender was able to inform Captain Noble I. Irwin, Director of Naval Aviation, of the situation—and that his bureau would cease development of aircraft radio until prospective aviators were schooled in the operation and maintenance of radio *before* they were exposed to the heady experience of flight training. Lavender was almost thrown out of the office! Captain Irwin eventually simmered down; but most important, pilot candidates were soon trained to radio (among other things) before they were allowed to sit in a cockpit.[15]

During the initial planning of the NC flight, Towers decided to eliminate all radio equipment.[16] This was by no means a decision rooted in ignorance or stupidity; it was simply an ingrained habit. The chances

45

are that 99 out of 100 aviators of the same generation would have done the same—but with less thought than Towers gave to the subject, which was a real problem. Aboard the NCs, 260 pounds was allowed for the complete radio plant, and although its weight as actually installed was reduced to 250 pounds, this nevertheless could be traded off for 41 gallons of gasoline, which represented 30 minutes flying time. When weights in an airplane became a problem in this era, the first item thrown overboard was *always* the radio. However, Captain Stanford C. Hooper, head of the Bureau of Steam Engineering's Radio Division and the master builder of Navy radio during its pioneer years, convinced Towers that this would be an error.[17] Accordingly, radio was included in the NC transatlantic flight and Lavender was ordered to Rockaway in March.

At Rockaway, Lavender's problems proved to be less with the equipment than with its installation in the aircraft and the final adjustments. These difficulties were due to the NCs' design and to last-minute changes in the engine configuration during the final rush to have the aircraft ready by May.

The NCs' transmitting and receiving set consisted of a 500-watt SE-1310 transmitter in a streamlined housing with a wind-driven generator on its forward end, mounted outside the hull on one of the engine struts. The unit weighed only 44 pounds, it worked well, and could transmit a signal 1,200 miles. But this transmitter's power depended upon the airplane's motion through the air to turn the propeller of its generator. When the plane was on the water, the "windmill" of its generator stopped, and this set was useless. Here a 26-pound, battery-powered 50-watt CG-1104 "emergency" transmitter took over the work; it had a normal range of 75 miles. The receiver was a Navy SE-950, and a radio direction-finding set (somewhat erroneously referred to in that day as a "radio compass") was installed in the hull's stern. In flight a 250-foot antenna was trailed from the hull; on the water a fixed antenna stretched between the "skid fins" near the tips of the upper wings was used.[18]

The ideal location for radio in the NCs was in the nose—away from the airframe's struts and wires and well forward of the engines with their vibrations and the electrical interference created by their ignition systems. But the nose compartment belonged to the navigator. The amidships spaces belonged to the pilots and fuel tanks. The only place left for the radio was in the stern compartment, where it was directly in the wake of the interference created by the center tandem engines.

Lavender had worked out these problems to his satisfaction aboard the *NC-2*. But the *NC-2* had its engines in tandem units out on

46

the wings, well away from the hull. When the NC's engine layout was revised in favor of a center tandem engine unit, with the engines almost on top of the radio room he had to begin all over again. The *NC-3* was the first to fly with the center tandem unit, but that was not until 23 April—only a week before the estimated takeoff date of 1 May. In the rush to fly load tests, determine fuel consumption, and iron out minor bugs in the airframe and engine installations, Lavender got very little time to adapt the radio to its new environment. The transmitter and receiver performed well, but the range of the radio direction finder was reduced from 50 to 15 miles. With time, this could have been corrected. But there was no time. This degrading of the RDF set's range would have its consequences for the *NC-1* and *NC-3* above the fog-blanketed Atlantic.

These radio tests, the improvisation of instruments and techniques for navigation, and the creation of an aerological service were only part of the preliminary requirements of the Navy's transatlantic expedition. Beyond these there was the organization of the NC Transatlantic Task Force itself, the creation of logistics to serve the task force and the aircraft, and the determination of the NC boats' transatlantic configuration and its refinement. These requirements were met with the expeditions' final preparations.

Gaar Williams Cartoon
The Indianapolis News, 19 May 1919

Final Preparations

The uncertainties that afflicted those primitive days of aerology, aerial navigation, and aircraft radio communications, not to mention the aircraft and their engines themselves, all called for an emergency backup system that would provide, in the event everything went wrong, a means of rescuing a crew forced down at sea. The NCs' backup system was vitally necessary to weather intelligence, it served the needs of navigation and communications, and it could function as a rescue system.

This system was criticized in 1919, and occasionally over the years in the half century since, as being bizarre, extravagant, "unsporting," or typical of American "over-organization." The object of these criticisms was the fleet of almost a hundred ships that provided logistics support to the NC flight, including the five dozen destroyers that maintained stations at 50-mile intervals along the track of the flight.

It deserves appreciation, however, that it was one thing to take off from Newfoundland and aim an airplane at the 36,000 square miles of Ireland, which had England and Scotland a few miles away as a backstop. It was a far more ticklish problem to zero in on the 890 square miles of the Azores Islands whose terrain is distributed unevenly among nine specks spread over an expanse of ocean that is as large as Ireland. If a pilot missed the Azores his next landfall was 900 miles away at Funchal in the Madeiras, and there was no hope of making that. In any case, the NC flight was not a "sporting venture"; it was a national undertaking. The Navy had an obligation to look after its men and aircraft, and to provide the expedition with every possible assurance of success. If anything less than the most was done to further its success, and the flight failed in its objective, it would be very difficult to justify the project to Congress and the taxpaying public. Even before the flight took off, a few noisy voices of some small minds in Congress were carping that the flight was a waste of the taxpayers' money on a frivolous stunt. After all, what ordinary person would ever want to *fly* across the Atlantic?

The planning for the task force to support the transatlantic flight was put in the hands of Captain Harris Laning, a brilliant staff officer who had been Assistant Chief of the Bureau of Navigation during the war.[1] Occurring as it did in the midst of an indecently hurried demobilization, the organization of the NC task force was not a simple job. Base ships had to be provided along the route to service the flying boats, and destroyers had to be found, made available, and modified to serve as ocean station vessels. The minelayer *Aroostook,* the NC base ship for Newfoundland and England, was rushed into the Norfolk Naval Shipyard to be outfitted with tankage for 5,000 gallons of gasoline, the means for carrying two small, single-engine Curtiss MF flying boats, and to have enlarged berthing and messing spaces installed to accommodate aviation personnel. Similar alterations had to be made in the old cruisers *Baltimore* and *Columbia,* and the destroyer tenders *Melville* and *Shawmut,* the base ships for Halifax, Horta, Ponta Delgada, and Lisbon, respectively.

The alterations to these few large ships were relatively simple as compared to the arrangements that had to be made for a fleet of sixty-six destroyers. All of the destroyers had to be scheduled for shipyard availability to be outfitted with an SE-950 aircraft radio receivers for communicating with the airplanes, each set being carefully tuned to 1512 and 1905 meters. And fifteen of these destroyers had to be rigged with special aerological equipment for weather reporting. These weather ships also had to send some of their officers and men ashore to attend a cram school that taught them how to become aerographers in five days. To keep this task force steaming, a schedule was set up for the tankers *Hisko* and *Houma* to supply bunker oil at Newfoundland, the Azores, and Lisbon, and for the *Maumee,* which was rigged for refueling at sea, to replenish the destroyers on their ocean stations.

While these preparations were being organized, Bellinger was ordered to the Naval Air Station, Hampton Roads, where he took charge of a unit of F-5L flying boats. During February and March these airplanes were used to fly navigation problems at sea, and they conducted radio and visual signal tests with the destroyers *Trippe* and *Wilkes.* While the ships steamed along a predetermined track 150 to 200 miles offshore, the F-5Ls navigated themselves to an interception. Later, the ships made smoke to determine the distance at which an airplane could sight it in varying weather conditions. At night, the same tests were flown with the ships using searchlights and starshells. Concurrently, an F-5L equipped with the new experimental geared-down Liberty engines became available for testing. Its tests were encouraging as regards low fuel consumption, and for this reason it was hoped to install engines of this type in at least one of the NCs before takeoff for Europe.

In the latter part of March, Bellinger left Hampton Roads in the company of Lieutenant Elmer F. Stone, with orders to make a survey of base facilities in Newfoundland. Elmer Stone was a Coast Guard officer and one of the founders of the Coast Guard's aviation service. In 1916 Stone convinced the Coast Guard that it would be to the service's advantage to have an aviator; he was sent to Pensacola, where on 10 April 1917 he won his wings to become Naval Aviator No. 38. During the war the Coast Guard was temporarily integrated with the Navy and Stone was assigned to the Bureau of Construction and Repair's Aircraft Section as an engineer and test pilot. Then and later, he was one of the best. During the transatlantic flight Stone would be at the controls of the *NC-4*.

On the afternoon of 26 March Bellinger and Stone were on the bridge of the destroyer *Barney,* watching her skipper, Lieutenant Commander James L. Kauffman, maneuver the ship's sleek 1,200 tons out of Boston Harbor, work her up to 25 knots, and lay her on a course for Newfoundland's Avalon Peninsula. It was a beautiful day of departure; it proved to be a nightmare of a voyage.

Richard E. Byrd's survey of Newfoundland during the summer of 1918 had recommended a seaplane base in the vicinity of Cape Broyle on the east coast of the Avalon Peninsula. However, summer is not the best time to evaluate seaplane base sites in Newfoundland. In the early spring of the year it could be supposed with great confidence that the east coast was jammed with ice blown out of the Davis Strait between Labrador and Greenland. So Bellinger was told to investigate the bays of St. Mary's and Trepassey on the south coast, which were in the lee of the ice floes.

Off Cape Breton Isle, near the entrance to the Gulf of St. Lawrence, the *Barney* found her passage blocked by a great ice field. Three hours were spent finding a passage around it. On the morning of the twenty-eighth, Cape St. Mary was in sight, but the bay was packed with blue Arctic ice; the floes were six to eight feet thick, the cakes fifty feet in diameter. Kauffman turned east for Trepassey and St. John's, but the U.S. consul in St. John's radioed the *Barney* that easterly winds had the entire east coast jammed with ice and the port of St. John's was closed. Kauffman took the *Barney* to Halifax, Nova Scotia, to wait for an offshore wind that would start moving the ice.

At 0911, 30 March, the *Barney* dropped anchor in Halifax, and here Bellinger and Stone first picked up the scent of "the enemy." Also in the port was the freighter *Digby,* a recent arrival from Placentia, Newfoundland, where she had landed Harry Hawker and Kenneth MacKenzie-Grieve with the Sopwith airplane in which they intended to fly the Atlantic.

During February and March, Hawker's Sopwith *Atlantic* was perhaps the most carefully watched airplane in the world. The newspaper press, of course, was generous with its treatment of Hawker's daring entry in the *Daily Mail* competition. Admiral Sims' office in London's Grosvenor Square was equally attentive, keeping Towers' office in Washington informed of Hawker's progress in England. Five days before the *Digby* made her landfall on the New World, the U.S. consuls in St. John's and Halifax had notified the Navy Department of the ship's expected arrival and of the aeronautical cargo she was carrying.

Bellinger made a point of visiting the *Digby* for a call upon her master. The *Digby's* captain told him that the British aviators "were very confident." That evening Bellinger wrote Towers, "We certainly have got to work at high pressure, else we are going to be left."

Perhaps spurred by his contact with the *Digby,* Bellinger decided that he had to get to Newfoundland immediately, and he left Halifax the next day by train for Sydney, where he hoped to connect with an icebreaker that would take him across the Gulf to Placentia. But his connections were bad, the ice was worse, and five days later he was back on board the *Barney.* Meanwhile, a westerly wind had started moving the ice out to sea and the *Barney* got under way for Newfoundland. St. Mary's and Trepassey were still blocked, but the *Barney* was able to pick a passage through the floes into Placentia where the aviators were put ashore to find their way overland.

After landing the aviators, the *Barney* tried to make a dash down the bay for the open sea, but was slowed by fog and then stopped dead by a wind shift that began packing the ice back into the bay. It was a wild and wearisome night, with extra-long watches on deck to fend ice away from the *Barney's* thin skin and the soft bronze of her propellers. The ship's anchor tended to drag on the poor holding ground; and when finally it held, its chain parted and the destroyer was adrift in the ice pack. With sunrise the fog burned away and the *Barney* was able to pick her way through the floes to the open sea, where she was met by a gale filled with snow and white water. All hands were very pleased when the radio crackled with word to pick up Bellinger and Stone at Trepassey— which was now open—and then return to Boston.

The trip to Newfoundland was not at all inspiring as to determining the location of a seaplane base—even a temporary one. Bellinger and Stone concluded:

Newfoundland and its surrounding waters represents the most unfavorable weather conditions for operations of seaplanes of any on the Atlantic Coast, and the harbors with surrounding hills are very unsatisfactory for making a getaway [takeoff] except when wind conditions are suitable. The harbors form a suitable anchorage for ships only under good weather conditions or during offshore winds not exceeding moderate force. Poor holding ground for anchorage is to be expected, due to rocky bottoms in most harbors.[2]

St. John's was adjudged too small; Placentia was too open for a safe anchorage; the 40 fathoms of water in St. Mary's Bay was too deep. There was no choice except Trepassey Harbour with its adjacent Mutton Bay.

Bellinger's and Stone's Newfoundland experience was a gloomy one. But upon arrival back in Boston they were handed an encouraging piece of news: On 27 March an inexperienced pilot had crashed Sundstedt's *Sunrise* during an exhibition over the Bayonne Yacht Club and the airplane was damaged beyond repair. One competitor was thus eliminated. Perhaps the next thirty days would eliminate the ice in Trepassey Harbour and set the winds to blowing the right way.

Meanwhile, back in Towers' headquarters on Consititution Avenue, the man with all the small headaches and more than a few of the big ones was Lieutenant Commander Albert C. Read, whom Towers had placed in charge of the flight's materiel. Albert Cushing Read graduated from the Naval Academy in the class of 1907, a class that included such names as Lewis H. Maxfield, Archibald Turnbull, Raymond A. Spruance, and Patrick N. L. Bellinger. At the Academy he acquired the peculiar nickname of "Putty" because his seemingly immobile New Hampshire Yankee face seemed to be made of such stuff. In fact, he was simply quiet, unassuming, and all business—which was demonstrated when he graduated fourth in a class of 208. These elements of personality, combined with his small, spare stature, seemed to put him a world apart from anything as daring as aviation. In 1915 he nevertheless volunteered for aeronautics, and on 17 March 1916 finished his flight training at Pensacola as Naval Aviator No. 24.

Read subsequently was ordered to sea aboard the airplane-carrying cruisers *North Carolina* and *Seattle,* where he labored with Bellinger, Kenneth Whiting, Dick Richardson and others, in the development of Richardson's catapult. Like many of the pioneer naval aviators, he was kept in the United States during the war to assist in the phenomenal wartime expansion of naval aviation. He never got overseas, but was given commands of the air stations at Bayshore, Long Island, and Miami, Florida. When the NC organization took to the air on its transatlantic flight, Read would be in command of the *NC-4.*

53

In the execution of preflight planning, it was Read's job to sort out, identify and see to the procurement of the flight's "horseshoe nails"—the hundreds of tedious and mundane items that could mean the difference between success or failure, or at least a stupid and maddening delay. In these labors he was assisted by Lieutenant (j.g.) Braxton Rhodes. When the *NC-3* took off from Jamaica Bay, Rhodes would be aboard her as engineer.

Their work consisted of rounding up a great miscellany of gear and seeing that it was ready for loading aboard the base ships during the last week of April. This gear included such items as twenty 450-pound mushroom anchors with double-cone buoys and 1,200 fathoms of half-inch chain for mooring the flying boats at Halifax, Trepassey, the Azores, and Lisbon; twenty-four leather flying suits with fur-lined helmets and gloves, goggles and face masks, each accompanied by a life-jacket; and 120 Navy emergency rations, consisting of 13 ounces of "bread-and-meat component" and four ounces of chocolate, packed in water-tight tins.

In the realm of more substantial hardware there were spare parts for the NCs' engines. The consignment to the *Melville,* base ship at Ponta Delgada, may be taken as an example:

5	high compression Liberty engines, complete with tools, spare parts boxes and hand starters.
4	complete sets of gears.
2	engine overhaul stands.
2	Bijur electric starters and ring gears.
6	wind-driven fuel pumps.
4	hand-operated fuel pumps.
6	gasoline valves.
100	feet of copper tubing (assorted sizes).
4	oil pressure gauges.
4	tachometers, complete with shafts.
4	tractor propellers.
3	pusher propellers.
2	radiators, one of each type.
4	starting batteries (12 volt).
4	ignition batteries (8 volt).
4	radio batteries (6 volt).

These engine parts sound familiar enough and a similar list for a liquid-cooled aircraft engine would read much the same a half-century later. However, the spares parts lists for the repair and maintenance of the NC boats' airframes have a definite aspect of quaintness to them; for example:

10 feet of throttle wire.
50 feet of safety wire (25' steel; 25' brass).
 2 small turnbuckles.
 5 sleeves.
 5 thimbles.
 6 feet of bottom planking, 8 " x ⅛ ".
10 feet of leading edges for wings.
 1 mitre saw.
 1 claw hammer.
 1 chisel.
 1 wire cutter (claw type).
10 feet of Rib T beams.
½ pound of clinch nails.
¼ pound of ¾" brass screws.
 2 yards of hull cloth.
 2 yards of plane cloth.
 1 roll of plane tape.
 2 spools of thread.
 1 package of needles.
 1 ball of wing lacing, waxed.
 1 quart of marine glue.
 1 bottle of shellac.
 1 shellac brush.
 1 complete set of carpenter's tools (aviation).

And it went on and on. Similar packages of spares for engines and airframes were put together for the *Baltimore, Aroostook,* and *Shawmut.*

Read's deadline was 20 April, when all the NC supporting gear was supposed to be on the piers at the Fleet Supply Base at the foot of Thirty-fifth Street, Brooklyn (near present-day Bush Terminal). Read saw to it that each consignment was carefully and conspicuously identified for the transatlantic flight by being stenciled with a beg red "TA" inside a circle. But the smooth flow of paper in and out of Read's office in room 3403 in Main Navy was one thing; the end of the pipeline in Brooklyn was something else—and for a moment it appeared bad. Read traveled up to New York on 15 April, and we have this transcript of a telephone conversation between him and Towers:

Towers: Are you going down to Rockaway tomorrow?
Read: I don't think so; I'm at the Fleet Supply Base and I won't be able to finish up today . . .
Towers: How do you find things at the Fleet Supply Base?
Read: They have a lot of material here, but no one seems to know anything about the aviation material.[3]

Within a very few days, however, Read and Rhodes had the

material located and were able to turn their attentions to the airplanes at Rockaway, and to the takeoff—only three weeks away.

While these logistics efforts were being brought under control, work was going forward on the airplanes. This proved to be more complex than anticipated. At the time of Towers' October memorandum only the *NC-1* was flying. Her performance was good, but required improvement, and this was fully anticipated when she was refitted with high compression engines. Meanwhile, calculations showed that by adding a fourth engine the aircraft's weight was increased by about 1,600 pounds, but it provided power enough to lift an additional 3,200 pounds, plus 4-engine reliability. With these gains in prospect it was decided to change the NCs from a trimotor design to a four-engine configuration.

The decision for four engines was by no means simple because it was felt that one arrangement of four engines should prove superior to another. By way of experiment the *NC-2* was completed with its four engines in tandem pairs; each tandem unit consisted of two Liberty high compression engines back to back, one turning a tractor propeller, the other a pusher propeller. It was planned that the *NC-3* would be built with three tractor units only, using the new geared-down Liberty engines or, if possible, new Curtiss-Kirkham V-12 engines in prospect. The *NC-4* would have four engines, two in a tandem tractor-pusher unit on the centerline over the hull, the other two being outboard tractor units. Meanwhile, the *NC-1* would be kept flying to collect flight data.

This engineering program was nice in theory and might have proved out in practice—if everything went well. But it became bogged down in production changes, labor problems at Curtiss, late deliveries of material by contractors, the confusion attending the great demobilization, and just plain bad weather that kept the *NC-1* and *NC-2* grounded at Rockaway. The Curtiss-Kirkham engines never became available; the geared-down Liberties did not have their bugs ironed out in time for the transatlantic flight. The *NC-2* did not fly until 3 February, the *NC-3* until 23 April, and the *NC-4* until 1 May—which was only eight days before they took off transatlantic. Meanwhile, many plans and schedules had to be changed, and quickly.

The trials and tribulations of the *NC-1* and *NC-2* illustrate the sum of the situation. The *NC-2* was originally built like the *NC-1,* as a trimotor, but with her center engine a pusher. Her pilots were still seated in the center engine nacelle, but now the engine was behind them. The purpose of this change was to give the pilots better visibility and to determine if this might provide a more efficient power arrangement. It did not, and the *NC-2* made only four flights in this configuration. Then she was confined to Rockaway's hangar from 18 February to 1 April while being converted to a four-engine aircraft with two tandem pusher units outboard between the wings. After this modification she became known as the *NC-2T,* the "T" for "twin tandem."

The *NC-2T* subsequently made twenty-five flights and demonstrated the NC boat's ability to get off the water at 28,000 pounds with four engines. But the twin-tandem engine arrangement proved to have serious shortcomings, if only because the rear engine and propeller are never as efficient as the forward unit in this configuration, even when both are giving their best performance. The propellers of the after engines were designed to operate in the propwash of the forward engines, but if a forward engine failed the after propeller was deprived of this airflow and its efficiency was seriously degraded. This in turn transferred too much of the flying load to the other tandem unit, which unbalanced the aircraft and made its control extremely difficult for the pilot. In addition to this, it was discovered that the after propellers were very vulnerable to spray during takeoffs and landings; their wooden tips and edges became so badly nicked that often both propellers had to be changed after each flight.

The shortcomings of a twin-tandem engine arrangement first came to light in technical data from France and England while the *NC-2* was being modified; but these data could not be confirmed by experience until the first week of April. Meanwhile, time ran out—completely. It became manifestly clear the ambitious prototype program to determine the "best" NC configuration could not be achieved before the transatlantic takeoff date.

It was finally decided to finish the *NC-3* and *NC-4* as four-engine machines, but with two engines in tandem over the hull and the other two engines as tractor units between the wings. At Richardson's insistence the pilots were removed from their lonely, vibrating eyrie in the center engine nacelle and were provided with cockpits inside the hull. This reduced the pilots' cockpit visibility but it made for much better communications between them and the navigator. This proved to be the NC configuration that flew the Atlantic.[4]

It may be wondered why the NCs' engineers did not suspend the engines between the wings in a straightforward 1-2-3-4 order as would be the case with four-engine airplanes of a later day. They dared not risk such an arrangement because of the lack of a full-feathering propeller, which would not be available until the 1930s. If an outboard engine had to be shut down, the propeller (made of wood and of quite fixed pitch) would keep windmilling, thus turning the engine's crankshaft and pistons. The resultant increase in aerodynamic drag would be phenomenal, fuel consumption would skyrocket, and the asymmetrical forces on an

57

airplane as large and so relatively underpowered as an NC boat could make the airplane almost impossible to control. Thus the NCs' designers sought to group their power units as closely as possible around the airplane's centerline.

While these decisions were being made, a near disaster struck the NC project.

During March the *NC-2*'s modification to a four-engine aircraft and the assembly of the *NC-3* filled Rockaway's hangar. The *NC-1* had to be left out of doors. On the afternoon of 27 March a gale hit the station while the *NC-1* was at anchor in Jamaica Bay, and the storm warning came too late to haul the flying boat ashore. The *NC-1* rode out the storm well; but during the night she dragged her 550-pound anchor inshore, where her port wingtip float fouled the ramp of the marine railway. The wingtip float finally carried away, which put the *NC-1*'s lower wing in the sea, where it was beaten to pieces by the surf.

When the *NC-1* was able to be hauled ashore three days later it looked as if she was out of the flight. Her lower port wing had to be completely replaced. Unfortunately, the Locke Body Company had delivered the last of the NC wings some weeks before and not anticipating any further orders had dismantled the jigs in which the wings were made. At this point a small, wiry, and softspoken lieutenant commander named Marc Mitscher, who had recently joined the NC unit as a prospective pilot, offered a suggestion. The *NC-1* had the lightest airframe and she was more easily converted to the center tandem engine configuration than the *NC-2,* so why not cannibalize the *NC-2* to make the *NC-1* flyable again. It was agreed that this was an excellent idea; but until the *NC-3* became available, the *NC-2* would have to be kept flying to compile engine and fuel consumption data, and to continue radio tests.

A few weeks after the *NC-1*'s mishap the Rockaway station had a distinguished visitor in the person of the 37-year-old Assistant Secretary of the Navy Franklin D. Roosevelt. Secretary Daniels had accompanied President Wilson to Europe, and Roosevelt was ostensibly representing the secretary's interest in the transatlantic flight. In fact, Franklin Roosevelt had a tremendous personal interest in the operation. He had for long been personally acquainted with John Towers, and when Towers encountered difficulties in obtaining immediate results from other parts of the Naval Establishment with respect to the flight's logistical needs, he always knew that he could depend upon Franklin Roosevelt to use his telephone as a scissors for cutting red tape.

Richardson showed Roosevelt the damaged *NC-1* and took him out to the parking apron, where the *NC-2T* stood at the head of the marine railway. Roosevelt showed the greatest interest in all phases of the projected flight, and when Richardson asked him if he would like to go for a flight in the *NC-2T,* Roosevelt accepted with the enthusiasm of a small boy. Richardson had not intended to fly that day because the weather promised nothing but rough air; but it seemed ungrateful to allow the Assistant Secretary of the Navy to return to Washington without a flight in one of the NC boats.

The *NC-2T* was warmed up, Richardson, Roosevelt, and Mc-Culloch climbed aboard, and the flying boat was lowered into the bay. Roosevelt climbed up into the pilots' nacelle directly in front of the center engine and sat between and just behind the pilots, where he could see everything. The flight was only nine minutes long; after takeoff they flew out to the Narrows, up New York Harbor, across Brooklyn, and back to Rockaway. According to Richardson it was a rough flight with turbulent air bouncing the airplane all over the sky; he and McCulloch had a constant struggle with the ailerons to keep the wings level. Roosevelt observed all this activity with great interest, but seemed to think that it was normal. Back on the ground at Rockaway, Roosevelt thanked each member of the NC flight crews for a great day. According to Richardson, the "great day" belonged to his officers and men. Everyone had become quite fatigued as a result of too many 12-hour days in getting the NC boats ready for the flight. The assistant secretary's visit created a tremendous boost in morale.[5]

On 23 April the *NC-3* finally got into the air; and on this same day the *NC-2T* was stripped of her port wings for the benefit of the *NC-1* and began her reign as Rockaway's "hangar queen." Most persons were pleased by this occasion, but Robert A. Lavender was not. With the *NC-2T* "written off," most of his radio work was for naught. And the aviators, the engine people, and the Curtiss people were so busy fussing over the *NC-3* that there was no saying when he could begin radio tests with the new NC configuration.

When the *NC-3* took off from Jamaica Bay for the first time, the target date for the NCs' departure was only a week away. The base ships were loading their gear for Halifax, Trepassey, the Azores, and Lisbon, and most of the destroyers were ready to sail for their ocean stations. There nevertheless remained much to be done at Rockaway. Among other things, the *NC-4* was not yet fully assembled. But a telephone conversation of 18 April between Towers in Washington and Richardson at Rockaway suggests that no one was much worried about their takeoff date slipping too far:

Towers: I received yesterday from Mitscher some nominations for engineers. Did you see the list, and have you any criticisms to make? They are in the order of Moore, Howard, Christensen and Kessler.

Richardson: I saw the list. They are pretty good. Kessler is awfully good, and you might switch him for one of the others.

Towers: What do you think about carrying five or six people?

Richardson: Still in favor of carrying six if sufficient lift is available. We expect to take No. 3 *[NC-3]* out soon, probably Monday [the 21st; in fact, the *NC-3* did not fly until the 23rd], and will know then just what we can carry.

Towers: I had a talk with [Lieutenant Commander Sydney M.] Kraus and Hunsaker about the revised figures, and they both agree that 28,000 [pounds] will put us across nicely.

Richardson: We had trouble yesterday with the twin tandem *[NC-2T]*, but do not expect it under the new arrangement.

Towers: What do you think of the prospective date to leave Rockaway?

Richardson: I think May 5th.

Towers: They're still adhering to May 1st down here.

Richardson: Well, that is a possibility, of course; but there are a good many things to be done yet.[6]

When John Towers put his telephone receiver back in its yoke after talking with Richardson, a short, heart-rending drama had just been enacted on the other side of the Atlantic that eliminated another competitor of the NCs.

On this same 18 April, at Eastchurch on the Isle of Grain in the Thames estuary, Major J. C. P. Wood and his navigator Captain C. C. Wylie, climbed into their Short S.538 biplane named *Shamrock,* which was a contender for the *Daily Mail*'s transatlantic prize. The airplane was a variant of the Short N.1B Shirl torpedo plane, and was distinguished by a huge belly fuel tank that carried almost 400 imperial gallons. Wood and Wylie intended to fly the Atlantic the "hard way"— from east to west, against the prevailing wind. On this day, however, they were merely ferrying their airplane to its starting point at Curragh, Ireland. All went well until 22 miles out from Holyhead, Wales, when their engine gasped and stopped on a vapor lock. They could not get it started again and had to ditch in the Irish Sea. In the relatively calm seas running the *Shamrock* proved to be quite seaworthy, kept afloat by her empty belly fuel tank. But when finally towed into Holyhead some 20 hours later, salt water had taken such a toll of the airplane's internals that an extensive overhaul was necessary. Wood and Wylie were out of the running.

When Towers and the men at Rockaway read in the next day's newspapers of Wood and Wylie's bad luck, they may have felt somewhat relieved. But only somewhat. Their transatlantic competition had proliferated considerably since Bellinger's trip to Newfoundland.

Not only were Hawker and Grieve and their Sopwith *Atlantic* in Newfoundland, but also Frederick P. Raynham and his navigator C. W.

60

F. Morgan with their transatlantic contender, a Martinsyde biplane named *Raymor*. By mid-April both airplanes were assembled and had been test-flown. Only bad weather was preventing the two British teams from jumping off for Ireland. Hawker and Raynham were nervously watching the weather reports with one eye and each other's flight preparations with the other eye—each flier being anxious to be first away. At stake was not only the £ 10,000 of the *Daily Mail* prize, but the immortal honor of being first to fly the Atlantic.

The teams of Hawker and Raynham by no means made the roster of transatlantic competitors complete. On 18 April Handley Page's entry in the *Daily Mail* competition, a stripped-down *V/1500* 4-engine bomber, was already three days at sea aboard the freighter *Digby*, en route to Newfoundland. The Handley Page team was headed by Rear Admiral Mark Kerr, who had hoped to fly the Atlantic with Gustav Hamel in 1914. Also by mid-April Vickers Aircraft, Ltd., had its converted *Vimy* bomber crated up and quayside in Liverpool, ready for loading aboard the Newfoundland-bound freighter *Glendevon*. The flight crew of the *Vimy* was John Alcock and Arthur Whitten-Brown, both former Royal Air Force officers. And there were three other substantial entries in the *Daily Mail* competition, each testing their aircraft and anxious to get it loaded aboard ship for the starting point in Newfoundland.

Boulton-Paul, Ltd., was preparing one of their P.8s, a civil version of the twin-engine Bourges bomber. The Alliance Aeroplane Company had built a special single-engine biplane named *Seabird* designed by J. A. Peters, who also proposed to be its transatlantic pilot. The Fairey Aviation Company had one of its excellent IIIc naval scout bombers, a twin-float seaplane, tested and ready for shipment to St. John's. None of these aircraft would ever get to Newfoundland, much less fly in the transatlantic air race.[7] But no one could know this during the last week of April 1919. To the men at Rockaway these entries only seemed to heap the odds higher against their chances of being the first across, and perhaps reduce their flight to the status of an obscure "also ran."

Even without these transatlantic expeditions being organized in England, the odds were already bad enough. Hawker and Raynham were ready to fly at a moment's notice. With receipt of an encouraging weather report they could be gone before the NCs left Rockaway, and across the ocean and riding in a triumphal motorcade through Westminister before the Navy planes even arrived in Newfoundland.

The NCs had a thousand miles to fly simply to reach their transatlantic takeoff point in Trepassey. There would be difficulties enough in just getting there.

61

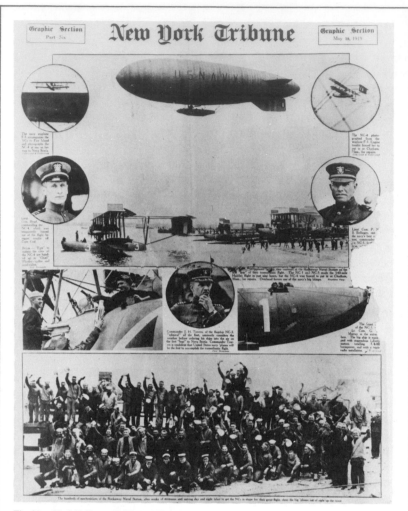

The *New York Tribune*, 18 May 1919

Getting There

When John Towers arrived at Rockaway on the afternoon of 23 April the *NC-3* had just made its first flight, the *NC-1* was being converted to the new four-engine configuration with the starboard wings from the *NC-2T,* and the *NC-4* was still in the process of being assembled. Any outside observer would find it difficult to believe that this scene of apparent confusion would be prepared to fly the Atlantic within a few days. Nevertheless, two weeks later the three NC boats made their takeoffs from Rockaway and by 15 May were poised at Trepassey, ready to jump off for the Azores. These weeks were filled with hurried preparations marked by human tragedy, near disaster and a rash of maddening technical difficulties that not only threatened the flight's success, but even the prospect of getting away from Rockaway.

The completion of work on the airplanes was simply a matter of time, but time was running out. Everything had to be rushed against the deadline of the first week of May because by the end of April the ships of the NC task force would be taking their stations at Halifax, Trepassey, and the Azores. The ships could not be kept there forever. By the last week of April the naval personnel at Rockaway were working a 24-hour day, with Curtiss operating two shifts of workmen on the NCs. There were many minor changes that had to be made in the *NC-3* as her flight testing progressed and these changes had to be worked into the *NC-4* and the conversion of the *NC-1.* This work went rather smoothly and on 1 May the *NC-4* made her first flight.

On Saturday morning, 3 May, the three NC boats were rolled out onto the parking apron and Towers mustered their crews to formally place the flying boats in commission. The flight crews were:

NC-3

Commander John H. Towers, commanding officer and navigator.
Commander Holden C. Richardson, pilot.

Lieutenant David H. McCulloch, copilot.
Lieutenant Commander Robert A. Lavender, radio officer.
Lieutenant (j.g.) Braxton Rhodes, engineer.
Chief Boatswain Lloyd R. Moore, engineer.

NC-4

Lieutenant Commander Albert C. Read, commanding officer and navigator.
Lieutenant Elmer Stone, U.S. Coast Guard, pilot.
Lieutenant Walter Hinton, copilot.
Ensign Herbert C. Rodd, radio officer.
Lieutenant James L. Breese, engineer.
Chief Machinist's Mate Edward H. Howard, engineer.

NC-1

Lieutenant Commander Patrick N. L. Bellinger, commanding officer and navigator.
Lieutenant Commander Marc A. Mitscher, pilot.
Lieutenant Louis T. Barrin, copilot.
Lieutenant (j.g.) Harry Sadenwater, radio officer.
Chief Machinist's Mate Rasmus Christensen, engineer.
Chief Machinist's Mate C. I. Kessler, engineer.

The ceremony was unusual; it was the first (and last) time in the history of the U.S. Navy that a group of aircraft was constituted as a division, the same as surface ships, and placed in commission as such.

Captain Power Symington of the Third Naval District read the Secretary of the Navy's orders that placed NC Seaplane Division One in commission. A bugler sounded "to the colors" and sailors aboard the aircraft hoisted the Stars and Stripes at the sterns, the Jack at their bows, and a commissioning pennant on their inboard wing struts. Then Towers read the orders that placed him in command of NC Seaplane Division One, and all hands were dismissed—to go back to work.

There was every cause for optimism this day. The *NC-4* had made her first flight the day before; the rehabilitated *NC-1* was being readied for flight on the morrow. The cruiser *Baltimore* had arrived at Halifax five days before and had sunk moorings for the flying boats. On this same weekend the great naval invasion of Trepassey was in progress with the arrival of the tanker *Hisko,* the destroyer tender *Prairie,* the mine layer *Aroostook* altered to service the NCs, and seven destroyers for the ocean stations. The weather reports looked good and everyone expected the flight to get under way on Monday morning, the fifth. The betting among Navy personnel at Rockaway was two-to-one that all the NCs would make Newfoundland; one-to-five against all of them making Lisbon; and even money that one NC boat would make England.

However, Monday's morning was only two hours old when all bets were off. For eight terrible minutes it appeared as if the whole flight might go up in smoke.

At midnight, Sunday, most of the Curtiss workers knocked off and went home, but a few remained to assist two dozen naval personnel with final adjustments to the NCs' engines and to get the aircraft fueled for Monday's departure. The fueling was being done from barrels, using portable electric pumps. At about 0215 Chief Machinist's Mate Rasmus Christensen of the *NC-1* stopped his work on the *NC-1's* starboard radiator, climbed down off the plane, and went to check the level of the gasoline drum that was being pumped. As he approached the drum, the pump's motor suddenly burst into flames and within a few seconds the drum was a pillar of fire.

Christensen shouted "FIRE!" and grabbed up a nearby fire extinguisher and played it on the drum. Others quickly arrived on the scene with more fire extinquishers. No one thought to pull the plug on the electric pump, or perhaps it was inaccessible because of the fire. In any case, while all hands were concentrating on the flaming fuel barrel the pump was still running, and unseen by the fire-fighters the discharge end of the fueling hose came adrift, sending a stream of gasoline across the hangar floor. It went up with a great WHOOOF, sending a sheet of flames under the *NC-1's* starboard wing and within reach of the *NC-4's* tail.

Aboard the *NC-4* Lieutenant James L. Breese, her engineering officer, was checking the forward centerline engine when he saw the first flash and heard Christensen's alarm. By the time he climbed down off the hull a sheet of flame was already under the *NC-4's* tail. He grabbed up a fire extinguisher and turned it on the fire.

Lieutenant Elmer Stone, pilot of the *NC-4,* was violating Towers' order that pilots were not to do any night work because he wanted them fully rested for the flight. But there were things that had to be done, and when they were important it was Stone's habit to do them himself. He saw the flash of fire reflected off the opposite wall of the hangar, and by the time he turned around to face it, flames were already licking the wings of the nearby *NC-1.*

Within the minute a dozen men were on the scene with fire extinguishers, and by the time the air station's regular fire-fighting crews arrived the fires were out. It was all over in eight minutes. No one was injured. But the lower horizontal stabilizer and elevator of the *NC-4* was badly burned, and the *NC-1's* starboard wing had its fabric completely burned away, its spars and ribs badly charred. The *NC-1's* starboard wing was a total loss.

A few hours of sandpapering, a bit of varnish, twelve square feet

65

of fabric, and a few quarts of dope would put the *NC-4* into flying condition within a day. But the *NC-1* seemed to be hopelessly out of the flight. Bellinger and his crew of the *NC-1* refused to accept the idea that they could be put out of the flight, and when Richardson arrived at the hangar at 0615 he agreed with them. After her storm damage of 27 March the *NC-1* had taken the *NC-2T*'s port wings; there was no reason now why she could not be made flyable again with the *NC-2T*'s starboard wings.[1]

When Curtiss workmen arrived at the hangar on Monday morning they had expected to prepare the NCs for flight and watch them take off for Newfoundland. The smoky mess in the hangar made them sick at heart. Instead of waiting around for their eight o'clock starting time as they usually did, they immediately turned-to on repairs to the *NC-4*'s tailplane and the removal of the starboard wings from the *NC-2T* and the *NC-1*.

It was a blue Monday at Rockaway, and it soon became a black one. During the afternoon Ensign Hugh J. Adams and Chief Machinist's Mate Harold B. Corey took off on a routine flight in an HS-1 flying boat. While turning in a steep bank over the air station, the plane lost flying speed, stalled, and came out in a shallow dive at 200 feet. Adams might have been able to pull out of it, but the 75-foot-tall mass of the gasometer used to store hydrogen for Rockaway's blimps was in his flight path. The little flying boat hit the steel frames of the gas tank's upper works and burst into flames. Fortunately for the air station, the airplane did not penetrate the gasometer and fire-fighting crews extinguished the fire in the wreckage quickly, or else the fire would have ignited the tank's hydrogen and there would have been a genuine holocaust. This accident, on top of the NC hangar fire, was not enough to constitute a bad day. A few hours later word came back to the station that two Navy trucks carrying sailors from Rockaway into New York City had become involved in a collision and two men were seriously injured.

To make things even bluer—certainly for the *NC-1*'s crew—on Monday evening Towers told the NC crews that the *NC-3* and *NC-4* would take off for Halifax the next day without the *NC-1*. Bellinger and the *NC-1* would follow on Wednesday or Thursday, or whenever they could get away. To make matters even more depressing, it rained that evening at Rockaway.

Towers had his two aircraft ready to go at 0430 on the dark, wet and starless morning of the sixth. If a person chose to extrapolate the local weather conditions to the eastern seaboard between New York and

Halifax, the chances of takeoff did not seem good. A messenger arrived with a premature telegram for Towers from Assistant Secretary of the Navy Franklin D. Roosevelt:

> CONGRATULATIONS ON SPEEDY REPAIRS. THE NAVY WISHES YOU AND YOUR OFFICERS AND MEN ALL SUCCESS IN THIS FIRST ORGANIZED EFFORT TO CROSS THE ATLANTIC [BY] AIR. I WISH I WERE WITH YOU.[2]

Towers wished that he had as much luck with weather as he had with repairs. Word came from stations up the coast that the local rain conditions had expanded to cloak the whole New England coast with poor visibility. Towers waited three hours for a change, then announced that the takeoff was postponed.

This news cheered Bellinger and his crew of the *NC-1,* but no one else. No one knew it on this sixth day of May, but this was the beginning of many long weather watches by the NC fliers. This is the explanation why the NC transatlantic flight—which in fact was a series of seven flights—required eight days to reach the Azores and another ten days to reach Lisbon, and a total of twenty-four days between Rockaway and Plymouth. Every time the airplanes stopped they required some time-consuming servicing, and by the time they were ready to go the weather had changed; then they had to wait, wait, and wait some more.

Wednesday's weather continued bad, but reports from the Midwest indicated that the rain and fog should be moving offshore by Thursday. Meanwhile, the *NC-1* had another close brush with destruction. Electric landing lights were not used aboard aircraft until the late 1920s; the NCs were equipped with a pair of flares hinged on their bows to provide illumination in assistance of a night landing. These flares were ignited by a push-button located all too conspicuously in the navigator's cockpit in the nose. According to Read, this button had an almost fatal attraction for the "I-didn't-know-it-was-loaded" type of person, and on Wednesday afternoon just such a person decided to test this attractive button. The flares went off with a WHOOSH, shooting two brilliant streams of fire across the hangar, setting fire to nearby paint stores. Once again Rockaway's fire-fighters (who were getting plenty of experience these days), had the situation quickly under control. Happily, and luckily, there was no damage to any of the aircraft.

This moment had scarely passed when a muffled cry from the flight apron announced another crisis. Machinist's Mate Edward H. Howard, who was working on the *NC-4's* engines, turned around in a split second of thoughtlessness and put his hand into the blurred arc of the after propeller. His left hand was promptly chopped off at the wrist. Gripping his bleeding stump, Howard slid down over the *NC-4's* hull and ran to a nearby automobile, gave the driver directions to the air station's hospital, and told him to get moving. This was a terrible experience for Howard, and for more reasons than one. He not only lost a hand, but his opportunity to make the transatlantic flight; and he had been a machanic with the NC boats since the initial trials of the *NC-1*. In the hospital he pleaded with Read that if the flight was delayed a few more days, his stump would be healed and would be able to go. But a transatlantic flight of 1919 had no place for a one-handed man, and Howard was replaced by Chief Machinist's Mate Eugene S. Rhoads.

The only good thing about Wednesday was that the new engines installed in the *NC-3* tested out well; and the test flight of the *NC-4*, for which Howard had been tuning her engines, went smoothly. The best news came in the evening when the 2100 weather report forecast good flight conditions for the next twelve hours.

When reveille sounded at Rockaway on Thursday 8 May, the NCs' crews had been up drinking coffee and checking their aircraft for a couple of hours. The sun crawled up from the swampy wastes of what is today John F. Kennedy International Airport to illuminate a slightly hazy day; its exaggerated light of early morning made the bright yellow wings of the NC boats shimmer like gold. While mechanics swarmed over the NCs' engines, the blimp *C-4* was hauled out of her hangar and took off for a flight to New Haven to drop leaflets to promote the sales of Liberty Bonds for the current "Victory Loan" campaign.

While the local weather was good, weather reports from Halifax, where Dr. Alexander McAdie was serving as aerologist aboard the base ship *Baltimore,* were discouraging. Takeoff seemed doubtful until 0920, when reports of clearing came in from stations up the coast. At 0930 Towers gave the order for takeoff at 1000.

Aboard the three aircraft their engineers checked the oil in their engines, primed their carburetors, and readied fire extinguishers in case of a serious backfire in starting. The pilots turned the individual ignition switches of their four engines to "on," closed the master switch to the 8-volt ignition system, and one by one closed the switches to the 12-volt starting motors. As the engines coughed to life and filled Rockaway's waterfront with noise, the engineers inside the NCs' after compartments checked their tachometers, oil pressure gauges, and the temperatures of their oil and cooling water.

As the three big boats stood perched at the heads of their marine railways with their engines ticking over to warm up, only about five hundred persons had gathered on the parking apron to witness the takeoffs. Among the spectators was Captain Noble E. Irwin, Director of Naval Aviation, Commander Arthur T. Atkins who had nursed the NCs' engine problems from beginning to end from his desk in the Bureau of Steam Engineering, and Commander George C. Westervelt. It was a day of mixed feelings for Westervelt. He was not only a Construction Corps officer but an aviator too; he had been in on the NC development from the very beginning and he desperately wanted to be a member of the flight. Captain Irwin told him that the flight crews would be line officers only; however, between Rockaway and Trepassey the *NC-3* and *NC-1* could carry an extra man and Irwin offered one seat to Westervelt. The transatlantic flight was one thing, a joyride to Newfoundland was something else, and Westervelt asked that the seat be given to Ensign C. J. McCarthy who had so much to do with working out the NCs' four-engine configuration, among many other things. This morning McCarthy was pulling on a leather flight suit before joining Bellinger abroad the *NC-1*. The extra space aboard the *NC-3* was given to Richard E. Byrd, who would have an opportunity to check out his navigation procedures as far as Trepassey.

Before boarding their planes, the three aircraft commanders were asked for statements by the press. Towers told them:

> I have been in the flying game too long to venture a very strong prediction regarding the result of even short flights. However, we are ready, and if the power plants hold out, I know of nothing which will prevent us from reaching the other side.
>
> I have been asked many times if we are going into this venture from patriotic, scientific, or sporting standpoint. There is little patriotism connected with the lucky chance to be a member of the over-overseas *[sic]* crew. Everyone in the air service of the Navy is anxious to go, for it will be good sport, though in no way a sporting venture. It is a scientific experiment, and if we get no further than Rockaway Point, the undertaking will be worthwhile for the reason that we have made big strides in the heavier-than-air machines.
>
> The Navy Department and the entire field [the Rockaway Air Station] have worked untiringly and have left nothing undone to equip the planes for the long flights. We are going to do our best. Guesses aren't worth much, but if you want mine, here it is: we'll get there![3]

Albert C. Read of the *NC-4* had some poigant observations to make about navigation and the possibility of weather afflicting the flight:

> Whether we get there or not, we are going to get some fun out of it, especially the commanding officers, who are also the navigators. The trip will be a most unusual and interesting problem in navigation. If any of the machines do not arrive on the other side it will be on account of some entirely unpreventable failure in material or the unforeseen development of unfavorable weather conditions, matters which may happen regardless of the amount of care devoted to preparations.

69

We leave with the assurance that all hands are pulling for us. America is with us, and I believe all countries want to see this experiment a success. Good wishes help.[4]

The irrepressible Bellinger predicted:

With the help of God, and in spite of the devil—we'll get there![5]

At 0950 Towers and Read, both wrapped in the anonymity of their leather flight suits, climbed aboard their planes. Bellinger was a more conspicuous figure in his forest green naval aviator's uniform with a pair of golden wings above his left breast pocket flashing in the morning's sun. But once aboard the *NC-1* he shrugged himself into one of the bulky leather suits. Standing up in the circular cockpit in the *NC-1*'s bow, Bellinger waved to the small crowd and pantomined a hearty handshake to everyone. A voice in the crowd shouted "do you think you'll make it?" With a big smile and wave, Bellinger shouted back "SURE!"[6] Then the NC boats slid down the marine railways into the bay, and with Towers in the *NC-3* in the lead, they taxied away from the shore in a broad V-formation.

As the three flying boats moved down the glassy waters of Jamaica Bay, Towers stood up in his cockpit, turned around to face the formation, and raised his hand for takeoff. His hand whipped down at precisely 0959. Twelve throttles were opened in response to his signal and engine r.p.m. jumped from 1,300 to 2,800, and the three flying boats charged across the bay in the midst of great clouds of spray. Ashore the crowd cheered, automobile horns were blown, and above all came the wail of whistles and sirens on the air station.

The *NC-3* lifted off at 1000; the *NC-4* at 1002; and the *NC-1* at 1009.

After becoming airborne they slowly climbed to 2,000 feet, where they formed up in a shallow V that pointed eastward along the south shore of Long Island toward Montauk and for Monomoy Point at the southeast tip of Cape Cod. The formation was rather ragged as the pilots and engineers felt out their engines at different speeds. Aboard the *NC-4* there was particular apprehension; she had made her first flight only a week before, and because of bad weather was able to log less than five hours in the air. These first legs of the transatlantic flight—to Halifax and Trepassey—were also the *NC-4*'s shakedown flights. The *NC-4* had another problem in that she was slightly heavier than the other planes and had to be flown a little faster. In any case, Elmer Stone was a firm believer in the old adage that "speed is control," as was demonstrated

70

throughout the flight. By the time the three flying boats were approaching the island of Martha's Vineyard, the *NC-4* was well ahead of the other two, and Stone had to bring the *NC-4* around in a complete circle to get back in position aft of the *NC-3*'s port wing.

At Monomoy Point the flight swung north, passing to seaward of the Naval Air Station at Chatham, Massachusetts, on the eastern tip of Cape Cod. Their next landfall was Cape Sable at the southern tip of Nova Scotia, 250 miles away. An NC flying boat had a cruising speed of about 90 miles per hour, and 250 miles represented almost three hours flying time.

This was their first over-water leg, and between Cape Cod and Nova Scotia four destroyers were keeping station at 50-mile intervals in case the aircraft needed assistance. The first destroyer, the *McDermut,* came in sight at 1405. When the planes' engines were heard aboard the *McDermut* the ship began making smoke, alternating between black and white, and began steaming a course that pointed toward Cape Sable, thus acting as a 1,200-ton compass needle for the NCs.

The next station ship was the *Kimberly;* but before she came in sight the radios aboard the *NC-3* and *NC-1* sounded with troubled words from the *NC-4:* she had to shut down one engine, but was able to proceed on three. The *NC-4* slowly fell behind and was lost to sight.

As the *NC-3* and *NC-1* proceeded north, the sky ahead darkened with a squall. This was a cause for apprehension. The NCs had never been flown in truly rough weather. This was going to be a new experience, and not a pleasant one. With a weight of almost 16 tons and an airspeed of only 90 miles per hour, an NC flying boat was an unweidly thing to fly in rough air, not to mention bad weather. As they flew into the squall gusts slammed into the hull and wings, sending frightful shudders through the whole airframe. One wing would be thrown up and the airplane would fall off the other, and a minute or two would pass before the pilots had control. It always required four arms and two pairs of back and leg muscles to control an NC boat in these air conditions; and sometimes the sounds of two sets of teeth could be heard gritting above the noise of the wind in the flying wires.

In the *NC-3* Richardson and McCulloch took 30-minute turns at the controls. During the squall both men were required on the controls. Within 20 minutes the planes were through the squall and the air smoothed out until they came abeam of the broken coast of Nova Scotia. While cruising along at an altitude of 1,000 feet along the Nova Scotian shoreline, warm air blowing out of the rocky shore mixed with the cool air over the ocean to bounce the NC boats around the sky.

71

Richardson nevertheless professed to be pleased with the NCs' handling characteristics.

Halifax was in sight on the northeast horizon at 1940. From the flying boats' altitude the setting sun could still be seen to the west, but on the earth below, twilight had already crept across the provincial capital, and its harbor shimmered mirrorlike in the fading light. They had to land quickly or run the risk of alighting on an unfamiliar piece of water in the dark. The *NC-3* touched down at 1958; the *NC-1* followed 12 minutes later. Only after cutting their engines and being taken in tow by launches could the NCs' crews hear what a big day it was in Halifax: all the whistles, sirens and bells in the town and among the ships in port were sounding a welcome to the Navy's flying boats.

The *NC-3* and *NC-1* were towed up astern of the cruiser *Baltimore,* where fueling hoses were connected and the pumping of 800 gallons to each plane was begun. The engineers checked the levels in their engines' sumps to see how much oil would be needed for the flight to Trepassey. A launch took Towers around to the *Baltimore's* accommodation ladder, and he found Captain W. T. Cluverius standing on the quarterdeck at its head, waiting to welcome him aboard. Wat Tyler Cluverius graduated from the Naval Academy in 1896, a classmate of Thomas T. Craven and Henry C. Mustin, who were both closely associated with early naval aviation, Mustin being Naval Aviator No. 11, and in May 1919 was about to relieve Captain Irwin as Director of Naval Aviation. Perhaps these associations had something to do with the sober enthusiasm Cluverius displayed for aviation in 1919 and maintained throughout the 1920s and into the 1930s.

The first thing Towers asked Captain Cluverius was what news there was of the *NC-4.*

He told him that there was none.

Over the past six hours the *Baltimore's* radio had been in contact with four destroyers searching for the *NC-4.* The last station ship to have seen her was the *McDermut* only 100 miles off Cape Cod. The next station ship, the *Kimberly,* never saw her or even heard her engines nearby. Nor did the ships on Stations 3 and 4. Until this hour the destroyers had enjoyed daylight in their searches; with darkness it would be immeasurably more difficult. There was cause for concern. Considering the relatively small area in which the *NC-4* must have gone down, the aircraft or its wreckage should certainly have been found by now.

The search went on into the night without finding anything. It seemed as if the *NC-4* had disappeared.

Aboard the *NC-4* Breese the engineering officer and Rhoads the machinist had been keeping a careful watch on their engines since takeoff. The engines had only a few hours on them, and anything could happen. Every hour one of them picked up the engine log and a pencil and checked their gauges: port engine, 1,500 r.p.m.; oil pressure, 28; water temperature, 120°; and then the same for the starboard engine and the two centerline engines in tandem that were grinding away almost directly over their heads. Between hourly log entries their eyes swept the gauges every five or ten minutes. There was no need of their really reading the gauges; the positions at which the indicating needles should be pointing had long since become etched on the backs of their minds.

At 1350, just before the *McDermut* came in sight, Rhoads noticed the after tandem engine losing oil pressure. He told Breese, they shut it down immediately, and notified Read and Stone. An NC boat had no difficulty in flying on three engines, but she lost considerable flying speed as a result of the dead propeller's drag. At 1450, about halfway to the *Kimberly,* the forward tandem engine suddenly exploded in a shower of water and steam. This indicated a break in the wall between the crankcase and its waterjacket—and the absolute end of that engine.

With only two engines Read was faced with a forced landing. Herbert C. Rodd, the *NC-4's* radio officer, tried to get off a message to the other planes, but without the propwash of the forward engine his "windmill" generator could not turn up enough power. Rodd did not have time to ponder this problem; the next thing he had to do—and *quickly*—was to crank in his trailing antenna before the plane was low enough to drag it on the water, which would surely wrench it off.

Stone brought the *NC-4* down to an easy landing in a moderately rough sea. The forward engine was clearly a basket case, but Read hoped that repairs could be made to the after engine that would allow them to continue on to Halifax. While Breese and Rhoads turned-to on the engine, Read got out his sextant and took a sunline. They were about 80 miles off Cape Cod, which was 60 more than Read had reckoned. With darkness only a few hours away this was not very encouraging.

Meanwhile, Rodd was using the small battery-powered emergency radio in an effort to get word to the other planes or the destroyers as to what had happened to them. It was hopeless. No one was listening on his low frequencies. But he could hear the airwaves filled with traffic among the destroyers, to and from the *Baltimore* and various shore stations. They were all asking in a noisy babble what had happened to the *NC-4!* Rodd was unable to break through this gabby racket. Finally he tried sending an SOS. The *NC-4* was in no danger but Rodd was

73

confident that the urgency of the signal would silence all the jabber. But the searching destroyers were too interested in chattering among themselves; they asked each other if they had seen the *NC-4*, when, where, and where the aircraft might have come down, and they discussed methods of search. None was about to shut up so they could hear what the *NC-4* herself might have to suggest.

As the sun began settling in the west, Breese and Rhoads had long since decided that repairs to the after engine were hopeless, and Read had wearied of waiting for a ship to find them. He decided to taxi the *NC-4* toward Cape Cod. If no one found them en route they would at least be at the Chatham air station by morning. At 1700 the two outboard engines were started and they got under way.

At about 1930 the dim silhouette of a destroyer was sighted ten miles to the north. Read ordered the *NC-4* about and headed in its direction; but the ship suddenly turned away from them at high speed. Course was resumed for Cape Cod. Darkness brought a beautiful clear night full of stars and an almost full moon to illuminate the sea. After midnight the lights of a merchant ship were sighted; Read changed course to intercept it, but the ship's speed was too great. Then both engines stopped. This was perplexing at first; then it was realized that the gravity tank had run dry. In flight, a wind-driven fuel pump constantly pumped gasoline from the main fuel tanks in the hull to a 90-gallon gravity tank in the upper wing from which the fuel flowed by gravity to the four engines. When the gravity tank was full, the overflow was carried off through piping back to the main tanks; this line had a transparent sight glass in it so the engineer could see the overflow and know the gravity tank was full. This system worked fine in the air where the slipstream turned the fuel pump. On the surface, however, it did not work at all and the gravity tank had to be pumped by hand.[7]

The starboard engine was restarted and for twelve minutes the *NC-4* wallowed around in drunken circles until the port engine could be started. Then they were under way again. A few hours later, as the sky beyond the *NC-4*'s tailgroup began to pale with dawn, Highland Light on Cape Cod was sighted. All hands felt very good now; the Chatham air station was just around the corner. Below by his radio set, Rodd could hear the destroyers still chattering among themselves as they chased around the ocean on tracks more than a hundred miles off to the north.

At 0610 the *NC-4* was standing off the narrow, sandbar-fringed channel to the air station. As Read picked up his Aldis to blink a signal for a launch to tow them in, two HS-2 flying boats came roaring down the channel to takeoff on a search for the *NC-4*. As Read remarked later, their mission was accomplished before it had begun. Within a few minutes Chief Petty Officer Charles Devine was alongside in a sea sled, tossed Read a line, and the *NC-4* was towed into the air station.[8]

The crews of the *NC-3* and *NC-1* and all hands aboard the *Baltimore,* if not to say the whole Naval Establishment, were relieved and cheered when Chatham flashed the news of the *NC-4*'s arrival. But the cheering at Halifax did not last long. The *NC-3* and *NC-1* had been fueled from the *Baltimore* the night before; in the morning their engines started with difficulty and idled reluctantly. Inspection of their carburetors and fuel strainers showed dirt and water in the gasoline; hereafter, the NCs were refueled through chamois filters.

Aboard the *NC-1* Marc Mitscher and his copilot Louis Barrin had struggled with their aircraft all the way to Halifax. After the *NC-2T*'s starboard wings were installed on the *NC-1* there was no time for exhaustive flight testing, and the flight to Halifax revealed that the wings were not rigged correctly. All the way to Halifax, Mitscher and Barrin had to fight the *NC-1*'s desire to fly with her starboard wings low. It was impracticable to attempt correction of the wings' rigging with the airplane on the water; to leave it alone held the prospect of too laborious a flight for the pilots. Mitscher attempted correction of the condition by pouring about 80 pounds of water into the port wings' stabilizing wingtip float. If too much or too little it could be corrected at Trepassey; as it turned out, it was just enough to keep the *NC-1*'s wings level.

Aboard the *NC-3* Lieutenant Braxton Rhodes, her engineering officer, and Chief Boatswain Lloyd R. Moore were checking over her engines when they discovered cracks in the tips of one propeller. These were Olmstead propellers of a special design which proved to be remarkably efficient at the NCs' cruising speed of about 90 m.p.h. A precautionary inspection of the *NC-1*'s propellers showed that the two on her outboard engines were also cracked. Because of the epidemic proportions of the problem Towers decided to have all the propellers changed before takeoff from Halifax. There were enough spare propellers on board the *Baltimore,* but not enough propeller hubs to replace the special types used with the Olmstead airscrews.

Richard E. Byrd recalled that there should be some propeller hubs among the surplus stores left at the U.S. Naval Air Station at Halifax when it was decommissioned and turned over to the Canadians on 7 January 1919. Byrd had been the base's commanding officer during 1918. The Canadians were only too pleased to oblige, and a trip to the air station at Baker Point, with several hours of searching, turned up the vitally needed hubs.[9] The rest of the day was spent changing the propellers on the two planes, and by the time they were flight tested in the afternoon it was too late to take off for Newfoundland. Towers had no intention of risking a landing in the unfamiliar harbor of Trepassey at night.

When the sun rose on 10 May, the NC crews had been up for an hour, their engineers laboring over the engines. The night had been cold, the oil in the crankcases had thickened, and the engines started with difficulty. Aboard the *NC-3* the electric starter on the pusher engine stripped its gears; it would require at least an hour to replace. Bellinger in the meanwhile got his engines started and warmed up without untoward incidents, so Towers ordered him to proceed to Trepassey.

Meanwhile, the Cunard liner *Mauretania* slipped into the port to discharge passengers and mail for Canada. Among those who disembarked were two British aviators, John Alcock and Arthur Whitten Brown, who were very interested at the sight of the Navy flying boats in the harbor. Brown would have liked to talked over the navigation problems of the flight with the Navy fliers, but he and Alcock had to catch a train to Sydney where they would connect with the ferry to Newfoundland.[10]

At 0845 the *NC-1* roared off the water at Halifax. Six hours and 56 minutes later she touched down at Trepassey Harbour. Within a half hour of the *NC-1*'s takeoff a new starter had been installed in the *NC-3* and she, too, was in the air for Trepassey; but the *NC-3* continued to be afflicted by troubles.

About 30 minutes out of Halifax the oil pressure in the pusher engine fell from its normal 35 to five pounds. There were no signs of its overheating, but Moore promptly shut it down and Richardson landed at sea a few miles off Egg Island. On close inspection, Moore found the trouble in a strainer with too fine a mesh; it was suspected that the oil was still not warm enough to flow through it freely. Before the flight reached Trepassey, the engineers aboard all of the NC boats discovered that these strainers had to be removed. Further inspection, however, found cracks in the starboard propeller—one of the new ones that had just been installed.

They were only 35 miles from Halifax, so Towers decided to return to change propellers. To expedite matters, Lavender got on his radio, told the *Baltimore* that the *NC-3* would be alongside within 30 minutes, and to have spares ready for installation. The main radio set could not transmit without its wind-driven generator operating and was useless with the aircraft on the water; Lavender used the small battery-powered emergency set and found it quite satisfactory. A week later at Trepassey, however, any impression that the 26-pound emergency radio made by this practical demonstration was forgotten when it came time to lighten ship.

Richardson used all four engines for takeoff, but once airborne the pusher engine was throttled back to idling to permit it a further warmup. Back in Halifax they found the *Baltimore's* store of propellers exhausted. Expedients were now the order of the day and the starboard propeller was replaced by one from the forward centerline engine, and this one was equipped with one of the as-yet-uncracked Olmsteads that had been removed earlier. It was more important to have reliable propellers on the outboard engines as insurance against losing their services, because having to secure an outboard unit resulted in a terrible yaw that made the airplane extremely difficult to control. The propeller changes took two hours and by 1259 the *NC-3* was finally back in the air for Trepassey.

The five and one-half-hour flight to Trepassey was made without further incidents, but it was none too pleasant. A 35-knot crosswind out of the northwest made the holding of a steady course a continual struggle, and Richardson and McCulloch spelled each other at the controls at 20-minute intervals. It was anticipated that air conditions would smooth out over the Gulf of St. Lawrence, but it proved to be a fight all the way. At about 1800 they were circling Trepassey and were introduced to the difficulties of its harbor.

Trepassey Harbour is a sliver of water almost five miles long and about a half mile wide at its narrowest. At first glance it appears to be an excellent runway for seaplanes, but the "runway" runs almost northeast while the prevailing wind tends to be from the northwest. Richardson was beginning his letdown to the harbor from 2,100 feet when a powerful gust caught the *NC-3* and pitched her over on her port wing. He threw all of his 243 pounds into the aileron controls to get the wing up, but there was no response. The *NC-3* was falling fast and was on the verge of a spiral dive. Richardson pushed on the top rudder, but this reduced flying speed. Feeling the airplane teetering on the brink of a stall, he shoved her nose down into a shallow dive—and finally regained control. As he remarked later, the event occurred in a fraction of the time required to relate it; but it was a close moment.

The landing was not easy. Forty-knot winds were blowing over the range of 300-foot hills on the harbor's western shore. This was an excellent headwind for landing, but this required landing across the width of the harbor, which was less than a mile wide. Richardson came in from the east in a long, slow glide, periodically clearing his engines with short bursts of power, and touched down off Powles Point at the eastern tip of the harbor. The *NC-3* slammed into the crests of the swells, put her hull in the water, and charged across the bay in a great cloud of spray. Halfway across the harbor, with the shingled beach on the western shore rushing toward him at 35 feet per second, Richardson threw the controls hard over, putting the *NC-3* through a sharp right turn, and then ran up the length of the harbor with a crosswind of almost gale force on his port side. It took all the strength of Richardson and McCulloch on the controls to keep the plane on the water and to prevent the wind from getting under the *NC-3's* port wing and tipping the starboard wing into the sea.

In the midst of this struggle, Richardson was horrified to look through his spray-spattered lenses of his goggles at what appeared to be a large white ice cake in the dim light dead ahead. It was too late to do anything; collision was imminent. But the ice cake seemed to keep its distance. Upon lifting away his goggles, the puzzled Richardson was relieved to discover that the ice cake was merely the white wake of a motor launch speeding along ahead of them to be ready to take them in tow.

Aboard the base ship *Aroostook* the aircrews discovered that their experience between Halifax and Trepassey had been similar, only the *NC-1* had been spared a forced landing and any more cracked propellers. The *NC-1* had used a different landing approach to Trepassey Harbour, but it was equally as rough as the *NC-3's*. Everyone was sure that it was going to be even tougher to get out of the harbor, especially with a full load of fuel.

As for the NCs' propeller problem, Towers had radioed the Bureau of Steam Engineering for the urgent supply of complete sets of new propellers for all three aircraft. Towers wanted nothing more to do with the temperamental Olmstead airscrews; he wanted standard Navy propellers made of oak. They would not be as efficient as the Olmsteads, but they were far more rugged and would not reduce themselves to kindling between Newfoundland and the Azores.

When Towers' request arrived in the Bureau of Steam Engineering, it landed like a bomb on the desk of Lieutenant George S. Murray. There were only four NC boats, not just any propeller would meet their needs, and the spares at Rockaway would not meet Towers' requirements. The propellers would have to be manufactured!

Murray obtained an urgent requisition from Rear Admiral V. C. Griffin, chief of the bureau, and rushed off to the factory of the American Propeller Company in Baltimore, the manufacturer of Paragon propellers. It was Saturday morning when Murray arrived at the factory and in that day of the 44-hour work week, the workers were about to call it quits for the weekend. Spencer Heath, the president of the company,

78

did not have to plead with his men to stay once he made it known that the propellers were for the NC flight. Work began at 1300 Saturday, went on through the night and continued all day Sunday without a break. By 1900 Sunday the twelve 10-foot oak propellers were finished, but had to be left standing for the next twelve hours to let their varnish dry. Meanwhile, Murray arranged for their transportation to Newfoundland. On Monday morning the propellers, each carefully wrapped in several thicknesses of burlap, were loaded into a special railroad coach which was coupled onto an express train for Boston, where it arrived that evening. Trucks met the train at South Station and rushed the propellers to the Boston Navy Yard, where they were loaded aboard the destroyer *Edwards* which was lying singled-up with full steam on all four of her Yarrow boilers and her two Curtiss turbines slowly turning over. As soon as the propellers were secured on deck, the *Edwards* cast off and was under way for Trepassey.[11]

When the *NC-3* and *NC-1* arrived at Trepassey the ships of the NC task force had been in the port for a week. The tanker *Hisko* was the first to arrive, dropping anchor in Trepassey on Friday 2 May. The next day the repair ship *Prairie* and the minelayer *Aroostook* sailed into the harbor. When their hundreds of sailors swarmed ashore for weekend liberty they soon discovered that a Newfoundland fishing village with a population of about a thousand persons was not the greatest liberty port in the world. Within a few hours Trepassey had been bought out of cigarettes, chewing gum, candy and beer, and the sailors were disappointed by the lack of picture postcards in the town. When seven destroyers arrived in the port early on Sunday morning, there was nothing to be purchased in Trepassey's general store, and its proprietor was making up a rush order to his suppliers in St. John's.

In St. John's the Bioscope Theater was showing D. W. Griffith's epic *Birth of a Nation;* but St. John's was about 80 miles away, transportation was difficult, and the personnel of the NC task force had to be content with the rustic diversions of Trepassey. There was beer available in Newfoundland, otherwise prohibition and supposedly no hard liquor was to be had; but smugglers did a thriving business in supplying fire water from the nearby French islands of St. Pierre and Miquelon. However, the American sailors were by no means intent on pub-crawling and hell-raising in Newfoundland, and the fisherfolk of Trepassey were impressed when on Sunday the village's Roman Catholic church—the only church in town—was packed to overflowing at all its Masses.

Monday was marred by a gale that caused the *Hisko* and three destroyers to drag anchor in the harbor's poor holding ground and to be blown aground; but they were floated off by high tide with negligible

79

damage. The medical officer and dentist aboard the *Prairie* busied themselves by providing free medical and dental care to the villagers; more than 150 persons were treated. The dentist was especially busy because of the notoriously poor teeth among Newfoundlanders, which was owed to a diet consisting mostly of fish. And the *Prairie* sent her band ashore to put on musical shows and give concerts for the villagers and the hundreds of fishing people who flocked into Trepassey from communities along the coast.

Acquaintanceships between the villagers and the ships' officers and men sprang up during the quiet days before the NCs arrived. This cost the Navy at least a hundred pounds of lathe stock and copper and brass sheet as machinists turned out rings, bracelets, and other trinkets for local children. The villagers responded with home-cooked meals and fishing trips to nearby streams that were jumping with trout. A favorite place of the sailors was the home of an old woman who came to be known as the "ham and eggs lady"; she had the only place in town that offered cooked food for sale. In response to the sailors' quest for souvenirs, one enterprising villager went to St. John's and returned with 200 sealskins, which the sailors snapped up within a few hours at $4.50 each.

The Americans were amused and fascinated by the simple life in Trepassey, and the villagers' peculiar manners of speech, which were probably closer to the English of Elizabeth I than to that spoken in the twentieth century. The "Newfies" were equally amused by the Americans trying to pronounce the name of their village as *Trepp*-asee, *Tree*-passy, and even Treppa-*see,* and their seeming inability to pronounce it correctly as Truh-*pass*-ee.

The Newfies were intrigued by the activities of the aerologists aboard the *Aroostook* and their launching of pilot balloons several times a day. These fishermen knew the offshore surface winds of Newfoundland as well as the calluses on their hands, but the *Aroostook*'s aerologists introduced them to the vagaries of the winds in the upper air. They were fascinated when a southeast wind would carry a balloon off toward the northwest; then at an altitude of about 1,000 feet the balloon would suddenly slow, stop, and dash off toward the east! They were equally fascinated by teams of men who trooped ashore from the *Prairie* and *Aroostook* and had a great time playing a game called baseball. The NC flight was probably the occasion of the introduction of baseball to Newfoundland.

The residents of Trepassey were especially pleased when they discovered that Lieutenant Richard James of the *Aroostook* had been born in Trepassey thirty years before. He had been taken to the United

States as a child when his parents emigrated. It was a very small world after all.

Besides the Navy, representatives of the world's press had also moved in on Trepassey. The village had no hotel facilities, so the newsmen improvised by leasing a dining car from the Newfoundland Railways, which had a narrow gauge spur line that ran down the eastern shore of the Avalon Peninsula from St. John's that followed a twisting roadbed to terminate at Trepassey. The railroad coach was soon christened "NC-5," and the *Prairie*'s carpenters made up a sign that said:

Nancy Five
American Press Correspondents
U.S. Navy Transatlantic Flight
Trepassey, Newfoundland[12]

On 9 May its American tenants solemnly hoisted the Stars and Stripes on a staff affixed to the end of one of the coach's vestibules. It was a ceremony witnessed only by the newsmen, a few children, and a half dozen of Trepassey's wooden-collared goats.

The fifteen days between the arrival of the *Hisko* and the departure of the NCs for the Azores were unquestionably the most exciting days in the 335-year-old history of Trepassey. There had been no similar excitement since a pirate named Rogers burned the village and destroyed its fleet of 120 fishing vessels in 1726. But Rogers had been unable to establish the name of Trepassey as a world dateline. For a moment in 1919 the name of Trepassey was on the front pages of newspapers around the world, obscuring the datelines of New York, London, Paris, Tokyo, Moscow, and even Versailles.

There was no newspaper in Trepassey, but a poet who wrote for the St. John's *Evening Telegram* summed up the situation in rhyme:

The World awaits. The hemispheres
Are listening for the pulse that tells
"The flight is on!" and such a flight
Earth's all consuming watch compels.

Now Ariel lead the storms to rage
O'er unfrequented Arctic seas.
The while these hearts of courage strive
To live the dream of centuries.

The World awaits, the millions list
New tidings. And on many a strand
On stranger lips in accents strange
Is heard the name of Newfoundland.[13]

Among the men of the *NC-3* and *NC-1,* however, the name of the Azores was heard more frequently than that of Newfoundland. After all, they had gotten there. But John Towers could not be entirely happy. There was not only the problem of the flight to the Azores and that of the propellers, but the disturbing fact that not all of NC Seaplane Division One had "gotten there."

Towers' "lame duck" was still straightening out its mussed feathers back at Chatham.

THE CITY RECEIVED THEM WITH OPEN UMBRELLAS

THE DREAM AND THE REALITY

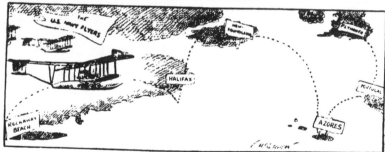

OFF ON THE FIRST HOP

John T. McCutcheon Cartoon
The Chicago Daily Tribune, 9 May 1919

The Lame Duck and
the Rubber Cloud

When the *NC-3* and *NC-1* arrived at Trepassey, the *NC-4* had been in Chatham for two days, where her troubles proved to be every bit as serious as anticipated. Her forward engine was a total loss, the after engine had to be completely overhauled, and this work would take several days. The American newspapers were quick to call the *NC-4* the "lame duck."

Also on 10 May the old cruiser *Chicago*, a ship of the original "White Squadron," steamed into the harbor at St. John's, Newfoundland, and the world learned of yet another transatlantic flight planned by the United States Navy. Aboard the *Chicago* was a contingent of officers and men in charge of Lieutenant Charles G. Little who were to service the airship *C-5*, which was to fly directly across the Atlantic from Newfoundland to Ireland. Little was assisted by Lieutenants Raymond F. Tyler and R. A. D. Preston, and Ensign Scott E. Peck, all significant pioneers in the Navy's efforts with lighter-than-air aeronautics.

Little and his group promptly made arrangements for the servicing of the airship on a cricket field near Pleasantville, a small community about a mile from St. John's on the shore of Quidi Vidi Lake. Mr. W. E. Bearns generously gave the Americans use of a house and a shed near the field for offices, a bunkroom, and to house their radio transmitter. Within a few days the area was stacked with hundreds of cylinders of hydrogen gas, drums of fuel, cans of oil, and a system of cables and ropes was staked out to moor the blimp. These preparations were watched with great interest by hundreds of spectators from St. John's and neighboring villages. Most of them imagined that the blimp was folded up in a crate aboard the *Chicago* and that it was going to be hauled out to Pleasantville to be inflated and rigged on the shore of the lake. They were disappointed when told that the airship was going to fly from the United States to Newfoundland.[1]

The Navy's plans for flying an airship transatlantic were conceived at the U.S. Naval Air Station at Cape May, New Jersey, shortly after the Armistice of 1918. When word leaked out of the Navy Department that a transatlantic flight was in the works by the NC boats, Ensign Charles E. Bauch and a few other junior officers suggested to Lieutenant Commander Robert R. Paunack, commanding officer of the station, that one of the new C-type airships should be capable of making the flight. Bauch specifically had in mind the airship *C-3*, which had recently been delivered to the station. On 8 February 1919, Paunack formally requested permission from the Chief of Naval Operations to make a transatlantic flight using the blimp *C-3*.

The Navy's C-type airship was a follow-up to its B-type, which was developed in early 1917. The B-ship was essentially a British design, a modification of the Admiralty's S. S. (Sea Scout) airship whose design John Towers had brought back from England in the form of rough sketches in 1916. The C-ship, however, was an all-American design, conceived and executed by the Navy's Bureau of Construction and Repair, and it was the Navy's first twin-engine blimp. The blimp envelopes were fabricated by the Goodyear and Goodrich rubber companies of Akron, Ohio, while the control cars were built by a subsidiary of the Curtiss Aeroplane and Motor Company.[2]

The C-ship's hull of rubberized cotton fabric was 196 feet long, 42 feet at maximum diameter, and had a nominal gas volume of 180,000 cubic feet. Inflated with hydrogen it had a gross lift of 11,650 pounds, 4,050 of which were disposable, and this could provide a nominal endurance of 31 hours, a range of 1,250 miles.[3] However, this was by no means the C-ship's limit, as was suggested by the flight of the *C-1* from Rockaway to Key West. The airship was refueled at Hampton Roads and Brunswick, Georgia, over this 1,500-mile track; but study of her fuel consumption data showed that this was unnecessary, and convinced the airship men of the C-ship's transatlantic capability.

The original planning at Cape May anticipated the airship refueling at sea from a series of destroyers; but as more experience was had with the *C-3* it was decided that only one destroyer in mid-ocean would be necessary. It was no great trick for a blimp to refuel from a ship at sea; the airship had only to descend within 100 feet of the destroyer and the two would cruise the same course while the airship's crew hoisted the fuel cans aboard. On 29 March 1919, flying the airship *B-3* out of Montauk, Ensign Scott E. Peck had demonstrated the feasibility of exchanging personnel between an airship and surface ship when he brought the *B-3* down over the submarine chaser SP-57; a jacobs ladder was put over the side and one of the ship's crew climbed skyward to join Peck in the *B-3*'s control car. Taking aboard fuel would be even more simple, and this was demonstrated on 7 February when the *C-3* began conducting a series of flight refueling experiments at sea with a submarine chaser off Cape May.

Encouraged by these experiments, on 12 February the *C-3* took off from Cape May with her normal load of 450 gallons of fuel on board and remained airborne for 33 hours and 16 minutes, flying a track of 1,400 miles, all the while maintaining cruising speed.[4] She was refueled once from a subchaser, taking aboard 125 gallons. Further calculations showed that by stripping the airship of its military equipment an extra 200 gallons of fuel could be carried, and a scheme was devised to use some of the airship's hydrogen as a supplementary fuel. With these modifications the *C-3* would have the 1,900-mile range necessary for a nonstop flight from Newfoundland to Ireland without having to refuel from a ship en route.

The Navy Department approved the proposed transatlantic airship flight, pending further tests with the *C-3*. However, the flight would not be made using the *C-3*, which was scheduled for transfer to San Diego, but by the new airship *C-5*, which would be made available for the transatlantic flight.[5]

The *C-5* was delivered to Cape May in early April and made her first flight on the twelfth, and on the twenty-eighth she was taken up on an endurance flight of 10 hours and 10 minutes. The fuel consumption data was conclusive: she could fly the Atlantic. On the same day that the three NC boats took off from Rockaway for Halifax, the *C-5* floated off the sandy airfield at Cape May, revved up her engines and was off to the Naval Air Station at Montauk, on the easternmost tip of Long Island. At Montauk she would top off her hydrogen lifting gas, her fuel tanks, and fly nonstop to Newfoundland.

When the *C-5* took off from Cape May for Montauk, Newfoundland and the Atlantic, she was under the command of Lieutenant Commander Emory W. Coil. His crew consisted of Lieutenant (j.g.) John B. Lawrence and Ensign David P. Campbell, copilots; Lieutenant (j.g.) Marcus H. Easterly; and Chief Machinist's Mates T. L. Moorman and H. S. Blackburn, flight engineers.

The *C-5*'s rubberized hull, envelope E-106, was fabricated by the Goodyear Tire & Rubber Company; her control car A-4126 was built by the Burgess Works of Marblehead, Massachusetts, a subsidiary of Curtiss. The standard C-ship was powered by two 150 horsepower Hispano-Suiza engines; but the *C-5* was equipped with a pair of the more rugged 120 horsepower Union engines. One of the engines was equipped with a special carburetor that would burn the airship's excess hydrogen, which was more economical than valving the gas to the

87

atmosphere, which was always necessary from time to time. And the C-5's normal fuel was doubled from 235 to 470 gallons.

The transatlantic attempt of the C-5 was a rather hush-hush affair, chiefly because no one could have a real index to the C-ship's capability until the C-5 arrived in Newfoundland. Only then could it be known with certainty that she had the ability to fly to Ireland; if not, then she would return to the United States.

One person who was not cut in on the C-5's operation until the last minute was Lieutenant Robert "Jiggs" Donahue, the commanding officer of the Montauk Naval Air Station. Donahue was a Coast Guard officer, Naval Aviator No. 54, and the Coast Guard's third aviator. In the summer of 1917 he had served with Byrd at Halifax and later became commanding officer of the Naval Air Station at Sydney, Nova Scotia, whose development was aborted by the Armistice. On this 8 May he was surprised by a phone call that told him the C-5 would soon be landing at Montauk and would require servicing.

It was an awkward moment for Donahue because his airship hangar was full. The brand new Goodyear airship B-19 filled half the hangar and the other half was filled by the envelope of the old Goodrich airship B-11. The B-11 had an accident a few days before and Montauk's riggers had her envelope inflated with air while they inspected it from the inside, looking for holes. With word of the C-5's imminent arrival there were sailors scurrying everywhere; the B-11's bag was hurriedly deflated, rolled up and stowed in a corner to make space for the transatlantic airship.

On Tuesday the thirteenth the C-5 made a short test flight from Montauk to New Haven and back, and on the fourteenth got under way for Newfoundland. The atmosphere at Montauk was "beat the NCs," and Coil told the press, "we will beat the seaplanes yet." Donahue shook hands with Coil, wished him the best of luck and told him that after he arrived in England, "shake hands with the King for me." "I will indeed, Donahue," Coil said; "and I'll shake hands with the Queen too!"[6] At 0800 the C-5's ground crew dropped their lines and pushed her into a dull, cloudy sky, where she pointed her nose across Block Island Sound for Cape Cod and points northeastward. Two and a half hours later the C-5 was plowing across the sky above the Naval Air Station at Chatham—where the NC-4 had taken off for Halifax only 57 minutes before.

When the NC-4 limped into Chatham, Captain Phillip P. Eaton, the air station's commanding officer, immediately put everything at Read's disposal. Eaton was a Coast Guard officer who learned to fly at Pensacola in 1917 where he became Naval Aviator No. 60, and the Coast Guard's sixth aviator. Within the hour, Eaton's machinist's mates were preparing to remove the centerline engines. Everyone was sure that there were big troubles in those engines, but four hours after their arrival they still knew nothing with certainty. At noontime Commander Kenneth Whiting in Washington phoned Read and we have this transcript of the conversation:

> Whiting: This is Whiting, Read. What was the trouble?
> Read: We lost all the oil from the engine.
> Whiting: How did it get out?
> Read: I don't know as we've not found out yet.
> Whiting: What's the arrangement of the vent pipes on the oil tanks? We used to have trouble with oil being syphoned out.
> Read: We haven't been able to find any leak. We're getting ready to take one of the motors out and overhaul the other one. The other people are taking a nap. We were taxiing fourteen hours.
> Whiting: Have you got all the assistance you need?
> Read: Yes, they're doing everything for us here.
> Whiting: There's nothing we can do for you here?
> Read: No, I don't think so. We will be here a couple of days and then join Towers. We will not need the destroyers if they've been recalled, as we'll go by way of the Maine coast.
> Whiting: Will you go straight to Trepassey or refuel at Halifax?
> Read: We will stop at Halifax to refuel.
> Whiting: Do you want anything from Garden City?
> Read: Haven't found that we need anything yet.
> Whiting: Have you talked to Mrs. Read yet?
> Read: No, will you please transfer me.[7]

The *NC-4*'s forward engine had reduced itself to a piece of junk; it was replaced by a new engine, but a low compression model. This was not to anyone's liking, but it would get the *NC-4* airborne again. At Trepassey it could be replaced by a high compression model from the *Aroostook*'s stores of spares. The pusher engine in the after part of the centerline nacelle had to be completely overhauled.

Breese and Rhoads, assisted by Chatham's engine repair force, put in four long days of work on the tandem unit. However, when the engines were ready to go on the morning of the twelfth, Chatham had been living for two days under a low ceiling of dirty clouds that were being pushed across the sky by gale force winds. The *NC-4* was weatherbound. When the weather began to clear on the thirteenth and the *NC-4*'s engines were started, the gears on the forward centerline engine's starting motor carried away. At this date these electric starters were unique to the NC boats and there were no spares at Chatham.

A radio call to Rockaway resulted in two new starters being put aboard an F-5L flying boat for air delivery. However, the F-5L could not arrive at Chatham before nightfall and it was regarded as too large an aircraft for a pilot unfamiliar with Chatham's channels to attempt a landing in darkness. So Chatham prepared a smaller HS-2 flying boat to meet the F-5L at Montauk. But while the HS-2 was on its takeoff run it hit a sand bar and stove in its bottom.

The Chatham air station also functioned as an airship base and inside its airship hangar were two brand new blimps, the Goodyear airships *B-18* and *B-19;* the latter had just flown in from Montauk. Airships were slow, but they did not have an airplane's problems in landing or taking off in darkness, which were considerable in 1919 when no airfield in the world could offer illumination beyond that provided by flares, barrels that burned a kerosene mix, or just plain bonfires. It was decided to send the *B-18* to Montauk, and within the hour she took off under the command of Ensign Karl Lange.

Only 20 minutes after the airship was under way for Montauk a radio call came into Chatham from the air station at Montauk that the F-5L had arrived, and its pilot was willing to fly on with the sorely needed spare parts and attempt a landing at Chatham, in spite of darkness. He was told to come on; and at 0030, aided by the light of a full moon, the big twin-engine flying boat put its keel down safely among Chatham's sand bars. Within the hour the *NC-4* was having her new starter installed.

When the sun came up on the fourteenth the *NC-4* was finally ready to go again. While Stone was turning over the engines the rotund shape of the *B-18* appeared out of the still darkened western sky, returning from her wild goose chase to Montauk.[8]

A six-minute trial flight displayed an ominous wobble in the forward propeller, and everyone suspected that it could result in another night of taxiing on the sea somewhere between Chatham and Cape Race. But they also knew that the storm that had delayed them at Chatham was also keeping Towers and Bellinger grounded at Trepassey. As the storm blew itself out over the Atlantic within the next 48 hours it would probably provide the *NC-3* and *NC-1* with a favorable forecast for flying to the Azores. After the flight, Read admitted that while at Chatham he was desperately afraid that they would miss the flight; and on this day he knew that if he did not hurry, the others would go—and they would go without the *NC-4.*

Read decided to risk the wobbling propeller. The *NC-4* could fly on three or "three and one half" engines; once airborne, the unreliable unit could be cut back to idling. They needed only to get to Trepassey, and there a new engine would be installed.

At 0907 the *NC-4* lifted herself off the water at Chatham and was on her way to Halifax. For about an hour of the flight she was escorted by a pair of Curtiss HS-2s from the Chatham air station. The flight was uneventful. The three destroyers on station between Cape Cod and Cape Sable rolled over the northeastern horizon like clockwork in one-two-three order; signals were exchanged, the ships passed below, and as mechanically as they had appeared ahead they slipped behind to be framed in the *NC-4*'s tailbooms for a few minutes before slipping over the horizon astern. Then at 1219 the dit-da-dits coming through the headphones that allowed Herbert C. Rodd to transcend his cramped space in the *NC-4*'s stern compartment spelled out a message from Washington:

WHAT IS YOUR POSITION? ALL KEENLY INTERESTED IN YOUR PROGRESS. GOOD LUCK. ROOSEVELT

Read dictated a message that Rodd tapped out through his radio key at 1221:

ROOSEVELT, WASHINGTON, THANK YOU FOR GOOD WISHES. NC-FOUR IS TWENTY MILES SOUTHWEST OF SEAL ISLAND MAKING EIGHTY-FIVE MILES PER HOUR. READ

Franklin Roosevelt's message created six big smiles aboard the *NC-4*. While the plane's engines were being worked over at Chatham her crew had been reading gossip in the newspapers about the "lame duck" and rumors that the Assistant Secretary of the Navy might withdraw the "troublesome" *NC-4* from the NCs' transatlantic flight. None of this made pleasant reading for the *NC-4*'s men while at Chatham; and if not demoralizing it was certainly irritating. Franklin Roosevelt's message off Cape Sable reassured all hands on this point. But first they had to get to Trepassey.

Four hours and three minutes after leaving Chatham the *NC-4* touched down in Halifax and was moored astern of the *Baltimore*. The propellers had no sooner rocked to a stop than Breese and Rhoads were up on her hull and out on the wings checking over her engines. The forward center Olmstead propeller was cracked at its tips; it was replaced by one of the still good Olmsteads left behind by the *NC-3* and *NC-1*. The starboard engine had been missing on three cylinders during the flight; its carburetor was taken apart and cleaned. In 1919 there was no such thing as Permatex gasket compound, nor even gasket materials that were impermeable to gasoline. Rubber gaskets were used in making up joints; they were soon eaten away by gasoline or turned into jelly by oil, and their shreds were forever plugging up carburetor jets or fuel lines. After each landing the NCs' engineers could count on a few hours of carburetor cleaning.

Aboard the *Baltimore*, Read was shown copies of recent weather reports and forecasts, and of the radio traffic between Towers and the destroyer tender *Melville* in the Azores. The weather over the Trepassey-Azores leg showed indications of clearing, and it appeared that Towers was planning to take off on the evening of the fifteenth or sixteenth. The *NC-4* could not be at Trepassey before late afternoon of the fifteenth, and even then she could not fly to the Azores until her forward engine was changed. Meanwhile, the *NC-3* and *NC-1* would be in the Azores. This worried Read, because if he missed Towers there was a possibility that the Navy Department would not let the *NC-4* fly to the Azores alone. As the *NC-4*'s crew worked over their engines that evening, they saw the chubby and content shape of a rubber cloud plodding across the eastern sky at 40 knots. It was the airship *C-5*. It seemed as if even that slow bag full of gas would beat them across the Atlantic.

All hands were up before the sun the next day. While starting engines the gears in another starter failed. This time, however, the spares did not have to be flown from Rockaway; they were on board the *Baltimore*. It was nevertheless a maddening experience that delayed takeoff by three hours. At 0953 the *NC-4* was off the water at Halifax. Less than an hour later the forward center engine began missing and its oil pressure falling. Stone landed the airplane in a moderate sea off of Musquodbolt Harbor.

Two and a half hours were spent on repairs. Decomposed pieces of rubber were found clogging fuel and oil lines. Trepassey, not to mention the Azores and Lisbon, seemed farther away then ever. By 1245, however, the *NC-4* was back in the air. The air over the Gulf of St. Lawrence was extremely turbulent and in spite of the combined efforts of Stone and Hinton on the controls the big airplane bounced and skidded all over the sky. But this rough air held a welcome tailwind that boosted the *NC-4* along at better than 100 miles per hour. The islands of St. Pierre and Miquelon slipped by below, and then the *NC-4*'s shadow was speeding across Placentia Bay to make a broad sweep over the Avalon Peninsula and come down upon Trepassey from the northeast, heading into the wind.

While flying across the peninsula Stone and Hinton looked off in the direction of St. John's and in the distance saw the airship *C-5* heading out to sea. Coil and his crew had evidently not wasted any time. The *C-5* was already on her way to Ireland!

The flight of *C-5* from Montauk to Newfoundland had been uneventful. Two hours and 10 minutes after takeoff from Montauk the

C-5 was over the air station at Chatham, where the *NC-4* had taken off only 57 minutes before. By 1710 the airship had overtaken the *NC-4* at Halifax, where the flying boat was moored astern of the *Baltimore.* The sun disappeared into the west at 1930 and the blimp plodded on through the night at her cruising speed of 40 knots. With daylight on the fifteenth the air became very rough, throwing the blimp up and down and yawing her to an extent that it was impossible to hold a compass course. Miquelon passed below and landfall was made on Newfoundland's Burin Peninsula. Here Coil changed course to take the *C-5* across Placentia Bay to the town of Argentia; but as they crossed the bay fog rolled in to obscure the shoreline.

Esterly had radio contact with the *Chicago* at St. John's and asked the cruiser to send out bearings for his radio direction finder. The radio bearings were followed until they no longer made sense; then Esterly and Coil realized that the radio compass was seriously out of calibration. Some hurried dead reckoning suggested that the *C-5* was somewhere over the extreme northern end of Placentia Bay. St. John's was off to the east so Coil turned the *C-5* across the fog layer in that direction. Within a few minutes she was flying over land, and the air conditions became very rough. Then a hole in the fog displayed a line of railroad tracks—an "iron compass" that would take them straight into St. John's.

Flying dangerously low, they followed the railroad line through the fog until they came to a fork in the tracks. Which way to go? There were a few houses at the rail junction and all of their inhabitants were out to see the gas-filled phenomenon that had droned out of the fog. Coil cut his engines and drifted down on the settlement. Within 60 feet of the ground he leaned out shouted "what place is this?" The answer came back, "Placentia Junction!" This was where the main line from the north branched out to Placentia in the west and to Harbour Grace and St. John's in the east. Coil and his crew waved an appreciative farewell to their guides on the ground and steered the *C-5* down the eastern branch for St. John's.

After leaving Placentia Junction the *C-5*'s navigation became quite simple. The air remained rough, but the fog began to thin and was soon burned away by the sun to create a bright day with sharp horizons. At 1100 the *C-5* floated in over St. John's, passing between Signal Hill and Cockhold's Head, to suddenly pop over a rise in the ground and drift down on her landing ground at Pleasantville. A crowd of thousands had gathered on the shores of Quidi Vidi Lake to witness her arrival.

By 1115 the *C-5* was in the hands of a ground crew from the *Chicago* who made her fast to the ground in the tackle of a three-wire mooring system. Coil and his crew climbed out of their control car to a tumultous welcome. The first person to step from the crowd to welcome them to Newfoundland was no less than Sir Charles Alexander Harris, the governor of the Dominion.

Nearby on the field, the Martinsyde *Raymor* of the *Daily Mail* contenders Raynham and Morgan flashed its brilliant scarlet and ivory paint job at the crowd; but on this day the *Raymor* had lost its magic. The Newfoundlanders had become rather accustomed to airplanes during the past sixty days; the airship, however, was a truly marvelous thing.

Coil and his crew were stiff, weary, and almost deaf after 25 hours of bucking through the air in the *C-5's* cramped, open control car with the two engines constantly beating on their ears. They were delighted to turn over the *C-5* to the care of Lieutenant Little and his crew and then be driven off to the *Chicago* for a hot meal and a few hours of rest.

The *C-5's* crew had good reason to be pleased with their flight thus far. They had been airborne for 25 hours and 50 minutes and had flown a track of 1,177 miles. Other blimps had stayed in the air longer, but none had flown as far nonstop. The *C-5's* average speed was only 45 miles per hour; but no one had ever pretended that a blimp was designed for speed. In any case, this was half the speed of the NC boats. Most encouraging was that they had consumed only 200 of their 500 gallons of fuel. They were now certain that Ireland was in range of their airship; and if the winds were fair they could even fly on to England or France. The experimental carburetor for using the airship's hydrogen was not altogether satisfactory. It was used for two hours during the flight and served its purpose of conserving gasoline and utilizing hydrogen that otherwise would have been wasted; but its use tended to overheat the engine.

When Emory Coil and his crew settled down in the comfort of the *Chicago's* wardroom the prospects of the *C-5's* getting across the Atlantic seemed excellent. Coil radioed Captain Irwin in Washington:

C-FIVE ARRIVED SAFELY AT ST. JOHNS AT 1400 HOURS GMT. TRIP A COMPLETE SUCCESS. READY TO PROCEED IMMEDIATELY UPON REFUELING AND A FEW HOURS REST FOR CREW. ALL CREW IN EXCELLENT PHYSICAL CONDITION. NO DIFFICULTIES WITH NAVIGATION EXCEPT IN MAKING ST. JOHNS UNDER ADVERSE WIND AND VISIBILITY CONDITIONS. REQUEST ORDERS PROCEED IMMEDIATELY UPON REMAINDER OF PROJECTED VOYAGE.[9]

Less than three hours later the *Chicago's* radio received an urgent and ominous message from Lieutenant Preston who was manning the field radio at Pleasantville:

CANT CONTROL MACHINE. MAY HAVE TO RIP.

All thoughts of sleep were swept away. Coil and his men dashed down the *Chicago's* gangway, hopped in a car and were off to Pleasantville.

From the moment she was secured to her moorings the *C-5* was trying to take off again on the 25-knot wind that swept through the valley that enclosed Quidi Vidi Lake. Lieutenant Little had 100 men from the *Chicago* for a ground crew and they were not enough to relieve the strain on her moorings and hold her steady while her envelope was replenished with hydrogen and her fuel tanks refilled.

The force of the wind increased and by 1420 two mooring lines had carried away and had been replaced; but the wind continued to rise, and the airship became uncontrollable. There were only two things to do: either start the *C-5's* engines and take her back into the air until the wind died down; or else pull out her ripping panel. A nonrigid airship has a special panel of fabric cemented along an otherwise open seam along the top of its envelope so the airship can be quickly deflated in an emergency. Little, however, had no choice. His machinist's mates had removed the engines' carburetors for cleaning shortly after the *C-5* landed; the carburetors were now in a dozen parts and it seemed unlikely that they could be reinstalled before everything got out of hand. If Little ripped the airship's envelope he would save the *C-5* to fly another day, but he would lose the transatlantic flight because replacement of the ripping panel required the shelter of a hangar and there were no airship hangars in Newfoundland.

By 1700 the wind was up to 40 knots with 60-knot gusts. Control of the *C-5* seemed hopeless and Little decided to rip the bag. The cord to the ripping panel was pulled—but the cord broke where it passed through the envelope into the gas space. Little, Preston, and a machinist were in the control car trying to cut through the tough rubber envelope with a knife so they could reach the broken end of the cord inside when a terrific gust shook the airship.

The *C-5's* 192-foot hull veered around with the force of the gust, wrenching at her moorings. Two steel mooring cables snapped. The manila lines began carrying away and she veered around completely, thrashing in the wind.

Little ordered everyone out.

By the time Little jumped from the control car the *C-5* was loose and already 30 feet in the air—with her nose pointed for Ireland. As

Little's weight went over the side the *C-5* ascended rapidly to 200 feet. Then she dropped to the ground with a crash, bounced back into the air and blew across the lake and disappeared over Signal Hill toward the Atlantic.[10]

The destroyer *Edwards,* which had just arrived in St. John's, was immediately ordered back to sea with instructions to shoot down the blimp. At 2010 a radio message from the British freighter *Clan Davidson* reported the *C-5*'s wreckage floating on the water at 47°50′ west, 50°37′ north, about 300 miles northeast of St. John's. By the time the *Edwards* arrived in the area at noon the next day there was nothing to be seen except a few small icebergs.

It was a bitter moment for the *C-5*'s crew. Their imminent prospect of a successful transatlantic flight was blown away by a 60-knot gust. It was a painful experience for Little, who was nursing a terribly swollen ankle as a result of his jump from the *C-5.* And it was a great disappointment to the hundreds of spectators at Pleasantville; when the *C-5* blew away, most of them thought that the flight to Ireland was on its way. But it was a tragedy for the family of a 14-year-old boy who was helping the *C-5*'s ground crew and was killed by a blow on the head when one of the mooring lines carried away.

In St. John's Cochrane Hotel, where Hawker and Raynham had their headquarters, and at Trepassey where the *NC-3* and *NC-1* were preparing to take off, there was a feeling that the *C-5* episode was too bad, but this was mixed with a definite measure of relief. The chance of being beaten across the Atlantic by a rubber cloud had been eliminated.

Within a few hours of the *C-5*'s loss, Coil radioed a brief report of the mishap to Captain Irwin in Washington. He concluded with a request that the airship *C-3* be immediately modified with Union engines for the purpose of flying directly from the United States to Europe nonstop, using the Chatham air station as the point of takeoff. He was convinced that the *C-5*'s performance between Montauk and St. John's proved the C-type's transatlantic capability and that it should be demonstrated. But it would require weeks to prepare the *C-3* and this would entail inconvenience and expense. Meanwhile, the NC boats took off for the Azores and it appeared that the Navy had its transatlantic "first" in hand. No one cared about seconds.

Emory Coil was thwarted from making his transatlantic flight in 1919, and three years later he was similarly thwarted from making another transatlantic attempt. In 1921 Coil was sent to England as a member of a complement that was to take delivery of the British airship *R.38* for the Navy and fly her to the United States. While undergoing trials on 24 August, the *R.38* broke up in the air and crashed; among the

16 Americans who died in the wreck were Emory Coil and Charles G. Little. No airship of the U.S. Navy flew the Atlantic until the summer of 1944 when, between 28 May and 1 July, the blimps *K-123, K-130, K-109, K-34, K-112,* and *K-101* of Airship Squadron ZP-14 flew from Argentia, Newfoundland, to Port Lyautey, Morocco, via the Azores, to establish a low-altitude ASW barrier over the Strait of Gibraltar.

While Stone and Hinton watched the *C-5* "flying" out to sea, down in the after hull of the *NC-4* Herbert Rodd already knew better. Radio traffic between the *Chicago* and the field at Pleasantville was filled with news of the blimp's mishap. But Rodd could not eavesdrop on the *C-5*'s troubles for long. He was more interested in an exchange of messages he intercepted between the destroyers *Buchanan* and *Walker* that indicated they were steaming to their ocean stations between Trepassey and the Azores. This was the first suspicion the *NC-4* had that the *NC-3* and *NC-1* were actually preparing to take off. When a message came from the *Aroostook* warning the *NC-4* to be on the lookout for two other aircraft on the water when coming in for her landing, their suspicions were confirmed.

Read quickly had Rodd call the *Aroostook* to have a spare engine ready for immediate installation after the *NC-4* was brought alongside. If the *NC-4* would have to fly the Atlantic alone, Read did not want her to be too far behind the others.

As Trepassey Harbour came in sight, Read could see the *NC-3* charging down the harbor at the apex of a white V of spray. Towers was taking off for the Azores!

But instead of lifting off the water, the *NC-3* slowed, stopped, wallowed in the waves and then began taxiing back to where she started. Something was wrong.

Stone dropped the *NC-4* across Mutton Bay, lifted her over the narrow Powles Peninsula, and at 1859 put her keel into Trepassey Harbour. Within a few minutes the *NC-4* was tied up astern of the *Aroostook.*

Now they had all gotten there.

John T. McCutcheon Cartoon
The Chicago Daily Tribune, 17 May 1919

"Let's Go!"

When the *NC 3* and *NC-1* arrived at Trepassey late in the afternoon of 10 May, they were no sooner moored astern of the *Aroostook* and *Prairie* than gangs of machinist's mates were swarming over them. Carburetors were removed for inspection and cleaning, sparkplugs were changed, thrust bearings oiled, crankcase oil changes, and a check was made of all the nuts securing foundation bolts and cylinder head studs. During the night a 60-knot wind lashed the harbor and sent the two flying boats plunging up and down at their moorings. The work nevertheless continued, and by sunrise all the NCs needed for their flight to the Azores was refueling—and a good weather forecast.

All this activity proved to be a case of "hurry up and wait." The morning of the eleventh put a brilliant sun on Trepassey, but storm warnings were up all along the eastern seaboard and reports from the Navy's weather ships on the Atlantic indicated unsuitable weather over the whole North Atlantic. The Navy's Atlantic weather surveillance had undergone a vast increase in scope since the first of May. Observations taken in Europe at 0100 and 1300 GMT were radioed to Washington where their data were integrated with American observations taken at 0900, 1200 and 2400 GMT. On 7 May five battleships with special aerological teams on board took ocean stations and began reporting at 0100, 0700, 1300 and 1800 GMT. Then on 10 May five destroyers with aerographers on board took station between Newfoundland and the Azores with a sixth on station among the islands, and they began reporting on the same schedule. All data went to the U.S. Weather Bureau in Washington where it was used to construct weather maps, and these were sent to the Navy radio station in Annapolis; they were then transmitted to the *Aroostook,* where Lieutenant Roswell Barratt and Willis R. Gregg of the U.S. Weather Bureau used them to make up their forecasts. Barratt and Gregg had no good news for Towers on this bright

Sunday morning; it was the first of five days that would keep the NCs weatherbound at Trepassey.

Meanwhile, Towers and Bellinger and their crews compared studies of their fuel consumption data from the flight between Rockaway and Newfoundland and computed and recomputed them against estimated tailwinds and headwinds that might be encountered and measured the results against the distances between Trepassey and the Azores.

The nine islands of the Azores are clustered in three principal groups along a general east-west axis of 280 miles. In the west and closest to Newfoundland are the tiny islands of Corvo and Flores with peaks that reach 2,500 and 3,000 feet into the sky. About a hundred miles east a central group includes the large islands of Pico, São Jorge and Terceira, and the smaller islands of Fayal and Graciosa. On the southeast shore of Fayal is the sheltered harbor of Horta where the old cruiser *Columbia* was stationed as a base ship. On nearby Pico there is a range of mountains that reaches up to 7,613 feet, which posed a formidable hazard to the NCs if they chanced upon the islands in a fog. About 130 miles east of the central group is the large island of São Miguel and its tiny partner Santa Maria. Of the principal islands of the Azores, São Miguel is the closest to Europe, and on its southern shore is the sheltered harbor of Ponta Delgada, where the destroyer tender *Melville* was stationed as the NCs' base ship.

From Trepassey to Corvo is 985 miles; to Horta, 1,110 miles; and to Ponta Delgada, 1,260 miles. Corvo was the NCs' landfall; Ponta Delgada was their destination, while Horta in between was regarded as an emergency landing facility.

Between Rockaway and Trepassey the NCs had averaged an 85-mile-per-hour airspeed and consumed about 85 gallons of fuel per hour. At 85 miles per hour the distance could be flown in 13 hours, and with the NCs' average fuel consumption, about 1,105 gallons (6,630 pounds) of fuel would be required. The NCs had demonstrated their capability to get off the water with 1,890 gallons (11,340 pounds), so theoretically the Azores were well within their range. However, averages can be deceiving when tossed into the no-holds-barred arena of reality. It had become painfully clear that a takeoff from the ideal conditions prevailing at Rockaway was one thing and that a takeoff from the cramped and narrow waters of Trepassey would be something else. What is more, the fuel consumption figures were no longer valid because the new propellers en route from the United States, although more rugged and reliable, were not nearly as efficient as the crack-prone Olmsteads; but by exactly how much, Towers could only guess.

100

It had been anticipated that the final fuel requirements might make it necessary to trade off the sixth man in the NCs' crew for an extra 30 gallons. Everyone was now relieved that final calculations made this appear unnecessary. But as a precaution, the spare parts carried aboard the planes were reduced to a minimum; anchors, towing gear, various tools, and extra rations were removed to lighten ship.

As Towers was handed bad weather reports by Barratt and Gregg every day, three or four times a day, he could find two consolations in them. The bad weather was giving the *Edwards* time to get to Trepassey with the new propellers, and it was also keeping his British competition grounded. In this second week of May the British transatlantic flight projects in Newfoundland all aimed at the *Daily Mail* prize—were beginning to multiply themselves by two.

On the same day that the NCs moored at Trepassey, the freighter *Digby* arrived in St. John's to discharge several huge crates that contained Admiral Mark Kerr's four-engine Handley Page *V/1500*.[1] Alcock and Brown were rattling over the northern part of Newfoundland in a railway coach, stopping at godforsaken places named Stephenville Crossing, Hattie's Camp, Gander Lake, Shoal Harbour and Holyrood—all of which would figure in the future history of transatlantic flight. But Kerr's airplane had yet to be hauled to Harbour Grace where it was to be assembled, and this was no small job; while Alcock and Brown's Vickers aircraft had yet to leave England.

These newcomers posed no immediate threat; the NCs could be in Lisbon even before their aircraft were assembled and test-flighted. The real competition remained Hawker and Grieve with their Sopwith *Atlantic* at Glendenning's Farm and Raynham and Morgan with their Martinsyde *Raymor* near Quidi Vidi Lake. With a break in the Atlantic's weather they could be off and away and in sight of Ireland when the NCs were only arriving in the Azores. So on this point, Barratt's bad news contained a small measure of good news for Towers.

The first days at Trepassey were pleasantly sunny and the daylight hours were warm; but when the sun dropped over the western rim the nights became bitterly cold and the mornings usually displayed a skim of ice on the fringes of the inner harbor. To prevent the oil in the NCs' engines from congealing into a sticky goo during these cold nights, steam hoses were led out of the *Aroostook* and jury-rigged to the engines' water jackets.

Towers, Bellinger, Richardson, and Mitscher took advantage of these days to make survey flights over the harbor in one of the two small single-engine Curtiss MF flying boats carried on board the *Aroostook*. Using this small airplane they were able to familiarize themselves with

101

the wind and water characteristics of the harbor without having to hazard one of the NCs. On the thirteenth and fourteenth, Trepassey became filled with fog, and there was no flying by even the MF boat. However, out on Trepassey's Meadow Point the fog failed to dampen the competition between the ships' baseball teams; the *Prairie* beat the *Aroostook* 4 to 1.

At noon of Wednesday the fourteenth, the fog began to clear; weather reports coming into the *Aroostook's* radioroom indicated that the storms over the mid-Atlantic were beginning to blow themselves out and the weather forecasts assembled by Barratt and Gregg began to brighten. It looked as if it would be possible for the *NC-3* and *NC-1* to take off that evening, but Barratt suggested that the next day's weather would be even better. Towers chose to wait, and for more reasons than the weather. The *Edwards* was expected in Trepassey the next day. What is more, the *NC-4* had left Chatham this morning; a 24-hour delay would give her time to reach Trepassey. If possible, Towers wanted all three aircraft of his NC Division to make the flight together.

The next day's forecast was indeed more encouraging. It was by no means the best, neither at Trepassey nor over the track to the Azores, but it was the best that the aerologists had been able to assemble since the NCs had taken off from Rockaway a week ago. At noontime Towers was pleased to see the *Edwards* steam through the narrows, come along-side and unload her precious cargo of Paragon propellers. The *Edwards* immediately got under way again, for St. John's; and before she was past Powles Head, machinist's mates were swarming over the NC boats, their wrenches hurrying around the bolt circles of the propeller hubs to remove the unreliable airscrews.

Just before noon Towers received word that the *NC-4* had been forced down off the coast of Nova Scotia. It looked as if the "lame duck" was not going to make it after all. Most of the destroyers had been on their stations between Newfoundland and the Azores for four days and the ones with stations closest to shore were now sailing to take their stations. The destroyers' fuel bunkers were good only for a week, even under low cruising conditions, and in a few more days the tanker *Maumee* would have to refuel them. But now there was word from the *Maumee* that she had a serious engine breakdown and was dead in the water while making repairs. Towers was squeezed between the deteriora-tion of the destroyers' fuel conditions and the capricious weather. There was fuel and reasonably good weather now; there might be neither in another day or two. He decided to go.

At 1700 the steam hoses were disconnected from the Libertys' water jackets, engines were started, the planes were cast off and began

102

taxiing around the harbor to warm up their engines. The day was still brilliantly clear, but there was a 30-knot westerly wind blowing across the harbor. The wind conditions were practically the same as those when the NCs arrived at Trepassey. But it was one thing to land a plane that had burned off most of its fuel at the end of a flight in these conditions, and a much tougher one to take off in the same conditions with a heavy load of fuel. To further complicate the situation, the sea was running heavy swells out of the south directly into the harbor. If in its takeoff run one of the airplanes went beyond the narrows and into the outer harbor, it would slam into a series of six-foot swells at high speed; combined with the treacherous crosswind, this would be disastrous. Earlier in the day, Towers, Bellinger, and Richardson had considered having the NCs towed out of the Trepassey Harbour, around Powles Point and into adjacent Mutton Bay, which offered a broad expanse of water that allowed takeoff directly into the wind. But the swells made this too hazardous. Takeoff would have to be made from the small inner harbor.

With Towers and the *NC-3* in the lead, the two flying boats taxied to the far north end of the harbor, slowed, and came about. Their engines roared to full power and sent them charging down the harbor in the midst of great clouds of spray. Ordinarily the spray would blow straight aft; but the westerly crosswind blew it across the aircraft, drenching their wings, carburetor intakes, and the pilots. In the *NC-3*, Towers stood high up in his bow cockpit, facing astern, in a futile effort to shield his pilots from some of the spray. For his troubles he only got soaking wet, and Richardson and McCulloch were only a little more dry. Less than halfway down the harbor the *NC-3* was planing on her step, but however hard Richardson struggled with his controls he could not wrench her hull free of the water's suction. As the harbor's narrows and the lines of whitecaps on the high swells beyond rushed toward him, Richardson chopped his throttles and the *NC-3* dropped her hull back into the water and wallowed among the waves.

Bellinger's experience in the *NC-1*, trying to take off in the *NC-3*'s wake, was equally as frustrating. At the end of their aborted takeoff runs, the two flying boats made a 180-degree turn and began to taxi back for another try. At this point the *NC-4* appeared in the sky overhead. Towers reluctantly faced reality. He and his pilots were soaking wet, and the same was probably true of Bellinger and his pilots. Even if they got into the air, it made no sense for them to spend a flight of 16 hours in the cold night air in wet clothing. The reward awaiting them in the Azores would probably be pneumonia. Towers told Richardson to head back to the *Aroostook* and signaled Bellinger to do the

103

same. The weather was supposed to be even better tomorrow. Then they could all fly together as NC Seaplane Division One.

After the *NC-4* had taxied up to her moorings astern of the *Aroostook* there was an exchange of congratulations and concern among the aircrews. The men of the *NC-3* and *NC-1* were pleased to have the *NC-4* back among them; the men of the *NC-4* were freshly aware of the problems in landing in Trepassey Harbour and were concerned by the other planes' inability to get off. However, they were nevertheless pleased by Towers' and Bellinger's inability to get off the water. Tomorrow would be different. Somehow, they would all get off together.

All night and through most of the next day machinist's mates swarmed over the *NC-4*. Chainfalls and stagings were rigged and the new engine installed at Chatham was removed to be replaced by a high compression model from the *Aroostook*'s stores. All of the *NC-4*'s propellers were removed and the new Paragon airscrews were installed; and the usual cleaning was given to fuel and oil strainers, the carburetors, and spark plugs.

Towers and his pilots spent the evening going over their fuel consumption figures again. The *NC-3* and *NC-1* had only 1,690 gallons (10,140 pounds) of fuel on board. Their ability to get off with this nominal load was puzzling. Then it was recalled that at Rockaway the NCs had always been refueled on their handling dollies ashore, and these held the aircraft level. In the water their hulls had a negative drag, floating with a nose-down attitude. The fuel gauges were near the after ends of the tanks, and with the airplane down by the bow they would indicate less fuel than was actually in the tanks. If each of the nine 200-gallon tanks was over-fuelled by only one gallon this amounted to 54 pounds; five gallons per tank was 270 pounds. Towers decided to reduce the fuel load of each airplane by 90 gallons (450 pounds). However, there is a touch of the abstract about the figures with which Towers was wrestling, because no one today knows (and perhaps no one even then knew) how many extra gallons were quietly pumped aboard by the machinists, as the saying goes, "for Mamma!"

All day Friday 16 May saw good weather reports continuing to flow into the *Aroostook*'s radioroom from the five meteorological destroyers between Trepassey and Corvo. These were the *Upshur, Walker, Meredith, Hopewell,* and *Philip* on stations 4, 8, 12, 16, and 20, respectively. The intelligence that they provided was supplemented by further data from the battleships *Utah, Florida,* and *Arkansas,* 600, 300, and 800 miles off to the north of the chain of destroyers, and the *Wyoming* and *Texas* on stations 300 miles off to the south. Aboard the *Aroostook*

Barratt and Gregg found that these data created a very favorable picture, and at 1400 they handed Towers a forecast that said "GO!" Their forecast was soon confirmed by a similar one received from the Weather Bureau in Washington.

In the morning, Richardson and some of the NC pilots had climbed into a motor launch and sailed down the harbor for a study of the seas running beyond the narrows. The view was not encouraging. Six-foot swells were still rolling up the outer harbor and the westerly wind was putting whitecaps on them. In spite of a good weather report, it looked as if they might not get off. But after lunch the wind died and the swells dissolved into choppiness. Then Barratt and Gregg appeared with their favorable forecast. Towers decided to go.

Shortly after 5:00 P.M.* the NC crews assembled on the *Aroostook*'s quarterdeck. Towers thanked Captain James H. Tomb for the ship's hospitality and enthusiastic cooperation. Tomb smiled, wished them all the best of luck, but made a bet with Towers that the 14-knot *Aroostook* would beat the airplanes to Plymouth. The NCs' men went to the gangway, saluted the officer of the deck, then the ensign at the ship's stern, and went down the ladder to the launches waiting to take them to their airplanes.

Standing in the navigator's cockpit in the bow of the *NC-3*, Towers waved a hand as the signal for Read and Bellinger and he shouted, "Let's *go!*" At his word the pilots started their engines—except the *NC-4*. Stone closed his starting switches, but nothing happened. The *NC-4* had had ignition problems during afternoon engine tests, but everyone was confident they had been squared away. Not so; and troubles such as this were becoming an old story with the *NC-4*.

Towers called across to Read, "How long?"

Read shouted back, "Ready in fifteen minutes, sir!"

Breese jumped the 8-volt ignition system into the 12-volt batteries of the starting motors, which put a plenty hot spark across the gaps. The forward centerline engine coughed to life with a belch of bluish smoke, and in a few seconds its twelve cylinders were rotating their propeller 1,300 times per minute. With the boost of an extra four volts the other engines followed suit. Meanwhile, the *NC-3* and *NC-1* had cast off from their buoys and were taxiing around the harbor to warm up their oil.

Towers gave the signal for takeoff.

---

* From here on in the text, local times will be cited in terms of A.M. and P.M. To keep the flight times straight, they will be cited in terms of GMT (Greenwich Mean Time), which was used throughout the flight in 1919.

105

Richardson opened his throttles wide and sent the *NC-3* plunging down the harbor, while he and McCulloch fought the westerly crosswind with their rudders and ailerons.

The *NC-4* roared off into the *NC-3's* wake, and Bellinger in the *NC-1* swung in behind the *NC-4* to bring up the rear.

As the *NC-4* lunged through the waves, Stone saw that Richardson was taking too long a run; he realized that Richardson could not get off the water before hitting the rougher water in the outer harbor. Read signaled Stone to keep going and at 5:37 he lifted the *NC-4* off the water and across Powle's Peninsula toward Mutton Bay. As the *NC-4* circled Trepassey her crew could see the *NC-3*, still on the water, turn around and taxi back for another try. Richardson tried again, but could not get off. Read expected the *NC-3* to make a third attempt, but instead she taxied back to the *Aroostook* where a launch came out to meet her.

Towers was still having weight problems. Before the *Aroostook's* launch had come alongside the *NC-3's* crew had torn up most of the hull's flooring. It was estimated that it was worth 50 pounds. More tools went over the side, along with spare oil and radiator water. Then Towers told Lavender to remove the CG-1104 emergency radio transmitter. Lavender protested; it weighed only 26 pounds and it was their only means of communication while they were on the water. Towers reminded Lavender that he was the commanding officer, the decision was his responsibility—and the radio went into the launch.

The bitter moment came when Towers had to tell Ensign Braxton Rhodes that he was going over the side as ballast. This came as no great surprise to Rhodes. Even before takeoff from Rockaway it was understood that, in a pinch, the sixth member of the crew might have to be left behind at Newfoundland. And he climbed into the launch. Less than 24 hours later Rhodes had good reason to regard this moment of expediency as a reprieve. In the hurried offloading of weights, someone accidentally put a five-gallon tin of drinking water over the side, perhaps thinking it was radiator water. It would soon be missed—along with the CG-1104 transmitter.

While the *NC-3* was lightening ship, the *NC-4* had made an 18-minute flight over Trepassey and environs to test out her new engine, and landed back in the harbor. More minutes passed while the *NC-4* and *NC-1* waited for the flagplane to get her weights squared away.

The *NC-3* finally got everything in order and taxied to the north end of the harbor, trailed by the *NC-4* and *NC-1*, and began her takeoff run.

At 6:00 P.M., 2200 GMT, after a takeoff run of 60 seconds, she was off, up and away.

106

The roar of a thousand voices cheering came across the water from the sailors lining the decks of the *Aroostook* and *Prairie,* echoed by 500 villagers and outport fishermen on the eastern shore. But they were all quickly drowned out by the ships' whistles and sirens.

The *NC-4* charged down the wake of her sistership and lifted off at 2205.

Bellinger ordered the *NC-1* about, and as the *NC-4* lifted clear Mitscher opened his throttles and took the *NC-1* roaring up to her takeoff speed. He lifted her off at 2210.[7]

Now the epoch-making event was really under way.

After becoming airborne the NCs did not circle the harbor nor attempt any flourishes; the aircraft were too heavily loaded with fuel for their pilots to think about such gestures, even if they felt that they could spare the fuel. They did well to get their unwieldly aircraft formed up in a ragged V-formation. With the warm, exaggerated light of the late day's sun gleaming off their golden wings, they flew off toward Mistaken Point, their point of departure for the Azores.

Back at Trepassey, Captain Tomb had already told his executive officer to get the anchors and buoys of the NCs' moorings raised from the harbor. Before the NCs were even halfway to the Azores, the *Aroostook* was under way for Plymouth to serve the seaplanes' needs in England. The *Prairie* remained at Trepassey as the NCs' communications center in Newfoundland and to refuel the fuel-hungry destroyers that would be steaming in from their ocean stations within the next 24 hours. Captain Tomb was confident that his wager with John Towers was a safe one; but it was one that he was more than willing to lose.

As the NCs faded into the darkness rising out of the southeast's horizon, hundreds of telegraph keys came down all over the world: *the flight was on!*

For more than a month the transatlantic flight had successfully competed with the Paris Peace Conference as the biggest story of 1919. In terms of front-page banner space and headlines the transatlantic flight preparations invariably beat out the old men who were muddling around at Versailles. Perhaps this was an omen of the future. The French wanted revenge; the British a balance of power; the United States wanted a ridiculously idealistic "Parliament of Man"; while the Russians—who were not represented at Versailles—wanted an equally ridiculous "World Revolution"; and the defeated Germans who pretended that they had never been defeated still wanted their arrogant "Place in the Sun." This was all too much for the exhausted and doddering nineteenth century men of Versailles to cope with, and they failed to give a modicum of peace to the second quarter of the twentieth century.

However, the adolescent airplane of 1919 grew to maturity by 1945, and the peace that the old men failed to achieve in 1919 has been enforced upon the world of the second half of the twentieth century by the airplane—through terror.

Such speculation was beyond the jaded minds of the men who ran the city rooms of the big American newspapers of 1919. Their job was to get the news on the street. And in 1919 the news did not go "on the air," it went *on the street.* Just as there were airplanes in 1919, but no airlines, there was radio but no broadcasting systems. Instead, big city newspapers put out a dozen or more editions a day, and an extraordinary news event called for an "Extra" edition. Even smalltown newspapers put out "Extras."

When the dit-dah-dit of the telegraph keys at Trepassey and St. John's transmitted word of the NCs' takeoff, editors all over the United States jumped out of their chairs. Coffee cups were, overturned, spittoons were knocked over, and cigars left to burn themselves out in their ashtrays as all hands rushed to prepare a new front page. The story was written, marked, set and cast; the presses were stopped, the new plates locked onto the rollers, and the big machines were set rolling again to run out a great web of paper chopped into pages and stuffed into folds with a front page that shouted: NAVY NC PLANES FLY TO AZORES. That they had not gotten there was immaterial. The truth might be straightened out in the next edition.

The 5:00 A.M. "Extra" of the conservative *New York Times* had a three-line banner eight columns wide that declared:

> ALL THREE SEAPLANES NEARING AZORES;
> NC-4 WAS 800 MILES OUT AT 3:06 THIS MORNING;
> HARTMAN APPEALS TO POPE TO SAVE GERMANY

This was pretty sober treatment as compared to the banners of most newspapers.

As the newspapers came off the presses they were thrust into the eager, competitive hands of a hundred or more tough, scruffy adolescent newsboys who rushed out into the streets shouting "Extra! Extra! Navy fliers cross Atlantic!" The price of their product was two or three cents.

The cry of "Extra! Extra!" was 1919's equivalent of today's "we interrupt this program for an important news bulletin ..." It told the man on the street that something BIG had happened. And there was no air conditioning in 1919, so on any day in May the windows of most office buildings would be open to hear the cries of the newsboys. Hundreds, then thousands of persons would rush forward with their pennies.

108

For the outlying areas of the city, bundles of newspapers were hustled aboard horse-drawn wagons (no fleets of trucks yet) for distribution in Brooklyn, Queens, and the Bronx, or Chicago's North Side and Hyde Park. In 1919, 1,600 mechanical horses lifted each of the NCs off across the Atlantic; but the ultimate means of news dissemination was by means of boypower and vehicles drawn by one horsepower.

While the world had not yet fully awakened to the beginning of the transatlantic flight, the heavily loaded NCs were flying low across the seas off Newfoundland. An aircraft compresses a wedge shaped "cushion" of air between its wings and the surface of the earth when flying at very low altitudes which creates what has come to be called a "ground effect." An aircraft can exploit ground effect either to save fuel or to maintain control of a heavily loaded or underpowered aircraft. Ground effect was not understood as such in 1919, but pilots knew from experience that a heavily loaded airplane should be kept near the surface after takeoff. When the NCs reached Mistaken Point, their point of departure from Newfoundland, they were flying at less than 100 feet.

When New York City's presses were beginning to roll out their first "Extra," the NC boats were almost a hundred miles out over the dark Atlantic. The destroyer Greer on Station 1 came and went, and as they flew past the Greer at less than masthead height, word of their passing was radioed on down the line.

Commander Raymond A. Spruance, commanding officer of the Aaron Ward on Station 2, gave a nod to his executive officer and told him to check the ship's preparations for the airplanes. Spruance knew that this young lieutenant from Oklahoma was quite an aviation enthusiast. While serving aboard the old airplane-carrying armored cruiser North Carolina in 1917 he had applied for flight training, but had been talked out of it by Captain Mark Bristol. But Spruance knew that his exec had not given up on aviation. The lieutenant's name was Joseph J. "Jocko" Clark.

Spruance told the officer of the deck to put the ship on course and the Aaron Ward was swung around to a heading that pointed her bows toward the Buchanan, 50 miles away on Station 3. Floodlights were turned on the eight-foot-tall numeral "2" on the Aaron Ward's fantail, while on the bridge the quartermaster of the watch switched on the ship's searchlight and turned its milky beam into the wind. The officer of the deck told the gunnery officer to begin the firing of starshells from the ship's 3-inch gun. As the starshells burst at 10,000 feet, the Atlantic was bathed in the ghostly white light of their burning magnesium. When the NCs radioed the Aaron Ward that her pyrotechnics were seen, the firing of starshells was secured and all eyes on board

109

scanned the northwest. A few minutes later the dim lights of the aircraft were spotted; and then the three flying boats roared by, the sounds of their engines almost drowned out by the *Aaron Ward's* whistle and siren. Spruance had his radio officer notify the *Buchanan* that the NCs had passed and were on their way, and on board the *Buchanan* all hands jumped to their stations to repeat the *Aaron Ward's* evolutions.

As the NCs roared over his ship at masthead height this evening, the thoughtful Spruance may well have been pondering the future of naval aviation. He was not an aviator, nor did he ever become one; but it was he who directed United States Naval Aviation to two of its greatest victories almost a quarter of a century later. It was Rear Admiral Raymond Spruance's Task Force 16 that destroyed the Japanese carrier fleet at the Battle of Midway, 4-6 June 1942, a work in which he was assisted by Captain Marc A. Mitscher, commanding officer of the carrier *Hornet*. On this night in 1919 Mitscher was on his way toward Station 3, wrestling with the controls of the NC-1.

Between this night in 1919 and others twenty-three years later there occurred a curious reversal of positions. On this night it was Spruance who was providing support for Towers and his men in the NCs. On the eve of Midway it was Vice Admiral Towers who had created Spruance's support, first as Chief of the Bureau of Aeronautics (1939-1942), and then as Commander Air Force, U.S. Pacific. And it would be Albert C. Read in the *NC-4* who, as commanding officer of the Pensacola air station during 1940-1942, supplied Spruance with most of the pilots who manned his planes during the fateful days of 4-6 June 1942.

What is more, two years later during the Battle of the Philippine Sea, 19-20 June 1944, Rear Admiral J. J. "Jocko" Clark, long since having won the golden wings of a naval aviator, would be commanding Task Force 58.1 of Admiral Spruance's formidable Fifth Fleet. On this exciting night of 1919, however, all these things were a long way off in an unforseeable future. And this night no one was trying to plumb the future any farther than the safe arrival of the NCs in the Azores—and Lisbon.

Aboard the NCs the flight was almost going like clockwork: the glow of starshell on the horizon ahead, acknowledgment by radio, the brightly lighted ship coming into sight with its number spread on the fantail, the upturned faces and waving hands that crowded the decks, the faint sounds of a whistle and siren as they flew by and a good luck message over the radio—then darkness, with another sudden glow of starshell dead ahead. And so it went through the night. Ironically, the NCs' navigational difficulties did not develop until daylight.

110

As the NCs overflew the *Aaron Ward* they were already having minor problems. Shortly after sunset, Read in the *NC-4* found that he was having difficulty keeping track of the *NC-3* ahead of him. Towers had not yet turned on his navigation lights. The *NC-4*'s lights had been burning since sunset at 2300 and Read could see the lights of Bellinger's *NC-1* straggling behind. The NCs had a single white light on the leading edge of the upper wing's center spar and the standard red and green lights on the port and starboard outboard wing struts. Stone and Hinton had difficulties in holding the *NC-4* down to the speed of the *NC-3*, and periodically they were unpleasantly surprised to see the *NC-3*'s tail assembly or her starboard wingtips shape up alarmingly out of the gloom. No one aboard the *NC-4* liked this. Read had Rodd raise the *NC-3* on the radio and asked Towers to turn on his lights. Lavender's radio key replied that the lights were "on" but were not working.

The *NC-3*'s lighting circuits had never been quite right; during the previous day's attempted takeoff they had become drenched with spray and after that everything was wrong with them. On this evening the navigation lights had been turned on for only a few minutes when the circuit went out and a few minutes later the lighting circuits inside the hull also failed. The indicating needles and the numbers of the pilots' instrument panel were luminous, but Richardson and McCulloch had to revive their luminosity about every five minutes with a flashlight. No one had any experience in flying the NC boats at night. In even slightly rough air it could be a difficult enough job in broad daylight to fly the big and relatively underpowered airplane on an even keel; but with the instrument panel virtually blacked out, the job teetered on the brink of the impossible.

The *NC-3*'s blackout continued to harass Stone and Hinton, who complained to Read. The *NC-4* had difficulty enough in flying at the *NC-3*'s slower speed without her pilots having to be on the watch against a collision. Read decided that the last thing a first transatlantic flight needed was a mid-air collision; the *NC-4* had thus far made most of the flight by herself and Read was confident that she could go it alone to the Azores. In any case, the three airplanes would probably rediscover one another at daylight. He told Stone to steer clear of the *NC-3* and forget formation flying.

Shortly after 2353 the dim shape of the *NC-3* was lost in the dark; but less than an hour later Stone was surprised to see her phantomlike mass reappear close aboard off the *NC-4*'s port side. This was too close for Read. He ordered a hard turn away to the right and Stone was pleased to comply. This was the last the *NC-4* saw of her sister ship until at Ponta Delgada four days later.

111

In the bow cockpit of the *NC-1* Pat Bellinger squinted into the wind at the black, star-filled sky ahead where the *NC-3* had melted away in the night. He could see the lights of the *NC-4*, but hard as he might have Mitscher and Barrin flog their four Liberty engines he knew that they had little chance of catching up. Bellinger might well have been amused at the newspaper press calling the *NC-4* the "lame duck." The *NC-4* had her troubles, but they were the troubles of any brand new aircraft. Newspaper reporters could not be supposed to know this. If anyone was flying a "lame duck" it was Bellinger and his crew. The *NC-1* was not only the oldest of the three airplanes, but she had originally been built and flown as a trimotor and altered to her four-engine configuration; she had been beaten up by a storm and almost destroyed by fire. What is more, since takeoff from Rockaway she had been flying on the wings of the *NC-2;* one of them had not been rigged correctly, and this was why the *NC-1* was dragging behind. For that matter, the *NC-1* was no longer the *NC-1* at all; she was really the *NC-1½!*

In spite of her straggling, all was well on board the *NC-1*. With the *NC-3* lost in the night and the *NC-4*'s lights getting dimmer as she drew away ahead, Bellinger and his crew became convinced that they would be making their flight to the Azores alone. But as Mitscher and Barrin were peering ahead, looking for the destroyer *Boggs* on Station 5, they were startled by a light flashing at them from almost dead ahead. It was Lloyd Moore in the after hatch of the unlighted *NC-3*, waving a flashlight to warn them away from a collision! Mitscher threw the *NC-1*'s controls hard over and turned away. After this near miss, all three aircraft proceeded independently.

A few miles ahead of the *NC-3* and *NC-1*, all was well on board the *NC-4*. The air was rough, the plane sometimes very difficult to handle, and Stone and Hinton spelled each other on the controls every 30 minutes. Down inside the hull Breese and Rhoads took turns at watching their instruments and the fuel overflow from the gravity tank. When the overflow became irregular they switched the fuel pump's suction to another main tank, which put another 200 gallons at the disposal of the four hungry Libertys. Each tank was good for about two and one-half hours. Breese and Rhoads took turns watching their instruments, otherwise sacking out on a pile of lifejackets spread on the deck for short snatches of sleep. Meanwhile, they were pleased to see their oil pressure needles riding at a steady 35 to 40 pounds. After so many difficulties between Rockaway and Trepassey they liked to believe that a run of good luck was with them at last.

The busiest man aboard the *NC-4* was Herbert C. Rodd who was tucked away in the hull's after compartment, crowded against his radio set and sending key. Born in Cleveland, Ohio, Rodd had become a radio hobbyist at an early age and in 1912 went to work for the Marconi Company as a radio operator aboard the ultimately ill-fated *Eastland,* a passenger ship that cruised the Great Lakes. On the gale-swept night of 10 November 1914, while chief operator aboard the *Lakeland,* Rodd became an "SOS celebrity" when the ship ran aground near Alpena, Michigan. Standing by his radio key, he guided a salvage tug through the snow-filled night which resulted in the *Lakeland* being pulled off the rocks before she was holed too badly, and the ship was towed safely into Port Huron.

Rodd was a shoreside operator of Marconi in Detroit when the United States entered the war. He joined the Navy and was immediately rated as an electrician's mate first class and was promoted to chief petty officer shortly thereafter. Most of his wartime duty was in the radio laboratory at the Great Lakes Naval Station; but after being commissioned as an ensign in the autumn of 1918 he was ordered to Norfolk, where he became involved with aircraft radio. Rodd's unusual resourcefulness with radio resulted in his being selected for the NC flight. On this night above the Atlantic, he was reflecting on how he anticipated getting a few letters written during this long leg of the flight, but the flood of dit-dah-dits in his headphones kept him tied to his key. A curious world wanted to talk with him and he enjoyed their company in his cramped cubicle of mahogany and spruce all the way to the Azores. During the *NC-4*'s fifteen hours between Trepassey and Horta, the only moments Rodd's fist was idle on his sending key were those in which he had to pause to receive.

Aside from Read, the aircraft commander and navigator, Rodd was the only man on board who had to be alert at all times. However, this was no problem for him because he not only enjoyed his work, he was absolutely absorbed by it. Hunched over the knobs of his radio, sending, receiving, or taking radio bearings, it was all wonderful to Herbert Rodd. He was especially pleased by the performance of his set as it had not been installed in the *NC-4* until 0330 on 6 May and he had been able to give it only one in-flight test on the seventh, the day before the flight took off from Rockaway.

Herbert Rodd was more than just a radio operator; he was not only the voice and ears of the *NC-4,* but as a result of the remarkable performance he was able to work out of his radio direction finder, he also proved to be the airplane's "eyes."

The *NC-3* and *NC-1* complained of considerable difficulties in getting even mediocre results from their radio direction-finding (RDF) sets. They felt fortunate to pick up a radio bearing signal transmitted from a station only 15 miles away. This was because of the electrical interference created by the ignition systems of the centerline tandem engines which were almost directly above the radio compartment. The shielding to prevent engine ignition systems from interfering with aircraft radios was a development that was not in hand until the latter part of the 1920s. The naked eye could see 15 miles from an altitude of 1,000 feet in even halfway decent visibility, so the RDF sets aboard the *NC-3* and *NC-1* were virtually useless. Herbert Rodd, however, was able to manipulate his RDF set to overcome most of the engines' interference. He coaxed his set to reach out for radio bearings 50 miles distant, which was the set's normal range; and by some means he was able to tease the set to obtain bearings at even greater ranges.

As the *NC-4* overflew the *Upshur* on Station 3, Rodd was pleasantly surprised to pick up a radio bearing on the *Crosby* 350 miles away on Station 10. This was probably owed to some freak atmospheric condition because nothing similar to it happened again during the flight. However, there is no question that Rodd was able to get an extraordinary performance out of the *NC-4's* RDF set.

At 0120 as the *NC-4* approached the glow of starshells floating over the *Boggs* on Station 5, Rhoads picked up the airplane's Aldis lamp and used it to inspect the outboard engines. An Aldis is supposed to be used for signaling, but the *NC-4's* engineers found its brilliant beam more useful for inspecting the wings, tail and engines at night. Rhoads moved its bright pinpoint spot over the propellers' arcs, along the engine cowls, their exhaust stacks, and the copper fuel lines leading to the engines, looking for the dark streaks of an oil leak or a glistening ribbon trailing aft that would betray leaking radiator water or fuel. An oil or coolant leak would eventually show itself by an increase in temperature and a drop in pressure on their gauges inside the hull, but not a fuel leak.

It was a fuel leak that everyone quietly dreaded. If not immediately detected, its first notice would be a sheet of orange flames when the hot engine exhaust ignited the vaporizing gasoline. Rhoads switched off the Aldis and dropped back down inside the after hatch. All was well.

At about 0030 the moon came up directly ahead. It was a huge thing, almost blood red, distorted and divided into three parts by the clouds fringing the horizons. As the moon rose higher, shrinking in size and transforming itself into a cold white disc, its pale light was welcomed aboard the *NC-4* and *NC-1*. It helped Read, Bellinger and their pilots to see the unlighted *NC-3* in case she wandered close to their tracks.

Aboard the *NC-3*, however, the moonlight served to further

114

complicate matters for Richardson and McCulloch. At first they welcomed the moon as a partial solution to their lighting problems. But during the first hour after moonrise, while the great orange disc loitered over the horizon, its soft exotic light only served to intensify the haze on the horizon, which made it almost impossible to determine if the *NC-3*'s wings were level. Until the moon rose well clear of the horizon Richardson and McCulloch had to fly wholly by instruments, with one man handling the controls and the other holding a flashlight beam on the instrument panel. Even as the moon climbed into the sky they discovered that its cold light only served to deepen the shadows in their cockpit, making the instrument panel harder than ever to read. Their flight continued by flashlight.

The bursts of starshells, the searchlight beams to windward, and the ships with their brightly lighted numbers came and went below. The night passed. At 0545, a few miles beyond the *Crosby* on Station 10, the sky began to pale in the east. At 0600 Rodd in the *NC-4* took radio bearings on signals from the ships on Stations 12, 13, 14, 15, 16, and 17. The signal from the *Stockton* on Station 17 was faint; but that from the *Hopewell* on Station 16, 200 miles away, Rodd was surprised to find very strong.

At 0645, from his perch in the *NC-4*'s bow, Read spied a ship below. At first he believed that she was a destroyer; but she was not making smoke, as the destroyers were supposed to do as the planes approached during daylight. Closer inspection showed her to be a merchant ship.

There was a hazard here in the NCs becoming overly dependent upon pilotage from destroyer to destroyer and not checking the destroyers' positions with their own navigation. During the night there was no difficulty in identifying the station ships; no other ships were about to fire off several rounds of heavy caliber pyrotechnics and have their searchlights pointed into the wind. During daylight, however, the station ships were not required to fire starshells and their searchlights were useless; their only means of marking their stations was by making heavy smoke as the aircraft approached. All ships make smoke from time to time, depending upon the talents of the fireman on watch; and in 1919, when most ships were still coal burners, they were highly disposed to making smoke. What is more, as dawn spread across the Atlantic the NCs were beginning to cross one of the principal transatlantic steamer lanes, and most ships tend to "blow tubes" at some hour between sunrise and eight o'clock in the morning. The operation of blowing tubes consists of sending jets of steam against the tubes in the ship's boiler to blow away the soot that has accumulated during the past twelve hours;

115

and all that soot blowing up the stack results in some very heavy smoke from the funnel. In sum, at this critical hour in the morning it would be easy for the NCs to mistake a passing ship for one of their station ships, especially if the visibility was poor. And the visibility was bad.

This was perhaps the greatest irony of the NC flight. The three airplanes surmounted the difficulties of their night flight from New-foundland to the Azores—which was imagined to be the most difficult—with relative ease. Their most serious problems came with the dawn, when the flight should have been an easy downhill run to the Azores made in broad daylight.

But there was nothing easy about it.

And there was precious little daylight.

116

Washington Times, 31 May 1919

Read, Rodd, Radio
—and Horta

As a vague daylight hinted at the morning of 17 May, it soon became obvious that immediately northeast of the Azores it was going to be a very gray day. At about 0700 Herbert Rodd suddenly felt himself becoming very sleepy so he got up and put his head out of the after hatch for a few minutes where the cold slipstream blew away his grogginess. Rhoads, who had been spread-eagled in sleep on the pile of lifejackets, rolled over to wakefulness, and Rodd assured him that everything on the engines looked okay. Back at his radio set, Rodd talked awhile with Harry Sadenwater at the key of the *NC-1*. Between replying to outside calls, the two radio operators had been keeping up a steady chit-chat all night. Sadenwater remarked that he was eating a sandwich which reminded Rodd that he was hungry. He asked Rhoads to see what there was left to eat. Rhoads returned with a sandwich and a thermos of coffee; but Rodd found the sandwich tasteless and the coffee stone cold.

By 0745 the *NC-4* had overflown the *Maddox* on Station 15. A few minutes later a dark wall of clouds full of rain appeared ahead. Read changed course in an effort to fly around it, but instead of rain he found that the clouds were degenerating into fog and that it was moving along the same track as the airplane. Visibility became almost zero, but within 30 minutes it cleared slightly and at 0830 the dim shape of the *Hopewell* on Station 16 passed below.

All was going according to plan. So far, so good—except for a disturbing increase in fog. There were only five more ships, another 250 miles, and then the island of Corvo would be in sight. But then the weather suddenly closed in on the *NC-4* and she was flying through a small, damp world of dirty gray in which the pilots could barely see their wingtips.

While the *NC-4* was leaving the *Hopewell* behind at Station 16, Bellinger in the *NC-1* was peering into the morning's haze to identify the *Cowell* on Station 14. All was well on board the *NC-1*. The *Maddox*,

Hopewell, and *Stockton* were overflown in mechanical 1-2-3 order and by 1050 Bellinger was straining his eyes against the deteriorating visibility, looking for the *Craven* on Station 18. Down in the *NC-1's* radio compartment, Harry Sadenwater was having no luck with his RDF set. While he, Lavender, and Rodd had practiced with the RDF set aboard the *NC-2T* back at Rockaway it had worked very well and they had obtained bearings at 40, 50 and even 60 miles. But with the new NC configuration and with the engines almost on top of his radio compartment he felt lucky to obtain RDF bearings at ten miles. This was of precious little use with the *NC-1* flying at almost 90 miles per hour because within six minutes of obtaining the bearing the *NC-1* had overflown the transmitting ship, assuming that the ship was within a ten-mile range in the first place. As long as the *NC-1's* engines were operating her RDF set was virtually useless.

As the visibility became thicker, Bellinger became concerned. All the station ships thus far had been almost directly overflown; but the *Stockton* was sighted 15 miles away off to the north. Bellinger could not be sure if the destroyer was off station or if the *NC-1* was off course, and with the weather as thick as it was it was hopeless to attempt a navigation sight. As Bellinger stared into the damp air whipping at his face, waiting for the shape of the *Dent* on Station 19 to appear on the gray seas below, the world around him suddenly lapsed into nothingness. *Fog!* Thick fog at that. Turning around in his cockpit he could barely see the engines 12 feet aft; the *NC-1's* wingtips and the after end of her hull were completely obscured.

In the pilots' cockpits, Mitscher and Barrin glued their eyes to their instruments. Their first concern was to hold the *NC-1* in level flight and their second was to keep her on her course. Their "instruments" for blind flying consisted of no more than liquid inclinometers, which were sluggish to say the least; but their sluggishness was less critical than the tendency of their bubbles to ooze back and forth and hunt over the length of their tubes in critical moments. By the time the bubbles quieted down to provide a reliable reading there was usually no longer any need of watching them. In 1919 there was not yet a reliable turn-and-bank indicator, much less an artificial horizon that would be familiar to the 1920s.

With only a slippery bubble for reference, over- or under-control by the pilots was commonplace, and the big clumsy airplane tended to yaw all over the sky and slip off into spiral dives from which recovery was difficult. The *NC-1* went seriously out of control twice, while flying in the fog on "instruments." Each time after the pilots had regained control, the plane had come about almost 180 degrees and was on a course back to Newfoundland. In the fog, it was no small job to bring the *NC-1* around through another 180 degrees and get her pointed back at the Azores.

Bellinger hoped that such terribly thick fog would be short-lived, but he was disappointed. He was sure that there were clear skies at a higher altitude, but he wanted to remain close to the surface so he would not miss the *Craven;* or, if he missed her, then the *Dent* on Station 19. But the strain on his pilots proved to be too great and he finally gave them permission to climb out of the soup. The *NC-1* topped the fog at 2,500 feet where the sun shone down on a great, lumpy cloudscape that rolled off as far as the eye could see.

The *NC-1's* troubles were by no means over; as they cruised along above the fog layer, Bellinger soon realized the fog tops were rising. Meanwhile, the *Craven* and the *Dent* were sliding by unseen somewhere in the gloom below, and the chances of their seeing the *Philip* on Station 20 seemed tenuous at best. At 1150 Bellinger tried taking a sunline with his sextant, but with the plane lurching around, the primitive bubble sextant was difficult to use. When he finally got a sight and worked it out to a line of position he refused to trust it. Meanwhile, the *NC-1* was roaring on across the lumpy gray carpet that obscured the sea.

By 1250 the *NC-1* had not seen the sea for two hours. This was much too long. Bellinger decided to drop down through the cloud layer with the hope that there might be a ceiling of at least 100 feet above the surface. His wildest hope was that after they broke out under the ceiling they would be looking at the four-stacked silhouette of one of the station ships. Their letdown was from 3,200 feet, and it was not until they were about 75 feet above the waves that they broke into the clear. And it was none too clear. Visibility was about a half mile and it was interrupted by patches of fog. This was of less concern than what met their eyes: there was no destroyer in sight—only miles of dull blue swells that rolled off into a gray horizon.

Two hours had passed since the *NC-1* missed sighting the *Craven* at Station 18. By this time Bellinger reckoned that they were somewhere in the vicinity of the *Philip* or the *Waters* on Stations 20 and 21. But if he was east or west of the line between the two destroyers he did not know. Somewhere out in the fog ahead were the destroyers and also the mountains of Corvo and Flores. The tallest masts on the destroyers were barely 90 feet tall—but Monte Gordo on the island of Corvo reached up 2,549 feet and Morro Grande on Flores was 3,090 feet tall. To see either of these suddenly pop out of the fog ahead could be disastrous.

Bellinger asked Christensen for the word on their fuel situation.

121

The chief machinist summed it up in terms of 200 gallons. This was about two and one-half hours' flying time, which was worth 225 miles. So there was fuel enough. The problem was that they did not know in which direction to use their fuel. They were lost.

Bellinger's only resource was Sadenwater's RDF set, which was useless in the air as long as the *NC-1*'s ignition systems were blanketing its reception. But if they landed on the water and secured the engines, then Sadenwater should be able to get some bearings. They could be back in the air for Horta or Ponta Delgada within 30 minutes of alighting.

Bellinger decided to go down.

At 1300 he told Sadenwater to notify all station vessels that they were landing in the fog somewhere near Station 21; he wanted all nearby ships to start transmitting radio bearing signals.

The sea appeared to be running with long, oily swells and held the promise of an easy landing. Marc Mitscher eased the *NC-1* down across the swells and put her keel into the seas at 1310. Her initial touchdown was good, but then she porpoised dangerously over two crests and stopped suddenly as her nose went down into a trough and plunged itself into the wall of a rising swell.

The last half of the landing was rough, but a careful examination of the *NC-1*'s wings, wingtip floats, and hull showed no damage. The engines were secured and Sadenwater set about getting his radio bearings.

Meanwhile, Bellinger and Mitscher began studying the seas running around them and they became uneasy. By softening the shadows on the sea, the fog had made the swells appear smaller than they were. From the air they appeared to be only 10 feet; on the surface they were no less than 20 feet—and with a 20-knot crosswind blowing through their troughs.

The *NC-1* was down, and she was going to stay down for awhile. Bellinger, Mitscher, and Barrin were sure that she was not going to become airborne again until the sea and wind conditions changed.

The *NC-3*'s troubles also came with the dawn. Through most of the night she had been flying between a mountainous terrain of cloud that blanketed the ocean and a ceiling of haze that by daylight transformed itself into a leaden overcast. Her flying above the cloud layer did not prevent her from fixing the destroyers because their starshells were fused to burst at 10,000 feet.

During the night the rising cloud tops kept driving Richardson to take the *NC-3* higher, and by dawn she was cruising at 4,300 feet. The *Bush* on Station 13 was overflown at 0623 when starshell from the

Cowell on Station 14 was already in sight. The clouds were thickening, the holes that revealed the sea below were becoming fewer, and the overcast was darkening, so Towers decided to check his heading with a close aboard sighting of the *Cowell*. A hole was found in the clouds and Richardson spiraled the big flying boat down through it in a series of wide, lazy circles.

According to Richardson, they flew out under the ceiling at 2,000 feet to find themselves in a strange, half-lighted room of enormous size, surrounded by a bright, silvery rim hung with patches of fog and a smattering of rain squalls. But the *Cowell*—whose starshell they had seen bursting only a few minutes before—was nowhere in sight.

Towers ordered the *NC-3* held to her course while Richardson jinked the big airplane around the curtains of rain and wads of fog that cluttered the cavernous space beneath the gray ceiling. The *Cowell* had evidently been passed, somehow; now they were looking for the *Maddox* on Station 15, which should appear out of the gloom any minute.

The silhouette of a destroyer was sighted on the horizon about 15 miles off to the south. Towers took it to be the *Maddox*, but her position surprised and disturbed him. He had been keeping the *NC-3*'s track parallel to the line of destroyers, but about a mile or two south of them. Finding himself north of the *Maddox*—and 15 miles north at that— meant that the wind must have picked up and had blown the *NC-3* off her track to a course diverging to the north. If Towers held to his course he was sure that they would never sight the *Hopewell* on Station 16, much less any of the other station vessels. To get back on the track of the station ships, Towers changed course 20 degrees to the south, expecting that this would bring the *NC-3* within sight of the *Hopewell* and directly over the *Stockton* on Station 17.

The ship that Towers identified as the *Maddox* was in fact the old cruiser *Marblehead* which was en route between Europe and the United States. The *Marblehead* had a silhouette that at a great distance could be mistaken for a flush-deck, four-piper destroyer. At this moment the *Maddox* was indeed somewhere directly ahead of the *NC-3*'s track, but shrouded by haze and rain. When Towers thus "corrected" his course with a change of 20 degrees to the south, he was in fact turning away from the chain of station vessels.

Now the *NC-3* was really off course.

The *NC-3* plunged on through the haze, fog and rain. Flying at 85 miles per hour and with the station ships 50 miles apart, she should have been overflying one of them about every 30 minutes. But an hour passed without a ship of any description being sighted.

At 0930 Towers had Lavender put out a general call to the

123

station ships that he was off course somewhere between the *Stockton* and the *Craven,* and requested them to transmit radio bearings and send up starshells. The starshell could have no illuminating effect, but it would create a lingering smudge in the sky.

The *NC-3*'s RDF set had an effective range of only 15 to 20 miles; beyond that everything was blotted out by the interference created by the engines' ignitions. There was a chance, however, that the poor visibility might be hiding a ship that was within the RDF's range; and there was a chance that freak atmospheric conditions might permit the instrument to penetrate the interference and reach out to its normal range of 50 miles. These were less chances than hopes; but unknown to the men of the *NC-3* their hopes of reestablishing visual or RDF contact with the surface ships were absolutely nil.

The station ships received only half of the message transmitted by Lavender. All they knew was that the *NC-3* was off course between Stations 17 and 18 and that she wanted radio bearing signals sent. After Lavender got off this part of his message, vibrations in the *NC-3* shook loose the radio generator's ground connection. This went unnoticed, and for the next four hours Lavender pounded his transmission key with increasing frustration. Half the Navy was out there, but nobody seemed to be listening to him. In fact, nobody could hear him.

The *NC-3* was now voiceless, and with the thick weather she was almost sightless. At 1100 she temporarily lost one of her pilots when Richardson dazedly passed the controls to McCulloch and collapsed from exhaustion. During most of the thirteen hours since they had left Trepassey, Richardson had been fighting the *NC-3*'s eleven tons through the air. Trying to keep this big sluggish airplane on an even keel through the night by flashlight, and in a swirling, amorphous world of cloud and rain since daylight, using the primitive instruments aboard the *NC-3,* was nerve-wracking and physically exhausting labor. Richardson slipped out of his seat and crawled down into the nose compartment where Towers gave him a dose of strychnine. In 1919 benzedrine, not to mention all the other "speed" drugs, had not yet come into use; instead, strychnine (ordinarily thought of as a poison) was administered in small doses to achieve a similar effect. Richardson was roused from his grogginess for awhile; but half an hour later Towers had to administer a second dose. Then he finally snapped back into shape, climbed up into his seat, and took the controls back from McCulloch.

Clouds above and fog tops below continued to crowd the *NC-3*'s passage. By 1200 Richardson was snaking the *NC-3* through a gray and white tunnel across the sky that wound around to left and right, up and down. Where blank walls appeared dead ahead there was no choice but to plunge through and hope that daylight would appear shortly on the other side.

At 1305 the sun appeared for a few minutes. Towers grabbed up his bubble sextant and got a sunline. A sunsight only establishes latitude; but this was one thing Towers wanted very much to know: how far south they were. When Towers worked out his line of position he discovered that it ran off to the northeast, directly through the island of Pico. With the *NC-3* bouncing around and the sextant's bubble "pumping" in its glass, Towers knew that his line of position could only be a close approximation. But the sun was gone before he could take another sight to check the first. Towers nevertheless ordered a 60-degree turn to the north. By flying up his line of position they could at least expect to sight the 7,600-foot peak that towered over Pico.

A few minutes later, Boatswain Lloyd R. Moore, the *NC-3's* engineer, crawled out from between the forward nest of fuel tanks. He told Towers that they had barely two hours of fuel remaining.

Two hours of fuel made for only about 170 miles of flight in an NC boat. Towers talked over the situation with Richardson and Mc-Culloch. If they landed on the sea they could stop the engines and get some reliable RDF bearings. If the sun came out, a reliable sunsight could be had.

Towers decided to take the *NC-3* down.

Richardson swung the *NC-3* around in a long, lazy arc to bring her around into the wind, and then eased her down through a series of thin curtains of fog until she was skimming the surface. The long and deep slate gray swells were not inviting; but they looked no worse than the sea in which Richardson had landed the *NC-1* off Barnegat. It could be done.

As the *NC-3* mushed through the air toward touchdown, Towers and his pilots suddenly realized that the sea was too rough—perhaps for landing, and certainly for taking off again. But their rate of sink was too great, and even in a light condition an NC's rate of climb was slow. If they shoved their throttles wide open to regain the air, they risked slamming into a wave at full power, which would surely knock the bottom out of their hull. They were committed.

Meanwhile, in the *NC-3's* after end, Lavender was rattling his radio key, calling to anyone who might be listening to tell them that the *NC-3* was landing to take radio bearings, and he gave their approximate position.

Everyone was listening for some word from the *NC-3*—aboard the ocean station vessels, aboard the *Columbia* at Horta, the *Melville* at Ponta Delgada, and all merchant ships in the area that had radios. But

125

no one could hear Lavender's messages. The *NC-3*'s generator cable was still adrift, which rendered her mute.

The *NC-3*'s keel sliced into the crest of a wave, her hull sank into it, then bounced off, zoomed across the following trough and touched down on the crest of the next wave. For a moment the flying boat seemed to come to rest, but the crest suddenly dropped out from under her. The *NC-3* still had some forward momentum and a bit of lift under her wings, and these carried her directly into the face of the next oncoming wave, which slammed down on her with a terrific force. The *NC-3*'s nose promptly surfaced, the wave gently lifted her over its crest and she skidded down the other side into its trough. The time was 1330. It was all over.

The *NC-4* was finding the weather no better; after overflying the unseen *Stockton* on Station 17 at 0845, the little visibility there was quickly degenerated into fog. From his perch in the *NC-4*'s nose, Read could not see his wingtips. They would have to climb above it, and Read motioned to Stone to take the plane up. But Stone had become momentarily disoriented in their formless gray world. A wing dropped. The big plane began to swing around in a spiral. Read felt the wind on his face quicken and he knew that they were slipping off into a spiral dive.

In the cockpit, Stone watched his altimeter slowly unwind and the bubbles in his inclinometers ooze back and forth across a quarter of their tubes where they shouldn't be. Occasional glimpses of the sun, which showed as a white spot in the fog, indicated that the plane was in a sharp turn. Otherwise, there were no external reference points; and the compass spun around crazily like a roulette wheel. Stone gradually regained control of the airplane; the altimeter steadied at 1,200 feet, and he eased back on his control column to start the *NC-4* climbing.

A soft pressure against the soles of his shoes told Read that they were climbing—out of this soft, damp realm of nothingness toward a world of some visibility. In a few minutes the *NC-4* broke into the clear and all hands were pleased and relieved by the glare of sunlight on the yellow wings. They were now cruising above a great sea of clouds. But the position of the sun suggested that they were flying in a wrong direction; and after their compasses quieted down it became clear that the *NC-4* was on a heading for New York!

Rodd got busy on his radio key requesting radio bearings while Read worked out a new course. While the *NC-4* was whirling around through the fog Rodd had missed the *Craven* on Station 18 reporting their passage; but the *Dent* on Station 19 informed him that they had overflown the *Craven* at 0945. By 1030 Rodd's radio bearings indicated that they were near the *Dent*, and the destroyer's radio operator told

126

him that although they could not see the *NC-4*, her engines could be heard somewhere up in the fog, off the ship's port bow.

Rodd was about to ask for more radio bearings when Read crawled out from between the fuel tanks. The NCs had an intercom circuit to link the navigator's cockpit in the bow with the pilots and the radio compartment, and when the NCs were flying very close together this circuit even allowed communications among the airplanes. It worked well aboard the *NC-3*, indifferently with the *NC-1*, and not at all aboard the *NC-4*. When Read wanted to talk with his pilots he had to crawl aft, write a note, and hand it up between the pilots' knees. When he wanted to talk with his radio officer he had to crawl the length of the hull on his hands and knees. Fortunately for Read he was a small man, which made his wriggling through the watertight doors and around the fuel tanks easier than it would be for men of Bellinger's or Towers' size. Read told Rodd that he wanted surface weather reports from the *Dent* and from the *Philip* ahead on Station 20; she was one of the destroyers equipped for weather reporting.

The *Dent* replied that it was very thick on the surface; but the *Philip* reported only mist. At 1113 Rodd raised the *Waters* on Station 21 offshore of Corvo, and she reported 10 miles of visibility. At first this seemed to be encouraging information but what it in fact suggested was that the *NC-4* was in a race with a fog condition that was moving out of the northeast across her path.

The *NC-4* was cruising at 3,400 feet between the lumpy fog tops that obscured the sea and the smooth base of a cloud layer overhead. From his perch in the nose Read could watch the *NC-4*'s dim shadow race across the irregular surfaces of the fog tops, disappear into their valleys, and then wildly dash up the opposite side. Off to the south a long sliver of blue showed itself between the fog and the cloud layer overhead, but in the east the weather was obviously thickening. The *NC-3* and *NC-1* were up in this same sky somewhere, but aboard the *NC-4* they seemed to be flying through a world that was all their own. It was a world without much endurance. The roar of the Liberty engines was a constant reminder that eight of the *NC-4*'s nine fuel tanks were empty and there was something less than 200 gallons remaining in the last tank. In less than two hours their flight from Trepassey would be over—in one way or another.

After overflying the *Dent*, Rodd had taken a radio bearing on the *Waters* and found her 25 degrees to the east of the *NC-4*'s heading. This told Read that they would pass south of Corvo without seeing the island and would make their landfall on Flores.

Three hours had passed since they had overflown the *Hopewell*

127

on Station 16, which was the last station ship they had seen; all the subsequent ships had been "seen" only through Rodd's radio. Now the *Philip* was somewhere abeam, hidden below the fog, and Flores was almost dead ahead. The island was not precisely ahead, but a few degrees off to the east because Read had no desire to be surprised by the all too solid mass of Morro Grande jumping out of cloud at him.

More minutes passed. Holes in the fog became more frequent. At 1127 Read peered down through one of the holes and noticed a strange discoloration on the sea. The water on one side of a thin white line of froth was darker than that on the other. It was a tidal rip. They were very close now, because tidal rips occur only close to shore.

Read looked again at the tidal rip and suddenly realized that the darker "water" was in fact land. What he mistook for a tidal rip was in fact a line of surf.

He was looking at the southern shore of Flores!

And hidden somewhere in the murk off his port wings was the deadly 2,549-foot peak of Morro Grande!

Read whirled around in his cockpit and waved excitedly at Stone, signaling him to make a turn away from the shoreline. Then he motioned for Stone to take her down, and ducked below to his chartboard to work out a course for the *Harding*, the first of four station vessels between Corvo and São Miguel.

Stone throttled back his engines and dropped the *NC-4* into a powered glide through the crack in the fog and came out over the sea under a 200-foot ceiling. As the *NC-4* sped along parallel to the surfline, all hands were cheered by the sight of a small farmhouse sitting among a quilt of terraced fields.

The worst seemed to be over for the *NC-4*.

Read had considered landing at Horta on Fayal; but Breese assured him that they had ample fuel to make Ponta Delgada. If the weather held out, they would be moored alongside the *Melville* in Ponta Delgada in less than two hours, and would be ready to jump off for Lisbon the next day.

At about 1205 the smoke of the *Harding* was seen ahead and three minutes later the *NC-4* roared over her decks at masthead height. Leaning out of the *NC-4*'s after hatch, Breese and Rhoads could see the destroyer's decks jammed with sailors who were jumping up and down and waving.

Rodd called the *Gridley* ahead on Station 23 for weather information: The reply came back: "no fog; visibility fair." This was good news, because after the *Gridley* there were only two more stations ships before São Miguel. However, when the *NC-4* arrived in the vicinity of the *Gridley* about a half hour later, the ship was nowhere to be seen. Fog had suddenly rolled in from the north and it was continuing to form, fast and thick.

As the *NC-4* sped toward the *Fairfax* on Station 24, the fog was not only thickening but the ceiling was beginning to lower. Stone was flying the *NC-4* right on the deck, with her keel barely 20 feet above the sea. The *Fairfax* had reported good visibility, but Read now realized that a sudden change had occurred, his *NC-4* was in a race with the fog—and the fog was winning. By the time they reached Ponta Delgada the port would probably be fogbound. He started to work out a dead reckoning course that would intercept the islands of Fayal or Pico when the mists suddenly cleared to reveal the southern shore of Fayal. Read immediately swung around to his pilots and signaled them to make a turn for land.

After a few minutes of following Fayal's mountainous shoreline, the *NC-4* rounded a point and in a bight of land ahead was the port of Horta. Stone throttled back and eased the big airplane down into the harbor. Immediately after alighting, Read looked around and realized that something was wrong. The harbor didn't look right. It was too small; there were no modern port facilities and the base ship *Columbia* was nowhere in sight. A glance was exchanged between Read and Stone; Read shook his head and pointed up for takeoff. Stone agreed by opening his throttles, and within a minute they lifted clear of the small fishing port of Ponta Ribeirinha.

Within five minutes they rounded Espalamaca Point and there was Horta, no mistake about it: a city terraced on a hill rising away from its harbor, a sixteenth century fort on the waterfront, and the pale gray shape of the *Columbia* riding to anchor offshore of the port. At 1323 the *NC-4* touched down at Horta. As she taxied up astern of the *Columbia,* three motor launches swarmed out to meet her; one of these had too much speed and not enough control, and gave the *NC-4* a rough bump with its bow. Read was furious when he discovered that the launch had punched a small hole in the *NC-4*'s bow, but at this moment he was too relieved by their safe arrival to vent his spleen on the boat crew. While the *NC-4* was being moored astern of the *Columbia,* the great wall of fog that had been racing down from the north moved in and clamped itself on the port. Another five minutes in the air and the *NC-4* would have been unable to find Horta.

After 15 hours and 13 minutes of tossing around inside the *NC-4*'s cramped hull, it was with the greatest of pleasure that all hands exercised their stiff joints and mounted the *Columbia*'s accommodation ladder. Herbert Rodd, however, was in no great hurry. Before he climbed out of his cubby hole he made a quick check of his radio. There was a slight coating of oxide on the sparking disc, and the set's stationary electrode insulator; he carefully wiped them off with an oil-dampened cloth. With that done he pulled himself out of the *NC-4*'s after hatch and boarded the *Columbia,* reminding himself to check the set's batteries later. Read did not permit smoking in the radio compartment, which was aft of the fuel tanks, and Rodd was anxious to get aboard the *Columbia* for his first cigarette in fifteen hours.

Aboard the *Columbia* her officers and crew were jammed around the rails, perched on turrets and guns, and clinging to every foot- and handhold that a gave a view of the quarterdeck, and the sailors were cheering and waving their hats. When Read and his men stepped onto the quarterdeck, Captain Harry L. Brinser, the cruiser's commanding officer, was there to give each of them an enthusiastic "Welcome aboard."

Stiff, tired and nearly deaf from the four Libertys beating on their ears, Read and his men were a bit dazed by it all. They knew that the transatlantic flight was important, but they were doing no more than what was expected of them. In any case, they were not yet across; the Azores were not Europe, Horta was still a long way from Lisbon, and two more legs had to be flown before they finally reached Plymouth. So they were a bit perplexed by all the excitement. They were truly perplexed when dozens of bouquets of flowers arrived on board from citizens of Horta, when a swarm of boats came alongside with Portuguese musicians who serenaded them, and by the radio and cable messages of congratulation from Europe and the United States that were already flowing into the *Columbia*'s radio room. It soon dawned on them that they were becoming celebrities.

After the initial pleasantries were attended to, the first thing Read asked Captain Brinser was when the *NC-3* and *NC-1* were expected.

No one knew.

The last word from the *NC-1* was at 1305; she was landing at sea somewhere near Station 20 and had requested transmission of radio bearing signals. The last word from the *NC-3* was a broken transmission at 1320; she was off course between Stations 17 and 18, and was landing at sea.

After that: nothing.

130

Washington Times, 20 May 1919

The Saga of
the *NC-3*

The *NC-3* and *NC-1* had alighted on the sea within 20 minutes of each other. Both Towers and Bellinger had allowed themselves to become overly dependent upon the station vessels; both had become uncertain of their positions on the track to the Azores, they were virtually lost, and had to land in order to straighten out their navigation. Both Towers and Bellinger and their pilots underestimated the sea conditions, and once on the water they could not get off again.

After the *NC-3* lurched to a stop and bobbed back to ride with the motion of the swells, Richardson considered the moment. It was he who had the most to say about the NCs' hull design, but now he wondered if he had designed it strong enough to withstand the impact of this landing. An inspection of the hull showed that a few longitudinals and frames had buckled, there was some leaking along the seams, but the *NC-3*'s hull remained quite seaworthy. Her superstructure told a different story. The impact had buckled the two steel struts that supported the forward end of the centerline engine unit; the struts were bowed out like the legs of an English bulldog and the engine was tilted down toward the pilots' cockpits. On smaller flying boats these struts supported only one engine and were made of wood. All hands aboard the *NC-3* were now pleased that it was felt necessary to use steel struts to support the NCs' tandem unit. The force of the landing would surely have collapsed wooden struts, hurtling the 1,300-pound engine unit down upon the pilots, and perhaps even through the bottom of the hull.

The *NC-3* was going to stay afloat. But with her distorted engine mounts she was not going to take off again, however calm the seas. The *NC-3*'s Atlantic flight ended at 38°11′ north, 29°22′ west; and at this same point her Atlantic voyage began.

In the fog-shrouded seas a few hundred miles to the north, the *NC-1*'s landing had been almost as rough as her sister ship's, but she experienced no damage. If the seas flattened out a bit, or if the wind

133

changed direction, Marc Mitscher was sure that he could get her back into the air. But the North Atlantic was determined to live up to its reputation as the cruelest sea; the *NC-1* was down and the Atlantic was not going to release her.

Dead in the water, the *NC-1* lurched around among the deep swells for a few minutes, then swung around into a flying boat's natural attitude on the water with her nose into the wind, and began to drift rapidly astern. The crossed wind and seas made for hazardous sailing, especially when the NC boat was not designed for sailing stern first. The wind was blowing the *NC-1* along the length of the swells; one minute she would be teetering on the crest of a swell, and the next she would be skidding down its slope into the trough broadside, to be lifted by the next crest—all the time moving at five to ten knots. Bellinger, Christensen, and Kessler rigged the plane's sea anchor and put it over the side to slow their drift; its wire cable promptly parted. Holes were punched in a bucket, it was made fast to a manila line and put over as a sea anchor. It held, and it checked the *NC-1*'s seaway, but not nearly enough. The flying boat's erratic passage continued to allow the sea to tear at her wings and tail. Within an hour of alighting, the ailerons and elevators had been carried away and a wingtip float torn off. The *NC-1*'s crew had long since forgotten about the possibilities of a takeoff; their concern was survival.

For four hours Sadenwater sat over the radio key of his CG-1104A emergency transmitter, trying to raise one of the destroyers. There was no response. But on his receiver Sadenwater could hear the destroyers chattering amongst themselves. At first they were asking the whereabouts of the *NC-1;* then Sadenwater was surprised to hear that the *NC-3* was also down. Sadenwater was experiencing the same frustrations that Rodd had off Cape Cod: the searchers were so obsessed by the mechanics of their search that they failed to listen in case the object of the search was yelling "help!" At about 1700 a destroyer finally acknowledged the calls from the *NC-1* and asked the aircraft to send a series of Vs so radio bearings could be taken on the signal. Sadenwater promptly responded; but after this there was nothing. Then his batteries went dead.

In anticipation of the batteries' exhaustion, the rest of the crew had rigged a piece of canvas into a wind chute to direct the propeller blast of the forward engine into the small propeller of the wind-driven generator of the main transmitter. The forward engine was started, its propwash blew through the wind chute, and all hands were delighted to see the generator start turning. This jury rig allowed Sadenwater to transmit for another hour—unitl the wind chute came adrift and blew into the generator's propeller, breaking its blades.

A spare propeller was installed, the wind chute re-rigged and transmissions resumed—until a heavy cross sea caught the *NC-1*, tipped her far over to starboard and sent her rushing down into a trough. The starboard wingtip float had long since carried away, and the *NC-1* heeled over so far that both of her starboard wings were in the sea. Except for the pilot at the controls and Sadenwater at his radio, all hands clambered out on the port wing to create a counterweight. This could not be done quickly; each man had to make his way through a tangle of struts and wires, and take care to put his feet down only on spars and ribs—otherwise he would plunge through the wing's fabric. The combined weights slowly righted the airplane; but after the emergency had passed it was discovered that someone had kicked the generator's propeller. It was broken. There were no more spares. After this the *NC-1* was silent.

A few minutes after this narrow experience, at 1740, the smoke of a ship was spotted across the crests. Bellinger had his pilots start the engines and they began taxiing across the almost mountainous seas in an effort to intercept the ship's course. It was a wild and wet ride for everyone except the pilots, because they were all out on the port wing, hanging on its struts, in order to keep the starboard wing clear of the sea. They seemed to be getting closer when the ship suddenly changed course. In the dim light of the fading day, no one could be sure if her course change had been toward or away from them. While they were trying to figure it out, fog closed in and the ship was lost to sight.

The disappointment was bitter. Everyone had been awake for more than 24 hours by this time; they were soaking wet, and some of them were wretchedly seasick. They had about five gallons of fresh water, plus the water in the engine radiators, a few soggy sandwiches and a half-dozen emergency rations. These could be stretched for a week, if necessary; but no one believed that the *NC-1* could remain seaworthy that long. When the port wingtip float carried away—and no one believed that it would hold up for more than a few hours—it would be impossible to keep the *NC-1*'s wings out of the sea. Then the *NC-1* would probably roll over on her side and capsize.

When morale was at its lowest a few minutes later, they were surprised to see a ship suddenly pop out of the fog only a few hundred yards away. She was the Greek freighter *Ionia* under the command of Captain B. E. Panas, outward bound from Hampton Roads, Virginia, with a load of coal for Gibraltar. And she was the same ship they had seen a few minutes before. The *Ionia*'s lookout had seen the torn fabric

135

of the *NC-1's* upper wing, reported it, and interpreted it as a distress signal. But as the *Ionia* had turned to investigate, the *NC-1* became lost in the fog.

Rescuer and the to-be-rescued were soon heaving up and down in the sea only 100 yards apart; but with the heavy seas running, it was not until 1920 that a satisfactory lee could be made and a boat put over the side. Even with the boat in the water, it was a tough job of seamanship to get the men off the *NC-1*. One minute the lifeboat and the aircraft would be alongside each other, and one man might be able to jump into the boat. In the next second the *NC-1* would be skidding down into a trough with the lifeboat riding a crest twenty feet above her. It would take another ten or twenty minutes for the oarsmen to maneuver the boat back into position off the *NC-1's* nose, and another man would jump. This went on for almost an hour.

By 2020 all hands were changing into dry clothing aboard the *Ionia*. Bellinger expected that Captain Panas had notified the Navy of their rescue, but the *Ionia* had no radio. When the *Ionia* sailed from Hampton Roads a week before, the NCs had just arrived in Trepassey; it was news to Captain Panas that the flight to the Azores was only now being made. After all, airplanes flew at great speeds; for all he knew the flight should already be in Europe. The captain agreed to change course and put into Horta, and to salvage the *NC-1*. By 2120 the *Ionia* had a towline on the *NC-1* and they were under way for Horta. Two hours later the towline parted. With the heavy seas running it was madness to attempt remaking the line in the dark, and Captain Panas decided to stand by the derelict until daylight.

At 0035 the destroyer *Gridley* under the command of Commander Frank Jack Fletcher appeared out of the gloom with her signal lamp flashing. Fletcher would also have a rendezvous at Midway with Spruance and Marc Mitscher twenty-three years hence. This evening Fletcher wanted to know if the *Ionia* had seen an airplane or two floating around the ocean. Captain Panas replied that he had found *one*.

Consideration was given to transferring Bellinger and his crew to the *Gridley*, but Captain Panas wisely chose to have nothing to do with that. The *Ionia* left the derelict *NC-1* to the care of the *Gridley* and put on steam for Horta, where she anchored at 1230 on 18 May.

A watch was kept on the *NC-1*; meanwhile the sea slowly beat off her wings and tailgroup. On the eighteenth, the *Gridley* turned the *NC-1* over to the care of the *Fairfax*, and while a salvage crew was attempting to put a towline on her, the wreck turned turtle. The *Fairfax*, however, was determined to bring in what remained—which was only the hull— and there ensued a two-day chase across the wild seas north of the

Azores. It was an interesting exercise in search and attempted salvage, but it achieved nothing else. At 1940 on 20 May the *NC-1* finally went to the bottom at 48°00′ north, 29°25′ west [1]

When Bellinger and his men were hoisted aboard the *Ionia*, they knew from Sadenwater's radio receiver that the *NC-3* was also down at sea and that the *NC-4* had arrived safely at Horta. After the *Gridley* came alongside, Bellinger queried her by blinker light: "Any word on Towers and *NC-3?*" Captain Fletcher replied: "Nothing."[2]

When the *NC-1*'s crew was rescued by the *Ionia*, Towers and his crew in the *NC-3* were still afloat. Unlike the *NC-1*, which had alighted only slightly off the track between Newfoundland and the Azores, the *NC-3* had overflown the Azores to westward and was drifting southwest of the islands—and no one knew it except the *NC-3*.

After Richardson had secured the *NC-3*'s engines, Lavender tuned up his RDF set and took some radio bearings. The *NC-3* was about 50 miles southwest of the channel between Fayal and Pico. This was galling information for Towers. When he checked this position against his hurried sunsight, he could see that his errors were inconsequential. If he had continued to fly up his line of position for only another 30 minutes they would have sighted the western shore of Pico. His bitterness was multiplied by five after he told the others.

The bitterness was compounded by the knowledge that the *NC-3*'s CG-1104A emergency transmitter was on board the *Aroostook* en route to Plymouth. Now they were voiceless when they needed to shout. Lavender and Moore set about rerigging the main transmitter's wind-driven generator on a strut behind the port engine. The center engines could not be used because of their weakened mountings.

While Lavender was at this work he discovered the ground cable that had vibrated loose. Had it come loose as a result of the landing shocks? How long had it been disconnected? Lavender did not find out until an hour later when he overheard an exchange between two destroyers that said the last word received from the *NC-3* was at 0914 when she asked for radio bearing signals near Station 17. For four hours he had been working his key for nothing. Small wonder that he received no replies to his calls.

The terrible realization for the men aboard the *NC-3* came when Lavender told them that everyone thought they were down somewhere between Stations 17 and 18, 150 miles northwest of Corvo. Lavender could hear the base ship *Melville* in Ponta Delgada directing destroyers to search grids northwest of Corvo which were almost 300 miles away from where the *NC-3* was drifting, only about 50 miles over the southern horizon from Fayal and Pico.

When Lavender finally got his CQ generator rerigged, he found the arrangement less than satisfactory. The mounts of the port engine were also weakened by the landing impact, the engine could not be run at full speed, and there was not enough propeller blast to turn the generator up to full power. Lavender estimated his transmission range at 30 miles. The closest ship was the *Columbia* in Horta, 50 miles to the north. In any case, Lavender soon discovered, as did Sadenwater, that the *Melville, Columbia,* and the searching destroyers were so busy chattering with each other that no one could hear his faint signals on 425 meters.

Towers quickly faced the fact that it was unlikely that the *NC-3* was going to be found, unless it might be by accident. A check of the *NC-3's* drift showed that she was being blown on a course to eastward that converged with the island of São Miguel 200 miles away. If the wind and sea held their velocity and direction, the *NC-3* could be standing off the breakwater at Ponta Delgada in two or three days. For food they had a few jelly sandwiches that were dry, others that were wet, some chocolate almond bars and their Navy emergency rations. It was dismaying to discover that the emergency drinking water had been put overboard at Trepassey, but there were about 11 gallons of water in the radiator of each engine. The radiator water tasted terrible; but this assured that it would last all the longer.

As the dull daylight dissolved into darkness a watch list was made up, each man taking two hours while the others tried to sleep. Richardson took the first watch. All hands had been awake since takeoff from Trepassey 24 hours before, all were exhausted, but sleep was an almost impossible luxury inside the rolling, pitching, and pounding hull of the *NC-3*. At 0800 the next day, as McCulloch was relieving Richardson from his second watch, a wave reached up and smashed the trailing edge of the port wing. A second wave carried away the wing's trailing edge up to the rear wing spar. The sea was rising, the wave crests growing higher, and they showed an increasing tendency to break over parts of the *NC-3*. Pitching back and forth in the deepening roughs, the *NC-3* now began to rock her tail into the seas. Damage to the wings increased.

As the seas smashed the wing ribs, the hitherto taut wing fabric crumpled and sagged into pockets that filled with water. Richardson and Moore climbed out on the wings and cut away their fabric, and even where the fabric was still intact they sliced holes in it. This allowed the sea to pass through the wings' structures and prevented water from puddling in the crumpled fabric. The lower wing had an area of almost 1,000 square feet and the water that could accumulate would amount to

138

several hundred pounds. Richardson was afraid that such weights would weaken the wing structure, overload the wingtip floats, or both, which would mean real troubles.

The *NC-3* was drifting backwards with her nose into the wind. This is a seaplane's natural direction on the water once its engines are secured; but it provides very little control and this small measure is difficult. The pilots had to learn how to "fly" backwards on the water, because sailing astern all controls had to be reversed. Their principal problem was trying to keep the *NC-3*'s stern straight into the seas. This was rather simple while ascending the wall of a swell; it became absolutely wild after topping the crest and the *NC-3* raced down into the trough on the other side. If the aircraft yawed too much to one side or the other there was a danger of putting a critical sideload on one of the wingtip floats. If one of them broke off, the *NC-3* would have nothing but stability problems.

The trouble came at 1130. Without any warning, the port wingtip float carried away. Now there was a definite danger of the *NC-3* capsizing; and if the other float carried away, the game would be up. Besides keeping a man on watch in the cockpit, now another man had to stand watch out on the starboard wing, secured to one of its struts, to prevent the port wing from putting itself in the sea.

Two hours later at 1350, land was sighted off to the north the dark blue peak of Pico that usually appears to float among the clouds, 7,610 feet above the Atlantic. However, the wind was carrying the *NC-3* off to the northeast, away from Pico. There were still 165 gallons of fuel on board and Towers discussed the prospect of using the engines to taxi to Pico. The fuel was enough for two hours' flying time; but it was decided that it was not nearly enough to taxi across 40 miles of rough seas, even if the *NC-3* could take the punishment. With only one wingtip float, the hull's leakage becoming worse, and the strength of the engine mounts being questionable, the idea was given up. In any case, Towers' reckoned that another 24 hours of drifting would either bring them up against the island of São Miguel or into the channel between São Miguel and Terceira, where there should be some shipping. If they drifted beyond that, in another 24 hours they would be in the steamer lane between New York and Gibralter. However, beyond the steamer lane there was nothing but a thousand miles of ocean before sighting Europe. No one wanted to think about that.

With land in sight, another effort was made to send off an SOS. The port engine was started, the generator set to turning up, and power came on the main transmitter. Lavender managed to get off two messages before the *NC-3* suddenly went wild. With only the port engine running, the plane was pulled around in a semicircle that swung her across the sea. The upset almost capsized the plane. The engine was immediately secured; radio transmitting was abandoned as too hazardous.

As Pico faded from view the light went out on another day. Two-man watches were kept through the night, with a third man being called out occasionally for extra weight to balance the port wing or to assist in bilge pumping. The bolts and turnbuckles on the wires bracing the starboard wingtip float were checked every 30 minutes and had to be tightened about once an hour. The wind shifted to the east during the night which told Towers that there was little chance of being swept between the two islands. Now the *NC-3* was headed directly for São Miguel. At 1015 on the nineteenth the mountains of São Miguel were in sight and each passing hour made the island more real; shortly after noon farmhouses, trees and vineyards were clearly distinguishable.

As the *NC-3* was slowly driven up on the island, it took all of the attention of her crew to hold her well offshore, against the wind. Towers and his men were too close to victory to have their aircraft swept into the surf and beaten to pieces on a rocky beach. A headland was passed in mid-afternoon and Ponta Delgada's breakwater came in sight. No one expected the *NC-3* to be this far east and as they drifted down on the port everything appeared to be quiet. However, listening on his radio receiver Lavender overheard an artillery battery of U.S. Marines some-where in the hills of São Miguel calling the *Melville* to tell the ship that they had spotted the *NC-3*. The *Melville* replied, "Look again; it can't be *NC-3*." The Marines were annoyed at having their word questioned; they told the *Melville* that it was a seaplane, a big one, and that it had "Threes" plastered all over it. After that, excitement reigned aboard the *Melville*. It was contagious, and within a few minutes it had spread to other ships in the port and into the city itself.

By 1625, the *NC-3* was standing off the entrance to Ponta Delga-da's breakwater and Towers was surprised to see the destroyer *Harding* steaming out of the port and bearing down upon them with full speed. The Stars and Stripes had been flying from the *NC-3*'s stern upside down as a distress signal. Moore rushed aft, hauled them down and hoisted them back right-side-up. At first Towers was pleased by the appearance of the *Harding,* but as he took in her frothy bow wave he shouted for all hands to stand up and wave—in an effort to warn her off. The *Harding*'s wake would be enough to swamp them. On the bridge of the *Harding* Captain Henry D. Cooke saw the men waving from the airplane and he took it as a sign of welcome. It appeared as if the destroyer put on more speed. Towers grabbed up his Aldis lamp and flashed a message telling the *Harding* to stand off and stand by; the

NC-3 would come into port under her own power. But it was too late. The *Harding's* 1,800 tons swept around the *NC-3* with a flourish that sent McCulloch and Moore scurrying out onto the wings, where they ran back and forth across the naked spruce spars in a frantic effort to keep the aircraft balanced.

Steering the *NC-3* to the entrance of the breakwater was a difficult and dangerous maneuver because she had to be turned crosswind, which put an increasing load on her starboard wingtip float. As she reached the breakwater, the struts on the float finally collapsed; the float carried away, but trailed after the wingtip on its bracing wires, and its drag was pulling the wing down into the sea. Moore dashed out with a pair of sidecutters and cut the float loose while McCulloch balanced the *NC-3* on the port wing, and Richardson climbed into the cockpit and started the center pusher. Fortunately, the wind was strong, and combined with the thrust of the after engine, it was enough to make the ailerons effective in stabilizing the aircraft. After the two outboard engines were started, control became even better. But the wind was off the port side, it continued to roll the plane to starboard, so Moore was stationed on the port wing as ballast.

As they swung into the harbor the wind increased, so Richardson turned over the controls to McCulloch and joined Moore. Lavender had no more need of manning his radio so he climbed out of his cubicle to see if he could be of assistance on deck. The engines had not been run in two days and when Lavender heard them start he was sure that they were the outboard engines only; he never imagined that the after pusher was running. As he climbed out of the after hatch and started forward, Towers gave out an unearthly yell that stopped Lavender in his tracks— just in time to prevent him from walking into the after propeller.

With Lavender on the starboard wing, Richardson and Moore on the port wing, and with all three of them running back and forth to keep the *NC-3* balanced in teeter-totter fashion, the battered flying boat taxied into the harbor.

All the ships in Ponta Delgada had hurriedly dressed ship upon notice of the *NC-3's* arrival, and Towers and his men found a riot of color flying from the rigging in the port to welcome them. As the *NC-3* sputtered up the harbor, all the ships in the port began sounding their whistles and sirens; then church bells joined the welcome. Swarms of sailors on the ships cheered and waved their hats while crowds of Portuguese joined in, waving hats, flags and scarves from the piers and rooftops and balconies of buildings near the waterfront.

Two motor whaleboats came speeding out from the *Melville;* Towers had requested them by blinker light so they would be available to get under each wing of the *NC-3* when her engines were secured. One of them dashed around astern of the *NC-3,* where it fouled its propeller on Lavender's trailing wire antenna that was still strung out, 200 feet behind the *NC-3.* The "rescuing" whaleboat drifted uselessly in the *NC-3's* wake. The other motor whaleboat came up under Lavender's starboard wing; "At last," he thought, "we're out of it." The sailor in the boat reached up to the wing, but instead of balancing it, he tore off a loose piece of fabric and put it in his pocket for a souvenir! In cold fury, Lavender glared down at him and shouted, "If you will be so kind as to help us secure this airplane, I'll give you every goddammed bit of fabric on it!" Abashed, the sailor grabbed the wingtip. But as he grabbed the starboard wing, other hands were pulling down on the port wing and the sailor was surprised to find himself lifted into the air with his feet dangling five feet above the harbor. When he let go, he was lucky to miss a wetting by dropping back into his boat, which almost capsized under his sudden weight. When Richardson, who was doing his own balancing act on the port wing, reflected on this moment, he was convinced that Mack Sennett could not have created more hilarious confusion with his Keystone Cops.

At 1830 the *NC-3's* 1,240-mile flight of 15 hours and 30 minutes, and her subsequent 53-hour voyage of 205 miles was at its end. When John Towers and crew stepped ashore, Ponta Delgada's citadel boomed a 21-gun salute in honor of their passage.[3]

Towers and his tired and dirty crew were greeted by the governor of the Azores and Rear Admiral Richard E. Jackson, Commander U.S. Naval Forces Azores. Then they were whisked off through Ponta Delgada's narrow streets to a reception at the governor's palace and were marched out on a balcony overlooking the main plaza which was packed with cheering humanity. Bands played, a parade marched in review, the crowds danced and sang in the streets; the *NC-3's* men wearily waved back. It was all very great; much more than anyone could even imagine while floating 50 miles south of Fayal, which was only 48 hours ago. But the greatest moment occurred when they were taken aboard the *Melville* where they were able to test out the hot showers, the sharpness of available razor blades, and the stiffness of the sheets in her bunks. They were allowed to log a few hours' sack time before having to attend a formal dinner in their honor that evening.

Aboard the *Melville,* Towers and Richardson had a few moments to take stock of the situation, and it was not entirely good. Captain Ward K. Wortman, commanding officer of the *Melville,* had given Towers a radio message from Secretary of the Navy Josephus Daniels:

I KNEW YOU WOULD MAKE IT. HEARTIEST CONGRATULATIONS ON YOUR PLUCKY AND SUCCESSFUL FLIGHT. JUST TOLD YOUR WIFE GOOD NEWS. CONGRATULATE OTHER COMMANDERS AND CREWS FOR SPLENDIDLY UPHOLDING NAVY'S TRADITIONS. CONFIDENTLY EXPECT AT LEAST TWO PLANES TO REACH ENGLAND ON SCHEDULE.[4]

Towers and Richardson probably grimaced at the secretary's last sentence. However, Daniels only knew that Towers and the *NC-3* had arrived in Ponta Delgada; he did not yet know the condition of the aircraft. Josephus Daniels' experience prior to Woodrow Wilson's appointing him to the cabinet was that of a North Carolina newspaper editor. Daniels was a shrewd politician, an able administrator, and one of the most pro-Navy secretaries the Navy has ever had, but he was ignorant of the powers of the sea.

The damage that the *NC-3* had experienced upon landing was serious, and it could have been repaired to make her airworthy again if she had been able to make port within the first six hours. But the remorseless beating she had taken during the past two days had transformed her into a wreck; and without the seamanship exercised by Towers and his crew she never would have made port. It was all too clear to Towers and Richardson that the *NC-3* was out of the running; and they were certain that this would be bad news for Josephus Daniels.

The situation was ironic. The *NC-3* had beaten both of her sister ships to Ponta Delgada, the jumping off point for Lisbon; but she was unflyable. The *NC-1* was gone. And the *NC-4*, which had flown successfully to the Azores, was still back at Horta, weatherbound.

Before heading for the festivities at the governor's palace that evening, John Towers more than anyone had cause to reflect upon the situation of the moment. He was not only aircraft commander of the *NC-3*, he was commanding officer of NC Seaplane Division One, and the successful conclusion of the transatlantic flight was still his responsibility. As far as the *NC-3*'s return from oblivion, there was more than enough cause for celebration. But as regards the transatlantic flight, it was only half done.

And now all their hopes were carried in one aircraft—the *NC-4*.

Many of us can remember the skepticism which greeted the first automobiles,

—but now no one marvels at transcontinental trips by motor.

Not so long ago the farmers around Dayton jeered at the experiments of the Wright brothers,

—but now English planes have flown to India, French planes to Madagascar, and an American plane 's the Azores.

Just now the same old skepticism greets the possibility of trans-Atlantic travel by aircraft,

—but in a few years it will be so common that we'll take it as a matter of course.

John T. McCutcheon Cartoon
The Chicago Daily Tribune, 19 May 1919

Beat the Yanks!

The celebrations in Horta and Ponta Delgada were bright and gay; the newspaper banners in the United States were big and black: NC-4 ARRIVES SAFELY; NC-1 CREW RESCUED; NC-3 SAVED!

The public enjoyed the moment. The NCs made far more interesting reading than the long gray columns that tried to render intelligible the seemingly endless bickering among the mustachioed old men in the so-called "Peace Palace" at Versailles. Most Americans were puzzled by the appearance of new names such as "Czechoslovakia" and "Yugoslavia." Many persons wondered what had become of Serbia; after all, it was an incident involving Serbia that had started the war in 1914. There was a Poland on the maps now, which seemed to be a good thing; but the new countries called Latvia, Lithuania, and Estonia were puzzling, and it was impossible to figure out why there was so much quarrelling over a tiny place called Danzig.

Americans who consulted their political atlases in 1919 discovered that their old maps no longer made sense. But so what? The war was over; the always quarrelsome Europeans could sort out their own mess now. The boys were on their way back from France, but best of all, America's airplanes were in the Azores.

When President Woodrow Wilson received word of the *NC-4's* safe arrival in Horta, he remarked, "I am very highly pleased."[1] When interviewed at his home in Dayton, Ohio, Orville Wright observed that "the Naval Aviators accomplished something really remarkable," and added that the remaining laps of the flight should be made with little trouble. Orville Wright had read a great deal of the sensational speculation in the press about transatlantic airlines in the near future, and felt obliged to throw cold water on it:

The thought of air lines is far fetched. The two drawbacks are the danger and expense. I doubt whether the present flight would have been attempted if

145

destroyers had not been stationed all along the route to assist in event of an accident. The air liner may come, but its advent is far removed.[2]

With his instinct for business and appreciation of publicity, Glenn Curtiss was completely uninhibited in predicting an immediate future for transatlantic aviation. He estimated that passengers would be flying the Atlantic within five years; and he assumed that the flying would be done in Curtiss flying boats.[3] A 20-year-old former Naval Reserve officer in New Haven, Connecticut, who had received his wings at Pensacola on 7 December 1918 to become Naval Aviator No. 1806, offered a more cautious estimate. Writing in the May number of the *Yale Graphic,* he observed that the flight of the NC boats "would demonstrate that a flight across the Atlantic Ocean is a perfectly safe and sane commercial proposition and not a gigantic gamble"; but he refused to predict when transatlantic passenger service would begin.[4] The young man was Juan T. Trippe, who eight years later would create an organization named Pan American Airways.

Secretary of the Navy Josephus Daniels, accompanied by Admirals David W. Taylor and V. C. Griffin, had just stepped off the Navy transport *Mount Vernon* in Hoboken, New Jersey, after a five-week tour of Navy facilities in Europe, when he was told of the *NC-4*'s arrival in Horta. Daniels was irritated by the newspaper reporters' frequent allusion to "luck" in the flight, and he retorted:

There is no such thing as "Navy luck." We have been working up this flight for two years; and as in other projects within its sphere of activities, what the Navy has done was due to a perfect system of cooperation.[5]

Most newspaper editorials were wild with enthusiasm; one from *The Brooklyn Eagle* was among the more sober:

We are nearing the day when the navigation of the Atlantic air routes will be a daily undertaking of many aircraft ... We shall see the day when the romance of Kipling's *The Night Mail* becomes a reality, when passengers may pass back and forth between Europe and America with a speed which will make that of the *Mauretania* seem a snail's pace by comparison. The next few days ought to tell whether American skill and daring will go down in History as having pioneered the way toward that amazing revolution in travel.[6]

Twenty years almost to the day would pass before a passenger could purchase a transatlantic airplane ticket, and that would be on a service created by Juan Trippe; but in 1919 it was nice to believe that it was "just around the corner." Meanwhile, an anonymous contributor to

146

the *New York Tribune* penned a few lines about the NC flight that were dedicated to the lost *NC-3* and *NC-1;* it took its title from John Towers' words at Trepassey—"Let's Go!":

> Would you touch the place where the morning lies?
> Go find the way with your new found eyes,
> If you know how the stormy petrel flies—
> "We know."
> Then over the sounded Caravel track,
> As East runs East by the Zodiac,
> New Worlds to Old Worlds—wing them back.
> "Let's Go!"
>
> In yonder dark where the lightnings play
> Find death and night—or life and day.
> The *Santa Maria* came that way.
> "We know."
> Come, follow the fathomless mystery
> Of the Skyward lanes o'er the fathomed sea—
> The "1" the "4" and the *NC-3*—
> "Let's Go!"
>
> And what if they vanish 'tween shore and shore,
> The "1" or the "3" forevermore—
> Still know you the course of the *NC-4?*
> "We know."
> While men are mortal and minds are meek,
> While hands still grope and hearts still seek—
> Still hear their questing voices speak:
> "Let's go!"[7]

However great the euphoria among the American public and the dancing throngs in Horta and Ponta Delgada, there was little with John Towers and his men of the *NC-3,* nor with Read and Bellinger and their crews aboard the *Columbia.* And although the news of the *NC-4's* successful flight, the rescue of the *NC-1's* crew, and the safe arrival of the *NC-3* created great excitement in the Navy Department, its members quickly sobered to the fact that all of their hopes were now in the *NC-4.*

There was no euphoria at all in St. John's Cochrane Hotel where Harry Hawker and Freddie Raynham were talking over the next day's weather forecast with their navigators. At tea time on Saturday, the seventeenth, word reached St. John's that the *NC-3* and *NC-1* were overdue, but the *NC-4* had arrived at Horta. The American newspapermen back from Trepassey greeted this news with a great whoop and holler and all kinds of liquor smuggled from St. Pierre and Miquelon appeared for a smashing party that evening.

Hawker and Grieve, with Raynham and Morgan, joined in the celebration, but their toasts were preoccupied with thoughts of the next

147

day's weather. The Yanks were in the Azores, but they could still be beaten across the Atlantic. The Britishers turned in early that night; but at Lester's Field and Quidi Vidi their ground crews were carefully preening the Sopwith *Atlantic* and the Martinsyde *Raymor* for a takeoff on the morrow.

Early on Sunday morning, the eighteenth, Lieutenant Laurance Clements, the Air Ministry's aerologist at St. John's, called at the Cochrane Hotel with good news for Hawker and Raynham. The bad weather over the Atlantic was breaking up. This is what both pilots had hoped for, had been expecting, but dared not depend upon. The weather over the track between Newfoundland and Ireland not only looked better than it had during the past three weeks, it actually looked good. What was more, the moon was still full to assist an overnight passage. No announcements were made, but the preoccupation of Grieve and Morgan with their charts led observers to feel sure that by Sunday's twilight both British airplanes would be gone.

Harry G. Hawker was an Australian who learned to fly in England in 1912, and the ink was hardly dry on his pilot's certificate when in October 1912 he won the Michelin Trophy for setting the world's endurance record of 8 hours and 23 minutes. A year later he set an altitude record by flying to 12,900 feet, and in subsequent years he became very well known in English sport aviation. During the war he was a test pilot for T.O.M. Sopwith's aircraft company. His navigator, Kenneth MacKenzie-Grieve, was not an aviator, but a former officer of the Royal Navy. Frederick P. Raynham's career paralleled that of Hawker's, but as a wartime test pilot for the Martinsyde company. Hawker and Raynham had been well acquainted with each other years before they met as competitors in Newfoundland. Raynham's navigator, C. W. F. Morgan, was also an aviator, having flown during the war with the Royal Naval Air Service.

As competitors for the *Daily Mail* prize of £ 25,000, it mattered not if either Hawker or Raynham beat the *NC-4* across the Atlantic, but there were strong nationalistic overtones to the transatlantic projects of 1919. In England a jingoistic press shrilled that it had to be a *British* aviator in a *British* airplane to make the first transatlantic flight and made the wild assertion that the North Atlantic's air between the United Kingdom and Newfoundland belonged to the British Empire. In the United States the press was almost as bad, and it was Josephus Daniels who rhetorically thumped the table with his remark that the Navy was "out to beat the world!" Hawker and Morgan felt very strongly about this; as Morgan told the press six days before the NCs took off from Rockaway:

148

If we are held here until the Americans arrive at Trepassey Bay, or even the Azores, we should still be able to get across before them. As the honour of the first crossing overshadows the London *Daily Mail* prize, for which Hawker and I are racing, I am sure neither of us will decline the issue if the Americans set out from here, whether stormy or fair.[8]

The British not only regarded the first transatlantic flight as an affair of honor, but had a peculiar way of looking at it as a sporting event of sorts. And to them the U.S. Navy's formidable organization was terribly "unsporting." A few days before the NCs took off from Rockaway, C. W. F. Morgan remarked on this with sarcasm to a reporter from the St. John's *Evening Telegram:*

At no time will they [the NC boats] be out of sight of a ship, as the American Navy is putting a ship every fifty miles of the way, which means that the machine will never be more than twenty-five miles from a ship. This eliminates any risk, and also does away with any need of navigation. The Americans might just as well fly the English Channel fifty times, an ordinary exploit these days. The flight [by the U.S. Navy] will prove nothing practically or theoretically.[9]

Hawker and Grieve felt equally strong about their American competition, even though the NC boats were not in the running for the £ 25,000 prize. And everyone at the Cochrane Hotel knew this as the four airmen quietly set about their preparations this Sunday morning.

Harry Hawker had arrived in Newfoundland with Grieve and their airplane on 29 March and the aircraft was assembled and test-flighted by 11 April. Meanwhile, Raynham and Morgan arrived, and they had test-flown their airplane by 16 April. After that the two parties studied their weather reports and each other's activities with suspicion. Finally a "gentlemen's agreement" was struck by which each agreed to give notice to the other when they proposed to take off; this took much of the tension out of waiting for the weather to change. At lunchtime this Sunday, Hawker gave "the word" to Raynham, and added an invitation to dinner in London on the evening of the nineteenth.[10]

The mid-afternoon sun gleamed brilliantly off the handsomely done buff paintwork of the Sopwith *Atlantic* when she was wheeled from her tent hangar on Glendenning's Farm. It was a magnificent day, with hardly a cloud in the sky, and it was difficult for the aviators to believe that this was the same Newfoundland in which they had been waiting for more than a month. Hawker and Grieve struggled into their specially made watertight flotation suits and climbed into the plane. On board was a small mail sack that enclosed a package of photographs for the *Daily Mail* and seventy-eight letters. Philatelists had paid the equivalent of $500 an ounce to have these few letters put aboard for the flight.

149

At 3:38 P.M. on the eighteenth, Hawker opened his throttle on the *Atlantic's* single 375-horsepower Rolls-Royce Eagle engine and the heavily laden biplane lurched forward. The field on Glendenning's Farm offered a run of only 400 yards, with a barrier of tall fir trees at the end of the track, but after a run of 300 yards the *Atlantic's* wings clutched the air. Hawker nursed the airplane over the tree line and then was careful to keep her close to the ground, almost hedge-hopping over the hills to the coast. As he crossed the coast he pulled a toggle that jettisoned his wheel landing gear, which relieved the *Atlantic* of about 200 pounds and a parasitic drag that increased her speed by 12 miles per hour; it also made the aircraft less hazardous to ditch at sea.

An hour later, on the shores of Quidi Vidi Lake, Raynham and Morgan climbed into their Martinsyde *Raymor.* The name of the air-craft was taken from the first three letters of her crew's names. Hawker and Grieve had an hour's head start on them, but the Martinsyde was a more carefully designed airplane; it had a greater wing area than the *Atlantic,* weighed about 35 percent less, and in spite of a slightly less powerful engine, it was the faster of the two. Morgan was confident that they would overtake and pass the *Atlantic* somewhere over the ocean during the 20-hour flight.

Raynham opened his throttle, the ground crew yanked away his wheel chocks, and the *Raymor* hurtled down the field. Her tail came up and she was at the point of lift-off when a gust of wind slammed into the airplane's side. The *Raymor* yawed and her landing gear slammed into the ground. The side-load was too great. The landing gear collapsed and the *Raymor* skidded to a stop amidst a cloud of dust and a crash of splintering wood. Raynham and Morgan climbed out of the wreck apparently unhurt, although it was later determined that Morgan had suffered serious head injuries. For the moment, however, they were both thankful that the crash had not ruptured their fuel tanks, which would have transformed the *Raymor* into their funeral pyre.

Raynham and Morgan were now out of the race. It was up to Hawker and Grieve and their *Atlantic* to "beat the Yanks."

Sunday at Horta was a gray day filled with rain, fog and 50-knot winds. The *NC-4* rode up and down on the waves and tugged at her moorings as the 14-foot swells rolled in around the breakwater. Aboard the *Columbia* Read and his men were pleased that their aircraft was still there because on the very day of their arrival at Horta they had come close to losing her. While the *NC-4* was being refueled, a sailor of the "I-didn't-know-it-was-loaded" type made his way to the navigator's cockpit in the bow and out of curiosity pushed the button on the landing flares. Once again there was a great WHOOSH and two brilliant streams of pyrotechnics went shooting across the harbor. Pyrotechnics and gasoline are a bad combination in any case, but in this instance it was fortunate that no gasoline had been spilled onto the harbor during the refuelling— or it might well have meant the end of the *NC-4.*

Read and his crew were resigned to the fact that they were not going anywhere until the weather lifted and the heavy swell conditions abated. It is of passing interest to note that these ocean swell conditions at Horta that delayed the 11-ton *NC-4* proved to be almost as great a hindrance to the transatlantic schedules of Pan American Airways' 41-ton Boeing 314 Clippers twenty years later.

On this morning of 18 May Albert C. Read was mulling over a radio message from Lieutenant Joseph B. Anderson, the aerologist aboard the *Melville* in Ponta Delgada. Anderson said that he could not foresee a break in the weather for at least 48 hours. It seemed like Chatham all over again. Read later remarked of these days at Horta, no doubt with the whole flight in mind:

I have never heard "patience" mentioned as one of the requisite qualities of an aviator's make-up. It should be. That quality has to be more frequently exercised and for longer periods than any others.[11]

Patience was probably one of Read's innate characteristics. If it was not, he had time to develop it at Chatham, Trepassey, Horta, and Ponta Delgada; in Portugal's Mondego River and again at El Ferrol, Spain. But on this Sunday neither he nor any of his crew imagined that all of nine days would pass before they would see the rooftops of Lisbon.

A wave of excitement swept through Horta when the freighter *Ionia* appeared out of the afternoon's fog to anchor in the port and disembark Bellinger and his crew from the *NC-1.* The Portuguese islanders were more than ready for another big public reception, but the rain kept these to a minimum. Aboard the *Columbia,* Read and Bellinger compared experiences and the crews swapped stories. On this day the *NC-3* was still drifting south of Pico, and the principal topic of conversation was what might have happened to Towers and his crew.

At suppertime, word came down from the *Columbia's* radioroom of Hawker's takeoff and Raynham's crash. It was estimated that Hawker should be over Ireland in about 16 hours and at his destination, Brooklands aerodrome outside of London, about three or four hours later. An air of futility slowly pervaded the *Columbia's* wardroom: two planes lost, the *NC-3* still unaccounted for, Hawker on his way, and the *NC-4* going nowhere for at least a couple of days. Everyone was sure that the

NC-4 would finish the last leg to Lisbon and fly on to England later; but it would be an after-the-fact demonstration that the flight could also be made with the best logistics support available. Yet the men in the *Columbia's* wardroom knew that it was flights such as Hawker's that proved nothing. If airplanes were going to fly the Atlantic on a regular basis someday, the flights would have to be made from one elaborate logistics system to another with a sophisticated communications network along the tracks between.[12]

Monday's rainy dawn failed to put much light on the port of Horta and it failed to put any light on the success or failure of Hawker's flight. The day of the nineteenth passed. Sunset came and went. Still no word. More than 24 hours had passed since Hawker and Grieve had taken off from Newfoundland; by this time their fuel was surely exhausted.

It was an overcast Monday at Brooklands aerodrome where an expectant crowd of several thousand persons had gathered by noontime in anticipation of hearing the sounds of Hawker's Rolls-Royce engine above the gray ceiling and then seeing the *Atlantic* sweep down out of the clouds to belly-in on the field. Afternoon came and went, the sun went down, the crowds went home, and Tuesday's dawn came 'round the clock. Still no word. There were reports that the *Atlantic* had been seen offshore of Ireland, overflying Ireland, that it had landed in some remote part of Ireland, but they were all spurious. Almost 48 hours had passed. Hawker and Grieve had to be presumed down at sea—or lost.

Hawker and Grieve had a radio aboard their *Atlantic* but it had a range of only 60 miles; in any case, no message was ever received from them. The *Atlantic* had fuel for barely 22 hours and now 48 hours had passed. Unlike the *NC-3* with her sturdy flying-boat hull, the Sopwith was a landplane with no provision for flotation beyond how empty her fuel tank might be at the time of ditching. Both Hawker and Grieve wore special watertight suits that assisted flotation and the turtleback of the *Atlantic's* fuselage was convertible into a small boat; but these were scant protection against the North Atlantic's cruel temperatures. Hawker and Grieve were gone.

Read and Bellinger and their crews had been speculating over the loss of the British fliers for only an hour or so when the *Columbia's* radio brought word of the *NC-3's* arrival in Ponta Delgada. It was pleasant to receive a bit of *good* news for a change. A bit later the day's forecast came in which indicated a break in the weather. This was good news too, because everyone had become rather weary of the *Columbia* and Horta.

Read had intended to fly directly from Horta to Lisbon, but with

152

word that the *NC-3* was in Ponta Delgada he changed his flight plan. The message from Ponta Delgada did not mention the *NC-3's* battered condition, and in their excitement at the news that Towers and his crew were safe, Read and his men assumed that the two aircraft would fly to Lisbon together.

Tuesday's flying weather was good, it was only 176 miles to Ponta Delgada, but Read had to wait until the afternoon before the swells rolling into the harbor had flattened out enough for a safe takeoff. The *NC-4* was off the water at 1239, Rodd quickly ran out his trailing wire antenna and began talking with the *Melville,* the NCs' base ship at Ponta Delgada. Then Rhoads gave Rodd a nudge and the radio operator turned around to see Breese with his face all lathered up and shaving from a mug of murky brown water. At first Rodd thought Breese was using coffee, but it was radiator water, freshly hot and drawn from the centerline engines.

The snowcapped peak of Pico passed abeam and by 1420 Ponta Delgada was in sight. Four minutes later Read was making the *NC-4's* nose fast to a buoy. When Stone cut his engines and their last sounds coughed away, all hands were surprised by the noise around them. The piers and seawalls were jammed with people waving and cheering, and thousands of pounds of good boiler water roared into the atmosphere as ships in the port tried to outdo one another with their whistles and sirens. There had not been as much excitement in the capital city of the Azores since the islands had been the crossroads of the Iberian empire's treasure convoys of yore, and the Portuguese were determined to make the most of it. Ponta Delgada's welcome to Towers and the *NC-3* was only for practice, but Read and his men aboard the *NC-4* were somewhat baffled; to them it seemed like an awfully lot of fuss for a flight of only 176 miles.

The first launch alongside the *NC-4* had John Towers on board. Read and his crew were shocked at how haggard Towers appeared; and it was only now that they discovered that the *NC-3* was little more than a derelict. Although the two airplanes would not be able to fly to Lisbon together it was automatically assumed that Towers would shift his flag to the surviving airplane and finish the flight with the *NC-4.*

Admiral Jackson, Commander U.S. Naval Forces Azores, met Towers and Read and his men at the boat landing where he introduced them to the governor of the Azores. Then the newsreel cameramen took over. Hustled into automobiles, the fliers were driven through the city's ancient narrow streets which were all hung with red, white, and blue bunting, to the Praca do Liceu and the governor's palace. Here Read had his first experience in "greeting the cheering populace" from a

153

balcony. By this time, the *NC-4*'s men were getting an idea that Ponta Delgada was only a dress rehearsal for even noisier and more elaborate receptions ahead.

The evening of their arrival was observed by a magnificent formal dinner; the wine flowed freely, there were many toasts, speeches, and dancing into the night. A good time was had by all—or almost all. The NC fliers' festivities were clouded by John Towers' anomalous position. The spectre at the feast was Josephus Daniels, sitting in the Secretary of the Navy's office more than 2,000 miles away in Washington, D.C.

Towers was an aircraft commander without an aircraft. His *NC-3* was not only unflyable, but was already disassembled for transportation back to the United States aboard the *Melville*. Towers was also the commanding officer of NC Seaplane Division One, and his orders of 18 April, signed by Franklin Roosevelt, emphasized that "as Commander of the NC Seaplane Division One of regularly commissioned seaplanes, your status will be the same as Commander of a Division of sea-going ships of the Navy."[13] Accordingly, Towers was at liberty to shift his command of the division to the airplane of either of the other aircraft commanders. Not just the United States Navy, but the navies of the world operated on this basis, and had done so for hundreds of years. No one among the *NC-4*'s crew was disturbed by this; it was a piece of bad luck that the *NC-3* was all beaten to pieces. John Towers was still their Division Commander, and they expected him to fly with them to Lisbon. Towers would not displace anyone aboard the *NC-4;* he would, in effect, be something of a passenger.[14]

Shortly after his arrival in Ponta Delgada, Towers informed the Navy Department of the status of the *NC-3* and the well-being of her crew, and concluded his report with "I will proceed to Lisbon in *NC-4*." Secretary Daniels, however, had other ideas. A former newspaperman, he was fascinated by the superficial contradictions in the *NC-4*'s success. There was the fact of the "lame duck" making good; and Albert C. Read being a small man, only five feet, five inches tall, gripped Daniels' attention. Here was an instance of the "little fellow" becoming the hero. The Navy Department had an aggressive postwar recruiting campaign planned and Daniels intended to use Read as a popular hero to demonstrate to the public that in the Navy "anybody could do it." This image seized his imagination; it was the stuff of a "good story," and he was sure that it would appeal to the man-in-the-street.

Later, there would be speculation that Towers had enemies in the Navy Department who convinced Daniels to "bump" him off the flight. After all, Towers had been closely associated with Admiral William S.

Sims' office in London for almost a year during the war, and the bitterness of the Daniels-Sims feud was notorious. But this was nonsense. On 21 May 1913, at the Navy's aviation camp at Annapolis, it was John Towers who had taken Daniels up for his first flight in an airplane; the eight-minute flight was made in the flying boat C-1 and the secretary enjoyed it greatly.[15] Josephus Daniels had only the greatest respect for Towers, or else he would not have put him in charge of the NC Transatlantic Project in the first place.

Daniels would later dress up his decision to exclude Towers from the flight to Lisbon in terms of "justice" to Read and the crew of the *NC-4*, insisting that if Towers flew with the *NC-4* one of her regular crew would have to be left in the Azores.[16] This sounded good but it was nonsense. Later yet, Daniels explained that he wanted to avoid a Sampson-Schley controversy as came to exist after the battle of Santiago. During the Spanish-American War Admiral Sampson commanded the Fleet but was absent from his flagship when the Spanish Fleet emerged from Santiago; it was Commodore Schley who supervised the slaughter of the Spanish ships—and for years thereafter the Navy was torn apart by a degrading public controversy over who deserved credit for the victory.[17] This also sounded good as regards the *NC-4*, but it was equally nonsense.

Daniels had a difficult time keeping his story straight over the years, but the truth of it is that Read's image appealed to the Secretary's imagination; he was certain that it would appeal equally to the public's democratic prejudices and that this would assist the Navy's postwar recruiting efforts.

The whole unfortunate affair might have been avoided if Admiral Jackson, acting upon the best of intentions, had not radioed Washington to ask permission for Towers to proceed in the *NC-4*. There was no necessity of this because Franklin Roosevelt's orders to Towers already made allowance for the possibility, but Jackson was unaware of this. It was Jackson's message that tipped off the secretary to the new details of the NC situation and inspired his intervention. On the evening of 20 May the *Melville's* radio operator brought the bad news to Admiral Jackson:

FOR COMMANDER TOWERS. YOUR 19220. SECRETARY THINKS BEST COMMANDER READ PROCEED IN COMMAND NC FOUR. THAT YOU REMAIN PONTA DELGADA AWAIT FURTHER ORDERS.[18]

Admiral Jackson took it upon himself to protest the matter to Daniels. And from London, where Admiral Harry S. Knapp's radioroom was monitoring all of the Navy's Atlantic radio traffic, Admiral Knapp took up Towers' cause by radioing Washington:

> PRIORITY. RECOMMEND THAT AS REGARD FOR HIS REMARKABLE ENERGY AND SKILL IN BRINGING NC THREE SAFELY INTO PORT, COMMANDER TOWERS BE AUTHORIZED TO PROCEED TO LISBON IN NC FOUR AS DIVISION COMMANDER.[19]

A message from London, Admiral Sims' former nest, may have served only to wave a red cape at Daniels. In any case, he was not about to be swerved from his original decision, and his reply was:

> WHILE SECRETARY RECOGNIZES FULL MERIT COMMANDER TOWERS SERVICES FOR WHICH HE SHOULD BE REWARDED, IN JUSTICE TO ALL CONCERNED, DOES NOT APPROVE HIS SAILING IN NC FOUR.[20]

And that was that—except for the gossips, rumor mongers, and journalists who would pick away at this unhappy moment for the next fifty years.

It was a bitter moment for Towers. The transatlantic flight had long since become one of his primary goals in life, dating from his association with the Curtiss-Wanamaker plans for the *America* in 1914. It was he who conceived the NC flight, led its planning, worked out its organization, and had led it thus far. It was no less a disappointment for the others; all of the NC flight crews felt that the politicians and the brass in Washington had swindled their Division Commander out of the honor that was his due.

John Towers could not know it in 1919, but this experience established a peculiar pattern for the rest of his Navy career. He expected with good reason to believe that he would succeed Rear Admiral William A. Moffett as Chief of the Bureau of Aeronautics when Moffett retired in October 1933. But Moffett's sudden death in the crash of the airship *Akron,* 4 April 1933, shattered this expectation. Towers was finally appointed bureau chief in 1939, and it was he who organized the wartime expansion of naval aviation. After 1942, as Commander Air Force, U.S. Pacific Fleet, he followed his creation to battle, organized its logistics, and was the principal architect of its strategy, all the while watching his contemporaries and juniors win the great tactical victories. When Towers finally assumed command of Task Force 38 in August 1945 all the victories had been won; only the Japanese surrender remained to be accepted. It was Towers' fate to be a primary organizer of naval aviation in World War I, the planner and organizer of victory over the Atlantic in 1919, and of naval aviation's victory over Japan during World War II—without being able to establish a bright spot for himself in the popular history books. Such is often the lot of the most determined and dedicated pioneers; and no *less* could have been expected of Naval Aviator No. 3.

Towers and the crews of the *NC-3* and *NC-1* received orders to proceed to Plymouth, England, on board the destroyer *Stockton*. Lavender and Sadenwater, however, requested orders back to the United States and they were transferred to the *Columbia*. The carcass of the *NC-3* was entrusted to the care of Moore and he and the *NC-3* went back to New York on board the *Melville*.

Aboard the *Stockton*, Towers was able to compare notes with her commanding officer, Commander Harry Baldridge. It was the *Stockton* that Towers had been looking for at Station 17 after he had been thrown off course to the south. Baldridge told him that the ship he mistook for the *Maddox* was probably the *Marblehead*, because the *Stockton* exchanged signals with the cruiser only a few hours before, and she was in the vicinity of the *Maddox* when the *NC-3* flew into the area. The *Maddox* was probably hidden by a rain squall.

From Captain Baldridge, Towers also discovered that the NC flight had not been made without loss of life. While the *Stockton* was on station waiting for the NCs to take off from Trepassey, one of her turbo-generators exploded; two men were seriously burned and Chief Machinist's Mate James Welch received a horrible abdominal wound. The *Stockton* did not have a doctor on board but within six hours the battleship *Montana* was alongside and Welch was transferred to her excellent hospital facilities. It was too late; three hours later the *Montana* reported that he was dead. Chief Welch's death made no headlines anywhere; but this was consistent with the universal anonymity of those who man the engine rooms of the world's navies. His death was nevertheless part of the price paid to get the NCs across the Atlantic.

The *Stockton* sailed for Plymouth at 1:05 A.M., 22 May. She was still under the immediate command of Admiral Jackson, and she was under way for only a few hours when orders were received from the Azores that diverted her to Lisbon. Admiral Jackson suspected that by sending the *Stockton* to Plymouth, the "gang" back in Washington was trying to cheat Towers out of the transatlantic flight's moment of triumph upon its arrival in Europe. He wanted to be sure that Towers, Bellinger, and the others were on hand to participate in the honors when the *NC-4* touched down at Lisbon.

In the early evening of 23 May the *Stockton* dropped anchor in the Tagus offshore of Lisbon's charming skyline, and Towers and his men were transferred to the cruiser *Rochester* where Captain Luther M. Overstreet, her commanding officer, was on the quarterdeck to welcome

157

them aboard. The *Rochester* was the flagship of Rear Admiral Charles P. Plunkett, Commander Destroyer Forces, Atlantic. During the World War, Plunkett had held a unique command in which his powerful fleet of 14-inch-gun men o'war operated hundreds of miles away from salt water and did all their "sailing" on steel rails. He had commanded the Navy's 14-inch railway batteries on the Western Front.

As Towers and Bellinger unpacked their gear on board the *Rochester,* they may well have exchanged some ironic remarks. Towers had lost his wager with Captain Tomb; the *Aroostook* had arrived in Plymouth six hours before this same day. But what is more, even sailing his *NC-3* backwards, he had beaten the *NC-4* to Ponta Delgada. Now he and Bellinger and their crews from the *NC-3* and *NC-1* had beaten the *NC-4* to Lisbon. An airplane was obviously not the quickest means of crossing the Atlantic in 1919. The *NC-4* was still back at Ponta Delgada—weatherbound again.

At daybreak on Wednesday the twenty-first, the day after her arrival at Ponta Delgada, the *NC-4's* crew were readying her for the flight to Lisbon. During the night floodlights had been kept trained on the flying boat while a Navy motorwhaleboat cruised around her to prevent the possibility of any harbor craft colliding with her—and to ward off souvenir hunters. All went well until the port engine was started; it was shy 300 r.p.m. and refused to come up to speed. In the small harbor, Read did not believe that there was room enough to get the airplane off the water except with full power. The problem was a stiff butterfly valve in the carburetor which was starving the engine. By the time this was determined it was too late to expect arrival at Lisbon before sundown and Read canceled the flight for that day.

The next day a 40-knot wind was pushing low clouds across a gray sky and the swells in the harbor were running ten feet high. Again, flight plans were canceled.

For five days the Atlantic clamped itself down upon the Azores with all of its malignancy, shrouding São Miguel in low clouds and dumping tons of rain on Ponta Delgada. Meanwhile, Bellinger and the crew of the *NC-1* had arrived from Horta aboard the *Gridley* and departed for Lisbon with Towers and the *NC-3* crew aboard the *Stockton.* Word came in from the *Fairfax* that the derelict *NC-1* had finally sunk, and a news bulletin from England announced that C. R. Fairey, Ltd., had withdrawn its seaplane from the *Daily Mail* competition.

On the twenty-second, heavy seas kept the *NC-4* clutching her moorings. In New York City a Franco-American hotel owner named Raymond Orteig announced that he was offering a prize of $25,000 for a nonstop flight from New York to Paris, or from Paris to New York.[21]

158

And in this May of 1919 a 17-year-old youth named Charles A. Lindbergh—who would win the Orteig prize eight years later—was deciding to give up farming as unprofitable and to attend the University of Wisconsin.

On the twenty-third, the big Atlantic swells continued to roll into Ponta Delgada's harbor. A radio message was intercepted from the American freighter *Lake Charlotteville*: she had found the wreckage of Hawker's *Atlantic* afloat at 49°40′ north, 29°08′ west. Its wings were completely smashed; only its almost empty fuel tank had served to keep the wreckage afloat. A bag of mail was found inside the fuselage but there were no signs of life.

The twenty-fourth came and went with more rain; and the pealing of church bells through the drizzle of the twenty-fifth announced that yet another Sunday had overtaken the NC flight. That afternoon the *Melville's* radioroom picked up the startling news that Hawker and Grieve had been found, and had just been landed in Scotland.

A few hours out of Newfoundland, Hawker's radio went dead; otherwise all went well through the first four hours. Then they flew into formations of towering cumulus clouds filled with turbulence and their struggle with the North Atlantic began. All through the night they dodged around the great cloud barriers, plunging through them blindly when no passage could be found around them. Sunrise came and the clouds continued to press in upon the little Sopwith's passage. Grieve checked his navigation and was dismayed to discover that during the night they had drifted off course 130 miles to the south. Then a vast cloud barrier loomed that reached across the horizon ahead, and from the surface to thousands of feet above the Sopwith's ceiling. Hawker plunged into the cloud to find a maelstrom of turbulence that threatened to tear the 6,000-pound airplane to pieces. He dove for the surface in an effort to fly underneath it—and then the Rolls-Royce engine sputtered and became silent. With the wind whistling ominously through the biplane's wires, they glided down through an eerie damp white world of nothingness toward the sea somewhere below. Hawker worked his throttle; Grieve pumped furiously on the plane's manual emergency fuel pump; it was futile.

The Sopwith broke out of the clouds less than 100 feet above a dark, gale-swept ocean. Hawker was preparing to ditch when the engine suddenly roared back to life; but when he looked at the engine's temperature gauge, its indicating needle was well over the danger mark. Its radiator's water had either boiled off or leaked away. Ireland was only 500 miles away, but with their engine running as hot as it was, the distance may as well have been infinity. During the next two hours they

159

flew back and forth across the steamer lane, nursing the engine and looking for a ship to ditch alongside. Now they were thankful that they had drifted so far south, because the drift had put them right over the steamer lane.

A whisp of smoke appeared on the horizon and the silhouette of a ship grew beneath it. Grieve fired off a Very flare while Hawker circled the ship. A man waved from its bridge; they were seen. Then Hawker brought the Sopwith down and neatly dropped her into a trough. For the next hour and a half they rode their derelict from trough to crest while the freighter appeared and disappeared across the slate gray waves as her crew struggled to get a lifeboat away.

The airmen eventually found themselves on board the Danish ship *Mary,* en route from Norfolk, Virginia, to Aarhus, Denmark. Captain Duhn of the *Mary* told them that they were at 50°20′ north, 29°30′ west, more than halfway to Ireland. However, the *Mary* had no radio so there was no way of telling the world that the aviators were safe. Thus for the next seven days as the *Mary* plodded along her great circle track across the North Atlantic, the world searched and wondered about Hawker and his navigator, and finally gave them up as dead. They came back from the grave on Sunday the twenty-fifth when the *Mary* came abeam of the Butt of Lewis at the top of Scotland. The Lloyds' Station there was thrown into a turmoil of excitement when a blinker signal from the *Mary* laconically reported: "Saved hands of Sopwith aeroplane." The station asked, "Is it Hawker?"; and the reply came back, "Yes!"[22]

The Admiralty was notified and the destroyer *Woolston* intercepted the *Mary* and took Hawker and Grieve on board. A few hours later they were landed in Thurso, Scotland, and were put aboard a train for London. When they stepped off their train in London's King's Cross Station they found a cheering crowd of thousands of persons awaiting their arrival. The press of humanity was so great the airmen had to struggle to get the door of their railway coach open. Then they were seized by a group of Australian soldiers who carried them on their shoulders to a waiting automobile.

When Harry Hawker learned that the *NC-4* was still in the Azores, he may well have felt the same irony as Towers and Bellinger. He had beaten the Yank airplane across—but without his aircraft.

NC-4 WINS FIRST OCEAN FLIGHT FOR AMERICA; 9¾ HOURS FROM PONTA DELGADA TO LISBON; HAWKER'S PLANE PICKED UP BY AMERICAN SHIP

HAWKER IN LONDON; TELLS REST OF STORY

Grieve Shares With Pilot Tremendous Ovation on Trip From Scotland and in Metropolis.

AVIATORS DECLARE GALE THEY MET WAS NO HINDRANCE

Would Have Completed Flight But For Boiling Water Trouble—Wireless Equipment Unsatisfactory—Details of Rescue.

Route of the NC-4 From Ponta Delgada to Lisbon.

NC-4 LEAVES AZORES 6:18 A. M., OUR TIME

Arrives at Portuguese Port at 4:02 P. M., Averaging Over 82 Miles an Hour.

START FOR PLYMOUTH TODAY WITH GOOD WEATHER

Lisbon Declares a Holiday and Cheering Thousands, Lining the Shore, Greet the Seaplane, While Bells Ring and Ship Sirens Shriek.

First Flier Across the Atlantic
Lieut. Commander A. C. Read

GERMANY DEMANDS LEAGUE EQUALITY

Answer to Allies Will Also Insist on Plebiscites in Disputed Territory.

TRUST FOR HER LOST FLEET

She Wants It Administered by Us and the World's Merchant Shipping Pooled.

Belgian Shuts Frontiers; Rumlls Troops on Leave

RIOTERS DAMAGE YALE BUILDINGS

Discharged Soldiers and Sailors Smash Windows in Attempt to Get on the Campus.

SEVERAL STUDENTS HURT

Trouble Grows Out of Remarks at Welcome—Home Parade Which Were Misunderstood.

FOREIGN REDS OUST BOLSHEVIKI

Chinese, Letts, and Finns Control Petrograd After Several Days of Fighting.

SOVIET CHIEFS IN FLIGHT

Bombardment from Sea in Direction of Petrograd and Kronstadt Heard at Viborg.

STRIKE IN CANADA SWEEPING WEST

Borden, in Parliament, Bids the Country Remember Labor Program at Paris.

ULTIMATUM FROM TORONTO

Calgary Postal Tieup Blocks Funds for Soldiers—Saskatoon Votes Strike, 5 to 1.

The New York Times, 28 May 1919

The *NC . . . First!*

When the sun finally managed to spread a dull daylight over the Azores on Monday morning of 26 May, everyone in Ponta Delgada was still talking about the rescue of Hawker and Grieve. News reports coming into the *Melville's* radio room said that Freddie Raynham was repairing his plane at Quidi Vidi and was still determined to fly the Atlantic; but Morgan had to be hospitalized and Raynham was looking for a new navigator. Admiral Kerr's huge Handley Page *V/1500* was still being assembled at Harbour Grace, and the freighter *Glendevon* had just arrived in St. John's with the Vickers *Vimy* to be flown by Alcock and Brown.

The only immediate competition the *NC-4* had from Newfoundland was the foul weather blowing out of the northwest. However, on the evening of the twenty-sixth, Lieutenant Anderson gave Read a forecast that indicated clearing during the night.

Read and his men were up early on the twenty-seventh for a getaway at first daylight. But again the port engine refused to come up to speed. Only the day before a brand new carburetor had been installed and the engine tuned; when Rhoads took it apart this morning he found its gasket shredded, plugging the jets. Two hours were lost while yet another carburetor was installed. Finally the *NC-4* had all of her engines running, and all idling nicely at 1,300 r.p.m.

All was well. Read waved his takeoff signal at the pilots' cockpits and Stone shoved his throttles open. The *NC-4* went roaring down the harbor, plunging through the swells at the head of a great cloud of spray. Lift-off was at 1018.

With the roar of the four Liberty engines around them, the *NC-4's* men could not hear the salute of whistles, sirens, and bells that filled the port at the instant daylight showed beneath their keel. In the *Melville's* radio room the operator's fist came down on a rapid series of signals and eight hundred miles away in Lisbon the *Rochester's* operator took up his pencil to copy them. The radioman handed the message to Captain Harris Laning, Admiral Plunkett's chief of staff, who read it with great satisfaction: The *NC-4* was off. Laning called a messenger and sent the dispatch to the officer of the deck. A few minutes later the *Rochester's* whistle and siren sounded across the city and was quickly joined by the *Shawmut's*. All of Lisbon knew what this meant: *"O hidroaviã Americano está achegar!"*

When Herbert Rodd felt the *NC-4's* hull come unstuck from the water, he put his head out of the after hatch to check on their altitude. Ponta Delgada was below and behind, slowly shrinking in size between the framing of the tailbooms. The island of Santa Maria appeared off to the right as São Miguel slipped astern. Both islands were easily identified in the poor visibility by the wads of clouds that clung to their mountaintops. As the *NC-4* climbed to 500 feet, Rodd ducked below, reeled out his trailing antenna, clamped on his headphones, and began warming up his radio. There were fourteen destroyers strung out between Ponta Delgada and Lisbon, with all of Europe beyond; there were all kinds of people to talk with this day.

Shortly after 1100 Read called Rodd over the interphone (which was now working) with a message for Admiral Jackson and the *Melville*. It is a classic example of the New Englander's art of understatement:

WE SEEM TO BE ON OUR WAY; THANKS FOR YOUR HOSPITALITY. READ.[1]

Then at 1110 Rodd began requesting weather reports from the station vessels. The replies came back from all the way down the line, and they were all good. Two minutes later the *NC-4* overflew the *Sampson* on Station 1.

About 25 minutes later the *DuPont* on Station 2 was in sight— but she was way off to the north and only her smoke was visible. Read checked his navigation. Either the *DuPont* was off station or he was off course. His check showed that the *NC-4* was on course. But a half hour passed and the *Cassin* on Station 3 failed to come into sight. Something was wrong. Read told Rodd to get some radio bearings.

Rodd called the *Wilkes* on Station 4. This was a piece of luck, because the *Wilkes* was one of the destroyers with which the NC crews had worked out their navigation and radio procedures in practices at Hampton Roads. Immediately the signals RC, RC, RC, FOUR; RC, RC, RC, FOUR, began ticking into Rodd's headphones. The radio bearing taken at 1220 showed the *Wilkes* slightly off to the left. As the *NC-4* flew closer the angle of subsequent bearings increased: at 1230 to 20 degrees, and at 1235 to 45 degrees. This told Read what he wanted to know. Course was

164

changed, and at 1250 the *NC-4* roared directly over the *Wilkes'* mast-heads.

Why his navigation had taken him on such a divergent course puzzled Read. An examination of his compasses provided the answer. The *NC-4's* compasses were in no way similar to aircraft compasses of only a few years later, which were self-contained units mounted flush into the instrument panel. The *NC-4's* compasses were simply boat compasses adapted to aircraft use and the instruments rode loosely in gimbals. Read discovered that his compass had been jarred out of position enough to create an error of eight degrees. He blamed this on the rough takeoff at Ponta Delgada, where porpoising across the swells must have bounced the gimbals out of their mountings.

While Rodd was taking his bearings on the *Wilkes,* more than 2,000 miles to the west in Washington, D.C., the House Committee on Naval Affairs was meeting with Josephus Daniels to discuss the Navy's requirements for the fiscal year of 1920. The committee's hearings were interrupted by Congressman Frederick C. Hicks (R., N.Y.) who announced that he had just received word from the Navy Department that the *NC-4* had overflown the *Lamberton* on Station 6, the weather was good and there was every prospect of the aircraft reaching Lisbon. As a member of the Naval Affairs Committee, Hicks had for long regarded naval aviation as his personal ward and had done much to further its cause. In 1919 his activities were by no means at their end.[2] Hicks obtained permission to be excused from the hearings for a few minutes and went on the floor of Congress to make the same announcement, where it was greeted with applause.

Hicks' injection of the *NC-4* into the committee room stimulated a long digression about the transatlantic flight. Congressman Fred Britten (R., Ill.) complimented Daniels on his decision to exclude Towers from the Azores-Lisbon stage of the flight. Britten was convinced that all honors belonged to Read and his men. This gave Daniels an opportunity to explain that if Towers went in the *NC-4* his weight might have overloaded the aircraft and one of the crew who had flown all the way from Rockaway would have had to be removed. This was by no means the truth, but the committee was satisfied and concurred in the secretary's decision, and Daniels was satisfied that he had done the popular thing.[3]

As the *NC-4* approached the *Robinson* on Station 7 she began to run into a patchwork of rain squalls. Rodd exchanged calls between Read and Commander George W. Simpson, commanding officer of the *Robinson*. The *Robinson* had served the *NC-4* between Chatham and Halifax, again between Halifax and Trepassey, and yet again between

Horta and Ponta Delgada; she was something of an old friend by this time. Simpson was pleased to show Read's message to his executive officer, Lieutenant Commander Frank C. McCord, and pass the word to his crew. A few years later Frank McCord would seek a career as a naval aviator; his career and his life would end as commanding officer of the airship USS *Akron*, when the airship crashed at sea on a stormy April night in 1933.

An hour later, east of the *Wadsworth* on Station 9, the day brightened and cleared; the wind began to fall off and the white caps on the sea below transformed themselves into long, glassy swells.

At 1700 Rodd tried to raise the *Shawmut* but could get no reply. Five minutes later the *Winslow* on Station 11 slipped by below. Then the *Rochester* called the *NC-4* with a message from Admiral Plunkett:

FINE WORK; COME ALONG.[4]

At 1750 Rodd finally managed to exchange calls with the *Shawmut* and 15 minutes later the *Ericsson* on Station 12 was overflown. An air of expectancy now began to fill the *NC-4*. Two more stations and there would be nothing more ahead of them except the coast of Portugal.

At 1835 the *O'Brien* on Station 13 came in sight, was overflown and was left astern. The executive officer of the *O'Brien* was a very interested spectator to the *NC-4*'s passage. In the years ahead he would have many things to say on the subject of aerial navigation. He was Lieutenant Commander P. V. H. Weems.

As the *O'Brien* slipped over the horizon astern, the *Rochester* called Read for an ETA. He replied:

EXPECT TO ARRIVE ABOUT EIGHT O'CLOCK GMT. PLEASE HAVE SEARCHLIGHT ON WATER TRAINED INTO THE WIND.[5]

Read was confident that this request would be executed smartly; the commanding officer of the *Shawmut* was Commander Damon E. Cummings, an old friend and classmate with whom he had graduated from the Naval Academy. Cummings' executive officer was Lieutenant Frank Wilbur Wead, not yet a naval aviator, but one who would become well known as such in the 1920s as a result of his work with the Navy's air racing teams, and later yet as a script writer of some of Hollywood's best aviation movies.

At 1900 the *McDougal* on Station 14 was overflown. Rodd heard her radio sending word of the *NC-4*'s passage to the *Rochester* and a few minutes later he noticed that the radio traffic among stations in Portugal and Spain suddenly became very active.

The *O'Brien* slipped off into the west; over the eastern horizon ahead was Europe. From his perch in the nose, Read leaned a little harder into the slipstream to squint at the haze along the eastern rim. Breese squeezed up beside Hinton in the pilots' cockpit for a better look; Rhoads manned the after hatch. Rodd remained busy with his radio key.

A half hour after leaving the *O'Brien* a dark, purplish line began to spread itself across the dusk gathering on the horizon ahead.

Read saw a small, diamondlike light flashing sharply in its midst.

It was the lighthouse on Cabo da Roca, the westernmost point of Europe.

The time was 1739.

A few minutes later the *NC-4* roared over the thin beachline backed by steep, jagged cliffs. In this moment it occurred to Read that "no matter what happened—even if we crashed on landing—the transatlantic flight, the first one in the history of the world, was an accomplished fact."[6]

As Stone eased the big airplane into a right bank and put her on a southerly heading parallel to the coast, Read ducked below to finish his report of the flight to Towers and the Navy Department. After their experiences in the Azores he knew that there would be precious little time in Lisbon to attend to paperwork, and he had been working on the reports, off and on, during the past hour. In anticipation of their reception aboard the *Rochester* Breese had already shaved. Rodd cranked in his trailing antenna and switched his set to the fixed antenna between the skid fins on the upper wings.

Lisbon had been anticipating the arrival of the NCs for all of nineteen days, and as the sun began to settle over the mouth of the Tagus this day, the city had been waiting for the *NC-4* for more than eight hours. It was 11:27 A.M. when the *Rochester's* whistle, siren and saluting gun announced the *NC-4's* takeoff from Ponta Delgada. In response to the signal, people ran out of shops and market places, cafes were emptied and by noon a crowd of several thousand persons had gathered along the waterfront, filling the capital city's Praça do Commercio, a magnificent public square that covers almost ten acres on the edge of the Tagus.

In the center of the Praça, under the bronze equestrian statue of the Portuguese king Dom Jose I, a detail of officers and men from the *Rochester* had set up a large blackboard to show the *NC-4's* progress past the fourteen station vessels. There were no walkie-talkie radios in

167

1919. Instead, a signalman was stationed on the seawall to link the *Rochester* with the blackboard detail on the Praça. Reports of the *NC-4*'s passage came into the *Rochester's* radio room at 30- to 40-minute intervals. They were given to a signalman on the cruiser's bridge who wigwagged the message to the man ashore on the seawall, who then set his flags in motion to relay the word to the blackboard detail set up in the shadow of Dom Jose I. When the signalmen went into action a hush came across the crowd until the message was chalked on the blackboard. Then it was relayed by shouts and cheers across the Praça: *"Estacão número quatro! A aviao passou a estacão número quatro!"*

When the number "13" was chalked on the board and the cry of *"Trece!"* roared across the Praça, the crowd went wild with excitement. Forty minutes later, no signalman was required to announce the *NC-4*'s overflight of the *MacDougal*. By prearrangement, the *Rochester* sounded her whistle and siren, and was immediately joined by all of the ships in the port. At 8:05 P.M., all of Lisbon knew that the *NC-4* had passed Station 14 and would be over the city in about an hour.

The sun was a brilliant red disc floating low in a brilliantly hued sky flecked with clouds above the Barre Norte when thousands of eyes began to strain toward the west for a first sight of the *NC-4*. The ships at anchor in the Tagus and along the quays were all dressed for the occasion; their hundreds of flags snapped in a 30-knot wind that flashed their colors against the exaggerated light of the sunset. In the city, the street lights were just coming on. The Navy artist Henry Reuterdahl remarked to the *New York Times* correspondent Walter Duranty that the scene was very much like a stage setting prepared by the Broadway impressario David Belasco for a happy ending to one of his productions.

"There she is!" cried a lookout aboard the *Shawmut*.

Eyes strained to find the airplane's silhouette in the riot of colors that filled the west.

For a moment it was regarded as a false alarm.

But there she was—a black speck among the oranges and reds over Punta da Laje at the end of the Tagus, and growing larger with the passing of each second.

Within two minutes the snarling of her four Liberty engines could be heard coming up the river ahead of her—and then they were drowned out by all the whistles, sirens, and church bells.

The *Shawmut's* searchlight snapped on and swung around to point into the wind.

Read made no flourishes. He did not have Stone circle the city. That was not the way of Albert C. Read.

The *NC-4* flew straight up the broad estuary at about 1,500 feet

168

until abeam of the Tower of Belem, and then began a long, easy let-down.

At 2001 (9:01 P.M. local time), the *NC-4*'s keel sliced into the Tagus; Elmer Stone eased her hull into the water and chopped his throttles.

As the *NC-4* touched down, the *Rochester* began firing a twenty-one-gun salute—an honor usually reserved for a nation's flag or its heads of state—and the old Portuguese man-of-war *Vasco da Gama* answered the salute, gun for gun.

A motor launch from the *Shawmut* sped out to meet the *NC-4* and led her to a buoy. A coxs'n threw a line to Read in the bow. Read lunged at it, but missed. His first words to the world upon completing this historic flight were "Try again! I slipped!"[7]

While the *NC-4* was being made fast to a buoy hundreds of motor launches, fishing boats, and sailing craft swam out of the dusk and began circling her, blowing whistles, ringing bells, their occupants waving hats and scarves, and all cheering. Read was alarmed by the sailing craft; their bobbing masts held a hazard for the *NC-4*'s wingtips, ailerons and her whole tailgroup. "Don't let those fellows come to close!" he shouted at the *Shawmut*'s boat crews; "If they foul her, there'll be damage done!"[8]

A launch from the *Rochester* arrived alongside to take Read and his crew to the flagship. Before leaving, Read cautioned the *Shawmut*'s men who would be standing watch aboard the *NC-4* during the night against the harbor's sightseers: "If they come too near, hit them lightly over the head; that will keep them away!"[9] Then they climbed into the motor launch and were off to the *Rochester*.

Darkness had covered Lisbon by the time the men of the *NC-4* were brought alongside the brilliantly lighted *Rochester* which had her crew manning the rails and yards. As Read and his men stepped out of the launch and mounted the accommodation ladder all hands began cheering. The quarterdeck was packed with officials of the Portuguese government, Lisbon's diplomatic corps and the admiral's staff.

As Read stepped onto the quarterdeck he saluted the Stars and Stripes which flew illuminated under floodlights at the cruiser's stern, and then saluted Lieutenant (j.g.) A. H. McCreery, the officer of the deck. He solemnly informed McCreery that he was Lieutenant Commander A. C. Read, commanding officer of the seaplane *NC-4*, and requested permission for him and his crew to come aboard. The O.D. promptly returned Read's salute and replied, "Permission granted!" Lieutenant McCreery found this evening so busy and so exciting that when he closed out his log of the watch he forgot to mention that the

NC-4 had arrived—and even that Read and his crew had come aboard![10]

When Read turned to the crowd around him and was searching for a familiar face, a forest green uniform broke from its midst, rushed up to Read and grabbed him by the shoulder and shook his hand. It was John Towers. As Towers turned to Stone, a deep roar rose from the hundreds of throats of the *Rochester's* crew. Then from somewhere behind the spectators the *Rochester's* Marine band struck up the Star Spangled Banner, and there was silence as the naval and military personnel froze to attention with a hand salute, while a searchlight snapped on to put its dazzling beam on the *NC-4's* men. According to Walter Duranty of *The New York Times:*

> It was a wonderful picture. In the foreground was the little group who had done what no man had ever done before, standing stiffly at salute in the dazzling brightness of a searchlight. Beyond them were rows of naval and military officers in uniform, and a dark mass of civilians, splashed with the color of women's dresses.
>
> On the left was the witchery of colored lights gleaming amid the bright-hued flags, and in the center and on the right background were sailors' faces—grave and reverent in homage to their country's national hymn—rising tier upon tier until lost in the darkness overhead.[11]

When the last note of the music faded off into the night, the officer of the deck ordered *"To!"* and all hands at salute snapped down as one. Then Admiral Plunkett stepped forward with Thomas H. Birch, the United States' Minister to Portugal, who presented Read and his men to Dr. Xavier da Silva, Portugal's Minister for Foreign Affairs, and Dr. Macedo Pinto, the Minister of Marine. In the name of the Portuguese government, Dr. Pinto decorated Read and his men with Portugal's ancient Order of Tower and Sword, established by King Alphonso V, thirty-three years before Columbus discovered America. The same honor was extended to Towers, Bellinger, and the crews of the *NC-3* and *NC-1.*

When the NC fliers had time to examine the beautiful design of their decorations, they discovered on them the words *Merito, Valor, Lealdade*—merit, courage, and fidelity, a very adequate sum of the qualities of those who manned the NC boats.

With the official ceremonies attended to, the evening passed on to a general reception and it was several hours before Read and his men were able to find their bunks aboard the *Shawmut.* As soon as Read could get away from the crowd gracefully, he located the *Rochester's* radio officer and gave him a message for Captain Ward K. Wortman, commanding officer of the *Melville:*

WE ARE SAFELY ON THE OTHER SIDE OF THE POND. READ.[12]

Read found the *Rochester's* radio room to be a rather frantic place this evening as messages of congratulation poured in from all over the world. The *Rochester's* radio officer had a bundle of messages for Read, but had singled out two in particular. One was from President Woodrow Wilson:

Accept my heartiest congratulation on the success of your flight, for yourself and your comrades, and the expression of my deep admiration. We are all heartily proud of you. You won a deserved distinction in adding still further to the laurels of our country.[13]

The other was from Secretary of the Navy Josephus Daniels who, as usual, was most emphatic with his congratulations:

The entire Navy congratulates you and your fellow aviators on your epochal flight. The ocean has been spanned through the air and to the American Navy goes the honor of making the first transatlantic flight. We are all intensely proud of your achievement and thankful that it has been accomplished without mishap to any one of the aviators who left our shores on the first air journey to Europe. To all of them, and to you, all honor is due.[14]

Back in Washington, Daniels was telling the press that "the splendid success of the Navy's fliers in the voyage to the Azores and Europe is only the beginning of experiments in the Navy." The Navy planned to develop its aviation in every possible way; there would be no stopping the Navy; United States Naval Aviation would go on progressing just as far as its funds and the Navy's genius would permit.[15]

Every time Daniels mentioned aviation his emphasis was on "Navy, Navy, Navy"—and with good reason in this May of 1919. Four months before, Brigadier General William Mitchell had swaggered down the gangway of the Cunard liner *Aquitania* to become the assistant director of the U.S. Army's Air Service. One of Mitchell's fellow passengers was Jerome Hunsaker, who was returning from an inspection of European aircraft facilities. Mitchell made no secret of his grandiose schemes for taking aviation away from the Army and Navy to combine them in a separate air force that would be a part of a marvelous bureaucratic empire which would also control civil aviation. The name of the empire was "airpower."

171

As Hunsaker listened to these ambitious schemes he came to suspect that Mitchell spelled trouble for the Navy, but in 1919 he never imagined how much. In April Mitchell appeared before the Navy's General Board, a group of senior flag officers who until 1947 advised the Secretary of the Navy on policy, and in this session Mitchell explained how armies and navies had been rendered obsolete; the future belonged to "airpower." Mitchell was still being relatively cautious in the summer of 1919, but Josephus Daniels knew that the noisy general and some of his friends in Congress were determined to take aviation away from the Navy and give it to a separate air force. What Daniels could not know was that this summer of 1919 marked the opening skirmishes of the sometimes bitter "Seven Years' War" between naval aviation and the zealots of "airpower."

The flight of the *NC-4* was not just an achievement of the Navy and naval aviation, it was an achievement of the United States. Josephus Daniels was at pains to make this clear in order to create an emotional amalgam in the public mind. The organization that planned and executed this remarkable transatlantic operation would not easily be disbanded and submerged in some new organization that had no historic laurels and boasted of "no traditions." Here Daniels was operating on very solid ground because nothing had created as much excitement in the United States since the Armistice. From faraway Denver the *Rocky Mountain News* declared:

Columbus achieved triumph over a vast expanse of uncharted sea; Commander A. C. Read overcame the tempests that blow over the seas and his name will go down in histories as the first who ever flew across those turbulent waters. After awhile, such flights will become commonplace, but the credit of the first accomplishment is to the glory of the Navy of the United States.[16]

When the *NC-4* arrived in the Azores, *The New York Times* observed that:

The American people, whose faith in their Navy never falters, for never has it failed them, are proud in knowing that the service has proved to be as daring and efficient in the air as it always is upon the sea, whatever the emergency. There is a thrill in the brave flight to the Azores that compensates for the rigors of the stern chase to place American aviation in the van, where it always should have been.[17]

And when the *NC-4* arrived in Lisbon, the *Times* added:

Our Navy has led the way in a work whose tremendous practical value will not wait long for demonstration.[18]

172

These were the kind of words that Josephus Daniels enjoyed reading, and they were typical of the hour. Other editorial comment was in a similar vein, but the *New York Herald* was speculative:

It may be that the time is not far distant when tickets can be purchased to London via "The Seaplane Express," equipped with bridal suites, deluxe drawing rooms, and dining saloons with the latest cuisine.

Why not? Commander Read's successful flight has opened up a vast field of speculation that may be a reality.[19]

In Washington, D.C., *The Evening Star* chose to set the American Eagle ascreaming:

American ability, American ingenuity, American thoroughness, American nerve have again come into their own. Epitomizing these inherent qualities of the American Navy, Lieut. Commander Albert Cushing Read of Washington, D.C., has blazed an air trail from the new world to the old, adding honor to his country, prestige to his service and fame to his name.[20]

In the Midwest, the *Chicago Tribune* drew a perceptive comparison between the *NC-4*'s success and the attempt by Hawker and Grieve:

Read and his fellows took the air after mature deliberation and with every wise precaution with the object of following an established course, of making scientific observations, of preparing data for future need, and of sanely developing overseas flying as a future reality; and Read was not a competitor for prize money.

Hawker flew for sport. Read flew for science. Read won. Had he not won he would still have given us much to think about and pore over and digest for the benefit of future fliers. Hawker lost. But still his feat is splendid, though it gives us nothing we had not already.[21]

In England, the *NC-4*'s arrival in Lisbon almost went unnoticed in the hysterical adulation that attended Hawker and Grieve's arrival in London on the same day. They had lost their race against the "Yanks," but the British press and public loved them all the more for their desperate attempt to score the historic "first" for the honor of England. The *Daily Mail* treated the *NC-4*'s arrival in eight inches, while seven full columns were devoted to Hawker. Even the staid London *Times* was swept away in the hysteria, giving one column to the *NC-4* and six to Hawker. There is an explanation for this that transcends nationalistic parochialism. After four long dreary years of war, the mud and blood of Flanders, Gallipoli, Palestine, and Mesopotamia had failed to produce a hero as heroes were understood prior to 1914. In 1919 the British press and public were starving for a hero. Hawker and Grieves' gallant attempt, their disappearance, and their dramatic "return from the grave" opened the floodgates on long dammed up national emotions.

At a luncheon gathering of 300 persons to honor Hawker and Grieve, sponsored by the *Daily Mail,* the ailing Lord Northcliffe who had posted the transatlantic prize could not be present, but he sent a message:

> Were I present I would like to raise my glass in congratulation of our American friends on their careful and characteristic preparations, and for their fine record-breaking flight to the Azores and Lisbon.[22]

However, his *Daily Mail's* prize for a nonstop flight between North America and the British Isles had not yet been won, and he added: "They have still left to us the problem of a direct flight from America to Europe."

Harry Hawker was not as gracious; the Australian aviator was still smarting at having been beaten by the unsporting aeronautical steamroller created by the U.S. Navy. When he got up to speak he ridiculed the *NC-4's* flight: with a chain of ships across the ocean shooting off flares and sweeping the sky with searchlights, the flight to the Azores was like "walking down Broadway," and this betrayed how little faith the Americans had in their engines. The luncheon guests were horrified and his remarks were received by a stony silence.[23]

The British press was very apologetic about Hawker's outburst and tended to attribute it to his being an Australian—who were more inclined to behave like a bull in a china shop than even the Americans!

One Englishman who was wholly out of sympathy with the popular hysteria was C. G. Grey, the waspish editor of the British aviation weekly *The Aeroplane.* Grey had an acid wit, could be outrageously biased, and his strong fascist sympathies led the British government to clap him into detention on the Isle of Man during World War II; but for more than a quarter of a century prior to 1939, his editorship served to make *The Aeroplane* the finest aviation weekly in the world. Grey had a great sense of history, and he remarked of the *NC-4's* flight:

> There is pure poetic justice in the victory being won by the Americans. After all, the first people to fly were the Wright brothers in 1903, on a machine of their own build with an engine of their own make. The first flights off and onto water were made by Glenn Curtiss in 1911, also in a machine and engine of his own production. And the first flying boat was designed and built by Glenn Curtiss in 1913, again with a home-made engine. Who therefore has a better right to be first across the Atlantic than an American crew on an American

flying boat with American engines? We may regret our own failure, but we cannot grudge America her brilliant success.

Nor was this the end:

> And now what next? The Atlantic has been crossed by air. We have lost the honour of being first across.
>
> There seems to be but a modified glory to be had in being the first to do a non-stop flight. So long as one can get from one place to another in any given vehicle, it matters little whether one stops for a drink along the way.
>
> After the first non-stop journey we shall begin to introduce an illimitable series of minor classes in the competition. We shall have the "first one man flight," then we shall have the "first flight with one engine," "the first flight with two engines" ... "the first flight with one passenger," "the first flight with ten passengers," "the first flight with a woman passenger," and so forth and so on, *ad infinitum*.
>
> The thing that really counts is being first across. And that honour has gone to America.[24]

This competition among "illimitable classes" is precisely how transatlantic flying came to develop, especially after its "barnstorming" period got under way in 1927. What interested Grey most, however, was the prospect of a regular transatlantic air service, and his observations on this point held another hint of prophecy:

> One swallow does not make a Summer and one trans-Atlantic flight does not make a commercial air service. We are still far from that regular service of aircraft across the Atlantic ... Such a service will come in due time, either by airship or aeroplane, probably by the former at first.
>
> When it comes it will depend for its success upon perfect organization and not upon slap-dash gallantry. So like the first crossing of the Atlantic it may fall to the skill and organizing power of America. If so, as in the present matter, honour be to whom honour is due.[25]

Several weeks would pass before Read and his men would read these press notices, in the scrapbooks kept by their wives and families. But before they rolled into their bunks aboard the *Shawmut* after the evening of 27 May, there was one thing of which they could be sure: Men would fly the Atlantic again—and again and again and again. They would fly it with much greater speed, in company, nonstop and alone, with passengers and carrying exotic cargoes that were impossible to define in 1919. They would fly at much great altitudes, in startling aircraft types that had not yet been conceived, and with comforts that in 1919 could only be imagined.

But no one else could ever be first.

A Curtiss Corporation advertisement for 1919

To Plymouth
by Seaplane . . .

While the press was reveling in its rhapsodic rhetoric, Read and his crew aboard the *Shawmut* were preparing for a day of ceremonies as guests of the Portuguese government, and looking after their *NC-4*. Arrival in Lisbon concluded the transatlantic leg of their flight, but their final destination remained Plymouth, England, more than eight hundred miles to the north. Plymouth was made the flight's terminal point because the NC boats could be disassembled for shipment back to the United States at the former U.S. Naval Air Station at Killingholme, and because it was a gesture of Anglo-American goodwill that would occur within a year of the three hundredth anniversary of the *Mayflower's* departure.

When Read and his men went on deck after breakfast they saw the *Rochester* getting under way for England with Towers, Bellinger, and their crews on board. They would see them again at Plymouth. At 9:57 A.M. the *NC-4* was towed up astern of the *Shawmut;* Breese and Rhoads went aboard her with a crew of machinist's mates for a check of her engines and to get her refueled. Herbert Rodd checked over his batteries and radio tubes. Meanwhile, Read and Stone were studying the isobars on a series of weather maps drawn up by Ensign Francis W. Reichelderfer, who was the NC flight's aerologist at Lisbon.

The 24-year-old Reichelderfer was the man with the most worries at Lisbon, because the successful completion of the *NC-4's* flight depended upon his forecast. When the *Shawmut* moored in Lisbon on 11 May, Reichelderfer promptly went ashore and introduced himself to the Portuguese Meteorological Office. The Portuguese were enthusiastic about cooperating with the Navy, but the first time Reichelderfer called them on the telephone he discovered that he had a language problem that he was unable to hurdle. Thereafter, he made daily trips ashore to the met' office to familiarize himself with local weather conditions before the NC boats arrived. Weather maps, fortunately, read about the same in any language.

The day after the *NC-4* arrived in Lisbon, John Towers summoned Reichelderfer to his quarters aboard the *Rochester* and told him how important it was for the *NC-4* to get to Plymouth and that her flight demanded the best forecast. Towers tended to place a good part of the blame for the losses of the *NC-3* and *NC-1* on inadequate forecasting, and this day in Lisbon he made it clear that there might be dire consequences to Reichelderfer's naval career if the *NC-4* met with a bad end en route to Plymouth.

This was a very uncomfortable moment for Reichelderfer, which may be difficult to appreciate a half century later; but in 1919 a naval officer with three stripes on his sleeve commanded the awe that only admirals have since 1945. Towers insisted on practically a 100 percent guarantee of any weather forecast for the flight. On one count this was extremely flattering; on all others it was absolutely impossible. However, given the ignorance in which the science of aerology was groping during 1919, Towers' order sounded only difficult, not impossible. And although Reichelderfer was a very worried ensign when he returned to the *Shawmut,* the vast ignorance of the day provided a substantial measure of bliss.

In the afternoon Read and his men went ashore, where they were received by President Canto y Castro of Portugal; the president had formerly been an admiral in the Portuguese Navy and was highly interested in naval aviation, so he and Read were able to indulge in more than polite small talk. Then they visited Lisbon's Town Council, which voted the striking of a special medal to honor the men of the *NC-4;* and by late afternoon they were back on board the *Shawmut.* The *NC-4* was checked over again to have her ready for the flight the next day; but Reichelderfer's forecast held bad terminal weather for Plymouth.

In the evening Read and his crew were the guests of honor at a magnificent banquet given by the Portuguese Navy. In the course of the evening, Minister of Marine DeMacedo Pinto made some remarks that held an element of prophecy. He observed that the U.S. Navy's use of flying boats pointed transoceanic flying in the correct direction, and he was sure that Hawker's misfortune proved the point. With respect to transatlantic air services of the immediate future, he concluded that "Lisbon is the ideal terminus for such crossings, as the wide, sheltered and well nigh landlocked expanse of the Tagus permits safe arrival and departure in any weather; the Azores, too, will make an admirable halfway station."[1] Twenty years later, almost to the day, Pan American Airways inaugurated the first transatlantic air services by airplane, using

Boeing 314 flying boats; their European landfall was Lisbon, and their flights were made via the Azores.

The following day there was further entertainment for the Navy fliers and a ceremony aboard the *Shawmut* in which officials from the city awarded Read and their men the city's medal. And the Portuguese Aero Club made Read a gift of a handsome silver plaque to commemorate the *NC-4's* flight. On this day, too, Reichelderfer had a favorable forecast for the morrow, and preparations were made for getting under way.

In the predawn of the thirtieth, Read and his men resumed their regular routine by being up well before reveille, and at 5:30 A.M. they boarded a launch that took them out to the *NC-4*. The engines were turned over one-by-one; Rhoads checked over his four wards carefully and found all well. Read cast off from the buoy.

Hinton wanted to make the takeoff and it made no difference to Stone, so he handed the controls to his copilot. Hinton taxied out into the estuary, swung around into the wind and opened his throttles to send the *NC-4* roaring down the channel. Lift-off came at 0529 (6:29 local), accompanied by the usual salutation of bells and whistles ashore. Hinton took the *NC-4* west, beyond the Tower of Belem, then banked her through a wide 180-degree turn and came roaring up the Tagus along Lisbon's waterfront. This was for the benefit of newsreel photographers who had complained to Read that they had been unable to get any pictures of the *NC-4's* arrival. In 1919 cameras were so primitive and film emulsions so poor that they were unable to seize action in the poor light of dusk. In order to have some footage, they asked Read to make a pass back up the river after takeoff, and Read agreed. The millions of movie-goers in 1919 who saw the newsreels of the *NC-4* "arriving" in Lisbon never dreamed that they were in fact watching her departure for Plymouth. But no matter; something was better than nothing at all. In any case, the hundreds of sailors aboard the *Shawmut* and the thousands of Portuguese who crowded the waterfront to witness the takeoff, more than enjoyed the *NC-4's* flyby.

Originally, there were no plans to have destroyers guarding the *NC-4's* flight along the coasts of Portugal and Spain, but Admiral Plunkett thought it a wise precaution and five ships were put on stations between Cabo da Roca and Cape Finisterre. To avoid confusion with the six numbered destroyers on stations across the Bay of Biscay between Finisterre and England, the coastal station vessels were given alphabetical designations, A through E. At 0635 Rodd called the *Conner, Rathburne* and *Woolsey* on stations A, B, and C for weather reports. The information was obtained with difficulty. These ships had been on European duty; they were not equipped with aircraft receiving sets and their operators had not been cued to the NC-4's radio setup until the last minute. Rodd called the Shawmut and requested her to order the destroyers to get their receivers carefully tuned to the NC-4's 425 meters.

At 0633 the Conner was overflown and all went well for another half hour when at 0705 a glistening feather of vaporizing liquid trailing aft of the port engine nacelle signaled a leak. There was no way of knowing if the silvery trail was fuel, oil or cooling water without sending a man out on the wing to get a taste of the stuff and Read thought this an unnecessary hazard. If it was a cooling water or oil leak it would eventually show itself by an increase of radiator and oil temperatures; if it was a fuel leak it would show up in a sudden increase in fuel consumption—or by fire, if any of the fuel touched the hot exhaust stacks. At 0710 Rodd called the Rathburne and told her operator to stand-by and listen closely for signals from his battery-powered emergency set if he sent the word "landing."

There was no point in taking chances at this stage of the flight. Read decided to land. A fair-sized swell was running below and Read was confident of being able to alight among them; but the experiences of the NC-3 and NC-1 were fresh in his mind and they raised the question that, once down, they might not be able to get off again. Read told the pilots to turn toward shore to find a stretch of smooth water and Rodd called the Rathburne: "We have gas leak on port motor and may land soon."

The smooth water came in sight a few minutes later in the form of a river mouth. When Rodd heard the engines being throttled back he quickly reeled in his trailing antenna and tapped out: "Landing! Landing! Sending on emergency antenna." At 0721 Stone had the NC-4 on the water and Breese and Rhoads had climbed out to check the engine. Rodd stuck his head out of the after hatch to discover, much to his chagrin, they were adrift in an estuary. If someone had thought to cut him in on the secret he would have been able to pass the word to the destroyers. Read came aft and told him that they were in the estuary of the Mondego River, off the town of Figueira da Foz.

Unknown to Read, the mouth of Mondego was studded with sand bars, and while taxiing upriver to more sheltered water they ran onto a bar at 0750 and found themselves stuck fast. With full power on the engines and all hands running back and forth on the lower wings to rock the hull, the NC-4 finally came off the bar. Meanwhile the engineers had discovered that the leak was in the engine's water jacket and had repaired it by pouring a can of "anti-leak" compound into the

180

cooling system. The *NC-4* was ready to go, but Read would have none of it until he could know how much water he had around her hull. Running on a bar at 80 miles per hour struck Read as a terribly ignominious way to end the *NC-4's* transatlantic flight. He had her taxied to the beach in the hope of getting some hydrographic information. Read, Breese, and Hinton promptly went ashore; Stone and Rhoads climbed up on the hull in the warm sun for a bit of sleep.

Meanwhile, Rodd was working his radio key, watching his batteries and reaching wit's end as he tried to contact the *Rathburne,* or anyone who might be listening for his feeble signals. No one was. It was the experience off Cape Cod all over again. The destroyers were so busy chattering with each other about the *NC-4's* possible whereabouts that they drowned out Rodd's small battery-powered set. Rodd could hear the *Shawmut's* radio pleading with the destroyers to quiet down, but with no results. Finally he recognized the "fist" of Ensign J. J. Dowd, an aviation radio officer aboard the *Shawmut,* when he took over her key. Dowd ordered the ships to shut up and listen. The *Woolsey's* operator duly acknowledged the order, but then felt obliged to fill the air for another five minutes re-transmitting Dowd's order. Rodd was furious; he later remarked, "His intentions were good, but we might have sunk several times during the five minutes which he occupied in so doing."

While Rodd was building up frustrations over his radio key, hundreds of citizens of Figueira da Foz and environs had gathered on the river bank to see the great *aviao* of the *Norte Americanos.* Among them was the Captain of the Port who introduced himself to Read as best he could. The language difficulty was gradually surmounted by Read and Breese pooling their sketchy knowledge of French, which the port captain spoke fluently. With the requisite hand gestures, smiles and shrugs, a form of communications was established. The most important information that the port captain had was that high tide would be at 1400, more than five hours away. This wiped out any hopes of making Plymouth before nightfall.

By 0918, almost two hours after the *NC-4* had alighted, the airwaves finally quieted down and Rodd was able to dash off a message from Read:

IN MONDEGO RIVER. MUST WAIT HIGH TIDE AT TWO GMT. SEAPLANE OK. CANNOT MAKE PLYMOUTH TONIGHT. REQUEST DESTROYERS KEEP STATIONS. WHAT IS BEST PORT TO NORTH TO LAND WITHIN 300 MILES? REQUEST REPORT SITUATION COMFRAN AND PLYMOUTH.

The *Rathburne* said that Rodd's signals were faint but readable and that she would be off the Mondego in an hour. Rodd tapped out "see you at

181

1030," unglued himself from his stool and climbed through the after hatch for some fresh air.

At 1035 the *Rathburne* arrived in the river and sent a boat ashore to see if Read needed assistance. He needed none, but asked the *Rathburne* to stand by. A few hours later the *Conner* appeared in the river— just in time to see the *NC-4* take off.

By 1300 the tide was clearly running into the estuary; the Port Captain had made it clear to Read where the channel was and Read ordered the engines started. At 1338 the *NC-4*'s hull broke clear of the Mondego River, Stone climbed to 1,000 feet, and pointed her nose north for Cape Finisterre. At 1440 the city of Oporto was framed in the interplane struts of the starboard wings and the *Woolsey* on Station C slipped by below. As the *NC-4* overflew the *Woolsey,* Commander William F. Halsey, Jr., commanding officer of the *Yarnall* on Station D, received a message from the *Shawmut* for relaying to the *NC-4:* "Best place north Mondego River is Ferrol and second Vigo." Halsey ordered immediate relay of the message and alerted his lookouts. At 1504 the *NC-4*'s shadow swept across Halsey's face.

As the *NC-4* left the *Yarnall* behind, Rodd received word from the *Tarbell* on Station E off of Cape Finisterre that she was leaving station and making for Ferrol, Spain; and word came in from the *Harding* on Station 1 in the Bay of Biscay that she, too, was making for the port. Rodd sent off an ETA of 1700 for Ferrol. The ports of Vigo and Muros slipped by off the starboard wings, Cape Finisterre came and went, and the *NC-4* slowly changed her heading to eastward, following the mountainous shores of Galicia. At 1630 the *Tarbell* and *Harding* were in sight, both making heavy smoke, and beyond them was the ancient, fortified seaport and naval base of El Ferrol.

With Ferrol in sight, Rodd hurriedly reeled in his antenna. At 1650 Elmer Stone eased the *NC-4*'s keel into the waters off Ferrol and then swung her about to taxi her between the ancient Castillos of San Felipe and De Palma that guard the narrow harbor entrance. Within twenty minutes of the *NC-4*'s touchdown the *Harding* steamed into the port and Captain Cooke put his vessel at Read's disposal. The *Harding* was no stranger to the NC operation; prior to 17 May she had been on Station 22 between Corvo and São Miguel, and it was she who stood by during the *NC-3*'s arrival at Ponta Delgada. With the arrival of the *NC-4,* Ferrol's waterfront was suddenly swarming with people. The Spaniards were surprised and delighted by the unscheduled visit of the great transatlantic flying machine. The Captain of the Port, accompanied by the British Consul, came aboard the *Harding* to pay his respects to the fliers, as did several other dignitaries of the city and the Spanish Navy.

Read was pleased and relieved that there were no ceremonies; everyone was able to get a good night's rest for the morrow.

Read and his crew were up for a very early breakfast the next day. The weather forecasts radioed from Reichelderfer aboard the *Shawmut* and from Roswell Barratt aboard the *Aroostook* in Plymouth were unfavorable. But the local weather looked fairly good and Read felt that the flight had dragged on long enough. The flight had taken most of May; it would look ridiculous if dragged out into June. He decided to go. At 0627 the *NC-4* was back in the air, pointed across the Bay of Biscay for the tip of Brittany.

The weather proved to be not just unfavorable; through most of the flight it was absolutely wretched. At 0645, immediately after takeoff, Rodd called the *Mahan, Gridley,* and *DuPont* on Stations 2, 3 and 4 for weather reports. The *Mahan* and *Gridley* reported good visibility; the *DuPont* said it was "fair" in her vicinity. At 0743 the *Mahan* was overflown, and then the horizons began to fill with fog. Rodd requested radio bearing signals from the *Gridley*. At 0758 Rodd's radio bearing showed the ship to be 30 degrees off to the right; another bearing at 0806 showed her 35 degrees to the right. Rodd passed the word to Read who corrected his heading, and at 0823 another bearing showed the ship to be 40 degrees off to the left. The *Gridley* was never sighted.

Hereafter, the weather became so thick that Read tended to rely almost wholly on Rodd's radio bearings to guide his navigation, and here Read became caught in an interesting situation. As the weather thickened with wads of fog and curtains of rain, Stone and Hinton, who were spelling each other at the controls at 30-minute intervals, tended to do their own "navigating" by way of flying around the patches of zero visibility. Read the navigator could not do any real navigating because he could not see anything, but as aircraft commander he was relying on the radio bearings provided by Rodd. Most of these could not be checked visually because only two of the six destroyers on station between Ferrol and Brest were sighted. Read tolerated the pilots' "navigation" for awhile, but he could not keep track of their continual jinking around rain squalls and finally had to insist that they fly the headings he gave them, regardless of bad visibility and rough air.

By 1145 the *NC-4* was over Brest, France, at the tip of the Brittany peninsula. When Americans of 1917-1918 sang George M. Cohan's rousing song "Over There," the *There* in the lyrics was initially Brest, the great port of disembarkation that served most of the American Expeditionary Force during the World War. In this May of 1919 Brest was functioning as the port of embarkation for most of those same millions, now en route back to the United States. Read signaled Stone to

183

take the *NC-4* low over the city, and a couple of orbits were made of the port to give the American troops a good look at their *NC-4*.

From Brest the course was almost due north to Plymouth. The *NC-4* sped across the tip of Britanny at less than 500 feet and hundreds of Breton peasants came running out of their cottages to look up in awe at the huge yellow wings that roared by overhead. Crossing the English Channel the visibility fell to almost zero and the pilots had to take the big boat down to within 50 feet of the surface in order to remain below the cloud layer. The rest of the flight to England was made practically on the deck. Rodd did not like this because he had to haul in his trailing antenna, which seriously degraded the range of his radio set. At 1251 Rodd looked out of the after hatch and spied a merchant ship in the haze. He ducked below and tried to raise her on the radio, but with no results. Most likely, as with the *Ionia* and the *Mary*, the little freighter carried no radio.

At 1310 a message from the *Rochester* said that the *NC-4's* radio transmissions were getting stronger. Then the fog suddenly thinned and the sun appeared overhead. Read had the *NC-4* taken up to 1,500 feet so Rodd could put out his trailing antenna, but this proved to be unnecessary: land was in sight almost dead ahead. Twenty-five minutes later the *NC-4* was circling Plymouth.

The city of Plymouth had been expecting the Navy's transatlantic flight for several weeks and had been actively preparing for the *NC-4's* reception since she had touched down at Lisbon. The *Aroostook* had been anchored in the port since 23 May, and excitement mounted when the *Rochester* dropped anchor off of Plymouth's ancient citadel at noon of the thirtieth. In anticipation of the *NC-4's* arrival, Mayor J. B. Brown had declared the thirtieth a city holiday; buildings were decorated with red, white, and blue bunting and American flags were in evidence everywhere. All the ships in the port, including harbor craft and fishing vessels, dressed ship and the Royal Air Force had a flight of three Porte/Felixstowe F.2A flying boats ready to meet the *NC-4* and escort her in. It was with the greatest disappointment that Plymouth received word of the *NC-4's* forced landing and that she would be staying overnight at Ferrol; however, this also meant that the city could have another holiday on the thirty-first.

Plymouth's historical ties to the New World were almost four hundred years old, and the port city was very conscious of them. It was from Plymouth that Sir Humphrey Gilbert sailed in 1578 to establish a colony in North America; from where Sir Francis Drake sailed on his voyage around the world in 1577; and from where the famous *May-flower* sailed in 1620. In 1891 the city had dedicated a handsome memo-

184

rial on a pier of the Barbican, the old part of the city overlooking Sutton Harbour, to commemorate the sailing of the *Mayflower.* In this summer of 1919 the city fathers looked forward to erecting yet another historical marker on their Barbican to mark the terminal point of man's first flight across the Atlantic.

The thirty-first dawned dark and wet with a heavy rain falling on Plymouth throughout the morning. It appeared as if the *NC-4* was going to have a miserable arrival until about noon, when the rain stopped and the sun came out; but a heavy haze clung to the horizons. A crowd of thousands of persons appeared with the sun and began to gather on the hillside beneath the citadel, and then the troopship *Indarra* arrived in the port, her rails jammed with the thousands of well-tanned faces of British troops returning from Mesopotamia. The *Rochester's* radio room was "tracking" the *NC-4's* passage through the reports of the station vessels; although most of the ships could not see the airplane they could hear her pass nearby. As the *NC-4's* radio signals became stronger, the *Rochester* called the Royal Air Force base and Major R. K. Kershaw led the three F.2A boats into the air to meet the *NC-4.* Kershaw's F.2A flew the Stars and Stripes from its port interplane struts and the British Union Jack from the struts between the starboard wings. The crowds in the port area became restless and every so often an excited shout would go up that the *NC-4* was sighted; but the sightings proved to be false alarms created by seagulls holding too steady a course through the haze.[2]

At 2:19 P.M. the *NC-4* suddenly appeared out of the haze at 1,500 feet, trailed by the British F.2As at a lower altitude. The spectators had no problem now in identifying the *NC-4;* she was immediately distinguishable by virtue of her "great size."

Read had Stone circle the harbor, overflying Drake's Island and the citadel; as she passed over, various colored Very flares shot up to mark her passage. From the harbor came the now familiar chorus of whistles and sirens and bells, with one of the loudest roars coming from the troops aboard the *Indarra.* Stone wheeled the *NC-4* around in a wide circle to eastward, then brought her around with her nose into the west wind for her letdown. At 1327 the *NC-4* joined her shadow on the waters offshore of the Corinthian Yacht Club—and the transatlantic flight finally came to its end.

The spectators on the heights of the citadel rushed down the hill toward the harbor to get a close look at the big flying boat, but the *NC-4* taxied on around a point to a stretch of water known as the Cattewater, where moorings had been prepared for her. Immediately, all the small craft in the harbor got into motion, but launches from the *Aroostook* and *Rochester* were already at the mooring, prepared to fend off sight-

185

seers. Read and his men turned over the *NC-4* to a crew of machinist's mates from the *Aroostook* and boarded the captain's gig from the *Rochester,* where they were received again by Admiral Plunkett.

Read and his five aircrewmen climbed aboard the *Rochester* to rousing cheers and the ship's band playing Sousa's "America Forever." After running the gamut of a reception they were finally able to leave for the *Aroostook* where they climbed out of their flying clothes and tested the ship's showers before being formally welcomed to Plymouth and England. Here, too, they were reunited with the personal gear that they had left aboard the *Aroostook* in Trepassey; for the most part this meant clean uniforms, which were very welcome by this date.

Joining Admiral Plunkett in his barge, Read and his men were sped across the harbor to the massive stone jetty on the waterfront of the Barbican, and here they climbed a series of stone steps to the monument that commemorated the *Mayflower's* departure. Read was a native New Englander of many, many generations, and he was surprised to discover that Plymouth, England, had its own Plymouth Rock. Among the official party that greeted them this day was Major Waldorf Astor, son of the Viscount Astor, and his American wife Nancy; she would subsequently become famous as the first woman elected to the British Parliament.

The NC fliers were greeted by Mayor Brown, who was dressed in his formal garb of cocked hat, a long, flowing crimson robe trimmed with fur, and a great gold chain around his neck. The mayor was attended by three mace bearers and the town clerk in a shoulder-length wig. Mayor Brown told the fliers:

> Plymouth is always a point of historic interest to Americans. The memorable sailing of the Pilgrim Fathers from this spot, though comparatively unnoticed at the time, was an event which has proved to be a point in history of immeasurable interest. Mainly out of that small beginning a mighty people has sprung up, and today, in most dramatic fashion, their descendants have crossed back to us in a way never dreamed of by our forefathers, and equalling in scientific development and daring the greatest imaginings of Jules Verne.
>
> Your flight today brings our two great countries together in the warmest fellowship. Gentlemen, I salute you and welcome you to England.[3]

At the conclusion of the brief ceremonies, everyone boarded automobiles and drove through the Barbican's narrow streets to the Grand Hotel in the newer part of Plymouth for luncheon. The streets were packed with people and the passage was difficult and slow. Even while the *NC-4's* men lunched in the hotel with the local dignitaries, a great crowd waited patiently in the street outside the hotel to cheer them again as they left.

The next day, Towers, Read, Bellinger, and their crews joined Admiral Plunkett and boarded a train for London. Upon arrival in Paddington Station they found the platforms packed with American soldiers, sailors, and Marines who grabbed up Read and his crew, hoisted them to their shoulders, and carried them through the station to the street outside where they paraded them up and down the streets. In the throngs at the station was Harry Hawker, who wanted to meet Read; but he never had a chance to get through the mobs of servicemen. The NC fliers were finally taken to the automobile that awaited them, but the American servicemen refused to allow it to be driven; they pushed it all the way to the Royal Aero Club where the Navy fliers were expected.

From the Aero Club they all drove out to the airfield at Hendon where an air show was in progress. The Americans were truly impressed by Lieutenant Frank B. Courtney's acrobatic demonstrations in a twin engine Boulton-Paul Bourges bomber, which included dives, spins, and even loops. This was extraordinary because the Bourges was considered a large airplane in that day; and what interested the Navy fliers even more was that a Bourges was to have been entered in the transatlantic competition of the *Daily Mail* prize. Interestingly enough, the pilot who demonstrated the Bourges bomber so dramatically this day attempted to fly the Atlantic himself eight years later, and again in 1928, but without success. Frank Courtney subsequently emigrated to the United States where the Curtiss-Wright and Consolidated aircraft companies were pleased to use his talents.[4]

After two more days in London the NC crews caught a boat train to Paris where they were met in the Gare St. Lazare on 4 June by Admiral William S. Benson, the Chief of Naval Operations. Admiral Benson took them to the French Ministry of Marine, and along the way the small, birdlike figure of Albert C. Read was immediately recognized and Frenchmen stopped to cheer him. In contrast to Read's physical appearance, Towers and Bellinger were simply two more tall, husky, typically American naval officers; so perhaps Josephus Daniels' intuitive assessment of the "hero" situation was correct after all. From the Ministry of Marine, Admiral Benson whisked the fliers out to the "Paris White House" where President Wilson was still laboring over the peace treaty. Wilson told them:

The entire American nation is proud of your achievement. I am glad to see you and to shake your hand, and I am glad to give you my warmest congratulations. I am happy to be able to say, personally, how proud I am of all of you. The whole of America and the Navy is most proud of your achievement. I am also pleased that you were able to keep your heads on land as well as on the sea.[5]

Precisely what that last sentence was intended to mean can only be left to speculation. Admiral Benson hurried the aviators from Woodrow Wilson's starched presence to introduce them to David Lloyd George, Georges Clemenceau and Vittorio Emanuele Orlando, the prime ministers of England, France, and Italy, who added their congratulations. It was a quick tour, and by noontime Towers, Read, Bellinger, and their men were back aboard a train speeding across Picardy for the Channel ferry and England, where they had an appointment the next day with the British Air Ministry.

On Friday 5 June, Read, the crew of the NC-4, and the other NC fliers were the luncheon guests of Major General J. E. B. Seely, Under Secretary of State for Air, in the House of Commons. Among those present was the immediate heir to the British Crown, the Prince of Wales, who is best recalled by history for his abdication in 1937, after which he became the Duke of Windsor. There was Major General Sir Hugh M. Trenchard, often referred to as the father of the Royal Air Force, which in the summer of 1919 was barely a year old; and his more thoughtful but less successful rival Major General Sir Frederick Sykes, who in 1919 was still Chief of Air Staff; and Lieutenant Colonel J. T. C. Moore-Brabzon, a pioneer of British aviation. Also present was Brigadier E. M. Maitland, who within a few weeks would himself fly the Atlantic to the United States—and back to England—aboard the airship R.34, thus making the first round-trip crossing of the Atlantic by air; and Major General Sir H. Sefton-Brancker, who would subsequently become Secretary of State for Air and eleven years later perish in the crash of the airship R.101. And there were several members of Parliament; most conspicuous among them was the former First Lord of the Admiralty, Winston S. Churchill.

The aircraft industry was represented by Oswald Short, Frederick Handley Page, T. O. M. Sopwith, and Colonel John Cyril Porte, the latter an old acquaintance of John Towers' when they were associated for a moment with Glenn Curtiss during 1914 in Curtiss's transatlantic flying boat project. Porte and Towers had much to talk about this day. Porte was a naval aviator who had been swallowed up by the new imperium of the Royal Air Force and he was unhappy. He was even less happy with the penny-packet mentality of new Air Ministry which had refused him the funds to support his Porte/Felixstowe "Fury" flying boat in making a transatlantic flight. The "Fury" was a huge triplane flying boat powered by five 334 horsepower engines; it had proved its

188

ability to get off the water at 33,000 pounds and Porte had great hopes for it, but he was being frustrated by a small-minded bureaucracy. Porte's brilliant mind still flashed from behind his weary eyes, but the frail shell that housed his effervescent intellect was fast failing him. His tubercular condition had grown immeasurably worse as the result of his wartime exertions, and within five months of this pleasant meeting with Towers, John Cyril Porte would be dead.[6]

Harry Hawker was unable to be present, but Commander Grieve was; he and Read were seated at the same table and found much to talk about on their common interest in navigation. In his after-luncheon speech, General Seely assured his guests that "there is no trace of envy on our part [cheers]. We recognize to the full that you have brilliantly succeeded where we gloriously failed." Seely's remarks reflected a growing consensus in the British press. After overcoming their initial disappointment at not being first across the Atlantic, there occurred a sudden appreciation of how nice it was to be beaten by the Americans, instead of by the aviators of some "foreign" country in Europe. Read responded to Seely with the observation that "The British people are good winners; but they are wonderful losers."[7]

The next day the NC fliers were entertained at lunch by the American Luncheon Club, a group of Americans living in London who got together for lunch once a week. Here the Navy men were reminded of the unpleasant fact that the 18th Amendment had been ratified on 29 January 1919, and what Josephus Daniels had done to the Navy on 5 April 1914, the do-gooders were now going to afflict upon the whole United States: Prohibition! Their hosts invited the NC fliers to come back to England at some future date and be their guests again, when they needed an "alcoholiday."

On the evening of 9 June, Towers, Read, and the crew of the NC-4 went to the Air Ministry where the officers were decorated with the Air Force Cross, which was for officers of the Royal Air Force; and Rhoads was decorated with the Air Force Medal, which was for noncoms and unrated men of the R.A.F. General Seely conveyed the regrets of King George V, that he could not be present to make the awards, and he apologized that he had only the ribbons to bestow, because the decorations were so new that the medals had not yet been struck. When he pinned the ribbon on Rhoads' blouse, he told Rhoads that he had the King's instructions to give Rhoads his special congratulations; His Majesty was sure that it was largely due to Rhoad's industry that the flight was a success.[8]

After London the NC crews returned to Paris where they were given a week's leave. But this soon palled on them. Like most Americans in France during 1919 they wanted only one thing: to get back to the United States.

189

Windsor McCay Cartoon
Washington Times, 4 July 1919

. . . And Home
by *Zeppelin*

In France the NC fliers took the usual tours of Paris; Herbert Rodd was especially interested in the Eiffel Tower, which is not only a Paris landmark but also houses a powerful radio transmitter and functions as the tallest radio mast in Europe. They toured the battlefields at Chateau Thierry and Belleau Wood, and by mid June were in the crowded port of Brest with freshly typed orders for transportation back to the United States aboard the transport USS *Zeppelin*. The name of the ship made for no end of puns and jokes. It was in Brest, on Sunday 15 June, that they received the news of Alcock and Brown's successful flight between Newfoundland and Ireland.

At 1:45 P.M. (1613 GMT) on 14 June, John Alcock and Arthur Whitten Brown lifted their twin-engine Vickers *Vimy* biplane clear of Lester's Field outside of St. John's, Newfoundland. Sixteen hours later, after what is probably the wildest and most hair-raising transatlantic flight ever made, they found the fields of Ireland below them. Alcock and Brown were flying for the *Daily Mail* prize, as was Admiral Mark Kerr with his four-engine Handley Page *V/1500* which was based at Harbour Grace, Newfoundland. The *Daily Mail* prize would go to the aircrew who was first to land *anywhere* in the British Isles, so Ireland was good enough. For all Alcock and Brown knew, Kerr and his big Handley Page had taken off shortly after he had heard of their own takeoff; if they flew on to England, Kerr following after them might still beat them to the prize by landing in Ireland. They decided to land immediately. The field below them near the Marconi radio station at Clifden, Ireland, looked like a solid meadow from the air. It proved to be a bog—and they nosed over on landing. But they were across, and their time was 16 hours, 12 minutes.[1]

Interviewed in Brest, Towers remarked that the flight of Alcock

191

and Brown was "a splendid feat." Read said that it was a "great stunt," and then added:

> While there is nothing which will add much information to the art of aviation as a result of the flight, it was a wonderfully nervy thing to attempt and a magnificent achievement. I have much admiration for the men who attempted the great feat in the face of such odds.[2]

The newspaper presses on both sides of the Atlantic were ecstatic about the flight of Alcock and Brown. The quick jump from Newfoundland to Ireland in 16 hours and 12 minutes was infinitely more dramatic than the *NC-4* spending twenty *days* to fly from Rockaway to Lisbon. However, there was some remark that although Alcock and Brown had made a daring flight, it was in fact less a transatlantic flight than one from the "American islands" to the "European islands," and from "no place" to "no place" at that. While it would have been startling only a few years before, in 1919 transatlantic flights should be made from one significant population center to another.

On Washington, D.C.'s Capitol Hill, a pudgy little freshman congressman named Fiorello LaGuardia hopped to his feet to praise the flight of Alcock and Brown. He insisted that the British flight eclipsed the *NC-4*'s and offered a resolution that would allow the President to award the Medal of Honor to the Britishers.[3] However, the congressman from New York was less interested in praising the British than he was in putting the Navy's flight at discount. As an Army aviator during the World War, LaGuardia had experienced a political collision with the U.S. Navy over aircraft procurement in Italy; the outcome had proved embarrassing to him and he had neither forgotten nor forgiven the episode. In 1919 LaGuardia was firmly and noisily in Billy Mitchell's "airpower" camp, working on schemes for a separate air force that would strip the Navy of its aviation.

The following day the NC fliers boarded the 12,450-ton transport USS *Zeppelin* and were on their way to New York. The *Zeppelin* was a German ship surrendered to the Allies after the Armistice and turned over to the U.S. Navy. She was commissioned at Portsmouth, England, on 29 March 1919 and her first commanding officer was Commander Theodore G. Ellyson, Naval Aviator No. 1.[4] One thing that Ellyson never expected from his Navy or aeronautical career was that he would some day command a German-built "Zeppelin"—much less the type of Zeppelin that he was given!

Besides the NC crews, the *Zeppelin* had on board 4,288 officers and men of diverse regiments of the U.S. Army, most of whom were

192

returning from occupation duty in the Rhineland. And there were 53 war brides and five children. The wife of Sergeant Hugh Clarke of Waynesburg, Pennsylvania, had borne a child only a few days before sailing, and the child was christened by one of the chaplains on board after the ship was under way. The *Zeppelin's* commanding officer, Commander William W. Galbraith, served as godfather, and the little girl was named Violet Zeppelin Clarke.[5] As long as she lived, Violet Clarke would never be able to forget where her middle name came from. It should be hoped that she did not grow up to be a chubby girl.

Between Brest and New York, Read, Towers, Bellinger, and other members of the NC flight crews gave several talks to the troops about their flights and other experiences. The USS *Zeppelin* had a ship's newspaper which was named *The Dirigible;* unfortunately, no copies seem to have survived.

The weather had been hostile to the NC flight to Europe, and it remained consistent in its malignancy during their return to the United States. It was pouring down rain when the *Zeppelin* picked up the pilot off Ambrose Light and steamed into the Narrows between Forts Hamilton and Wadsworth that guard New York Harbor. As the *Zeppelin* moved across the lower bay a score of submarine chasers, antisubmarine patrol craft, and Navy tugboats swarmed around her. Overhead, the blimp *C-4* from Rockaway tracked the ship's course and two F-5L flying boats wheeled around the gray sky. Then a DeHavilland DH.4 from the Army airfield at Mineola swooped out of the gloom and dove low over the *Zeppelin's* decks to drop six packets, each of which contained invitations for the NC fliers to attend a dinner in their honor.

As the *Zeppelin* approached the Battery, the submarine chaser *Herreschoff* swept in close aboard her. A newspaper reporter who had been a wartime signalman in the Navy wigwagged the transport that the NC fliers' wives were on board the *Herreschoff*. The tugboat *Manhattan* also met the *Zeppelin* off the Battery, and on board her were such VIPs as Glenn Curtiss, Rear Admiral Bradley A. Fiske, Captain Robert A. Bartlett, and Alan R. Hawley of the Aero Club of America, among others. These persons were present at their own initiative; they were not an official delegation. There was no official delegation to greet and fete the NC fliers because that custom, which became institutionalized in the 1920s, had not yet been invented.

As the *Manhattan* swung in close aboard the *Zeppelin* a soldier shouted down, "Has the United States gone 'dry' yet?" Captain Keane of the *Manhattan* waved a bottle of beer from the window of his pilot house and a great cheer went up among the troops that jammed the transport's rails. However, on this twenty-eighth day of June they had less than three days before the initial measures of Prohibition would attempt to "dry out" the celebrations of their homecoming.

The rain slowed to a drizzle as the *Zeppelin* was nudged into her berth alongside Hoboken's Pier 4. The ship's band was blaring away, but was encountering considerable competition from another band on the pier, and both were competing with the cheering soldiers on board and relatives ashore. The NC fliers were the first ashore, and when Towers led his crews down the gangway they were welcomed by Rear Admiral James H. Glennon, Commandant of the Third Naval District. While the aviators were standing at attention, waiting for the band music to stop so the admiral could begin his formal greeting, a small figure in naval aviation khaki separated himself from the crowd of spectators and joined the NC ranks, taking his place alongside Rhoads. The left sleeve of his blouse dangled loosely and there was no hand beyond its cuff. The crowd suddenly recognized him as Edward H. Howard and such a great roar of cheers went up that they almost drowned out the band.[6]

When the brief ceremonies were finished, the crowd swarmed in around the aviators and it was all of an hour before they could join their wives and friends who awaited them in nearby offices. Read remarked to the newspaper reporters, "Well, I went over in a seaplane and came back in a Zeppelin; that's some trip!" His only regret was that when the *NC-4* alighted on the Tagus the *NC-3* and *NC-1* were not with her. The only serious mistake he felt that he had made was in taking along a new uniform hat on the flight; between rolling around on the floorboards of the *NC-4* where it was often stepped upon, and its exposure to gasoline, oil and salt water, the hat was practically ruined. Read had nothing but disappointment for those who wanted to hear about the "excitement" of transatlantic flight. He told them, "My flight for the most part was quite a monotonous affair, it was simply the doing of the same things over and over again from start to finish."[7] This is an evaluation that has been echoed down the years since 1919 by most persons who have flown the Atlantic; both by pilots and invariably by the passengers.

John Towers told the press that "the principal lesson learned from the experiences of the NC expedition is the necessity of developing a radio direction finder for transatlantic flight, and . . . the establishment of a meteorological system by which weather in all quarters over the ocean may be reliably reported." He insisted that "meteorological stations will have to be set up all over the Atlantic before transatlantic flights will be commercially profitable." John Towers could not know it, but twenty-one years would pass before even the beginnings of such a system were created. It did not occur until January 1940, when at the

194

insistence of Jerome C. Hunsaker and F. W. Reichelderfer, President Roosevelt ordered the Coast Guard cutters *Bibb* and *Duane* to ocean stations between Bermuda and the Azores with U.S. Weather Bureau personnel on board. This was for the direct assistance of Pan American Airways' transatlantic operations. By that date Reichelderfer, who had worked up the forecasts for the *NC-4* at Lisbon, had been chief of the U.S. Weather Bureau for more than a year.

Towers saw no immediate future for the airplane in transatlantic operations, but he remarked, "The dirigible has a big future; until the seaplane is made larger, the dirigible will have the advantage in overseas flight."[8] Read agreed and added by way of emphasis, "Crossing the Atlantic by seaplane will not be profitable commercially soon; the dirigible will accomplish more along this line within the next few years."[9] In England, Arthur Whitten Brown shortly echoed their estimates with the pungent observation: "That the apparatus in which Sir John Alcock and I made the first non-stop air journey over the Atlantic was an aeroplane only emphasizes my belief that for long flights above the ocean the dirigible is the only useful vehicle."[10]

As if to prove the airplane pilots correct, four days later, on 2 July 1919, the British Vickers-built airship *R.34* took off from East Fortune, Scotland, en route to New York, where she moored at Mineola, Long Island, on the morning of the sixth. The *R.34* had on board a crew of 31, one American observer, a stowaway, two homing pigeons, and a tortoise shell cat named Woppsie. After spending four days at Mineola the *R.34* took off for Pulham, England, to complete the first transatlantic round-trip by air.[11]

When the American news media can no longer find anything "new" in a news event, its ever resourceful editors will invariably try to invent something. As a rule, the invention will have something to do with the unpleasant side of human nature. While the NC fliers were in England and France, the American newspapers busied themselves by contriving stories about a "feud" between Towers and Read. This was allegedly as a result of Towers attempting to "take over" the *NC-4* in the Azores; Daniels supposedly came to Read's rescue by excluding Towers from the rest of the flight, and seeing that Read was accorded most of the honors thereafter. When asked about this in New York, Towers retorted: "There was never the slightest foundation for the report, and I am glad of the opportunity of thus publicly denying it."[12] Read added, "It is all silly rot; and whoever thought up the story deserves a nice soft place in an institution for the feeble-minded!"[13] The feeble-minded would nevertheless enjoy playing with the shoddy invention over the next half century.

195

From Hoboken the NC fliers and their families took the Lacka-wanna Ferry over to Manhattan (there was no Holland Tunnel until 1927) and motored to their hotels. They were subsequently feted at a banquet given by Glenn Curtiss in the Commodore Hotel. It was a gala affair with the dining room having been made over at great expense to look like the cabin of some huge transatlantic flying boat airliner of the future. Irvin S. Cobb was the master of ceremonies and all the guests received a piece of fabric from the NC-4's wings as a souvenir. But that was that. There was no ticker tape parade up Lower Broadway followed by a big to-do at City Hall; this was an institution that awaited its invention by Police Commissioner Grover Whalen in the 1920s.

The NC fliers were quickly tossed into the dustbin for yesterday's heroes. On the day of their return to New York the American public was more interested in the final signing of the peace treaty at Versailles. It was the fifth anniversary of the fateful assassination at Sarajevo that provided the Teutonic Powers with the occasion for pursuing their disastrous "Place in the Sun"; and now the Great War was formally ended.

When John Towers mustered his officers and men in New York City's Penn Station for their trip to Washington, it was without fanfare. No one recognized them. And when they disembarked at the Capital's Union Station there was only a handful of friends and relatives to meet them.[14] Washington, D.C., was more interested in the Senate's hostility to Woodrow Wilson and the Versailles Treaty, the city's tense racial situation after a series of race riots, the necessity of a "gun control law," and the District of Columbia teetering on the brink of bankruptcy because Congress had once again forgotten to act on the District's budget for the next fiscal year.

On Monday 30 June, Towers, Read, and Bellinger reported to the Secretary of the Navy with their aircrews—including Lavender, Saden-water, and Moore, who had returned independently from the Azores. Josephus Daniels gave them his warmest congratulations. He told them that Congress was having a special medal struck to honor their flight. The medals would all be the same except that Read's would be in gold, Towers' and those of the crew of the NC-4 would be silver, and those awarded to the members of the NC-3 and NC-1 would be in bronze. A group photograph, including Daniels and his Assistant Secretary Frank-lin D. Roosevelt, was taken on the steps of the State, War and Navy Building, and then the historic NC group dissolved back into the Naval Establishment or civil life to pursue the remainder of their careers— where they became forgotten or discounted by the American public and by the world.

196

All the world loves a heroic figure, the single man who voluntarily struggles successfully to overcome some formidable obstacle in the face of great odds, and whose victory appears to benefit mankind. But there was nothing heroic in this popular sense about the Navy's transatlantic flight.

From David W. Taylor's brilliant conception of a self-ferrying transatlantic flying boat to the moment when Read and his crew flew the *NC-4* to her touchdown on the Tagus, it was vividly clear that this was less a transatlantic flight than a Transatlantic Flight Operation: the successful result of the highly organized labors of thousands of persons. Even aboard the *NC-4* no one man could be singled out as a "hero." For the most part they were professionals, and although to a man they had eagerly volunteered to be a member of the flight, they regarded their arrival in Lisbon as the execution of an assignment. It was their duty to be successful.

As the correspondent for the London *Times* remarked after interviewing Read and his men in Plymouth:

These American airmen are wholly without boastfulness. They look upon the transatlantic flight as a business proposition. The U.S. Navy decided to attempt to get three seaplanes across. They were chosen with their personnel. Detailed plans were made, safeguards were taken and no unnecessary risks were run. That is the beginning and the end of it. And the result is that the United States airmen have made history.[15]

And the London *Observer* added almost as a prophecy:

The very certainty and regularity of the American flight impaired popular appreciation of its true worth as a scientific achievement and example of the irrepressible spirit of venturesome humanity.[16]

The world of 1919 found little in the flight of the *NC-4* that appealed to the imagination. The spirit of Yankee nationalism was flattered, but Americans proved to be far more fascinated by the lonely lunge of Alcock and Brown. Newfoundland to Ireland in only sixteen hours—*just think of it!* However, the flight of Alcock and Brown gave a wholly false impression of aviation's capabilities in 1919, whereas the *NC-4*'s flight demonstrated all of the shortcomings of the airplane and the science of aeronautics, which were still manifest and manifold at that time.[17]

This was the greatest thing that was proved by the twenty days that the *NC-4* spent between Rockaway and Lisbon: flying the Atlantic, with even the best of all possible logistics systems, was a very tough

197

proposition. For all of the optimistic rhetoric that was thrown around in 1919 and for more than a decade thereafter, aeronautics in general and transatlantic aviation in particular still had a long way to go.[18] During the twenty years between the *NC-4*'s arrival at Lisbon and the beginning of scheduled transatlantic airplane services in May 1939 there were only 175 flights made across the North Atlantic, 142 by airplanes and 33 by airships. However, in making these flights only 87 airplanes and five airships were used.

All of seventeen years passed before a person was able to purchase an air passage on a scheduled transatlantic airliner, and that—as predicted by Towers, Read, and Brown—was aboard an airship, the German Zeppelin LZ-129, better recalled as the *Hindenburg*. During 1936 the *Hindenburg* lifted more than a thousand passengers between Germany and the United States.[19] Regular service by airplanes did not begin until three years later, when on 21 May 1939 the Pan American Airways Boeing 314 flying boat *Yankee Clipper* took off from Port Washington, Long Island, and flew to Lisbon via the Azores. Six days later on 27 May the *Yankee Clipper* roared back in from Europe, and when she alighted offshore of Port Washington it was twenty years to the day that the *NC-4* had arrived in Lisbon.[20]

However difficult the transatlantic air passage was, the vision of a great North Atlantic Airway was nevertheless clear in 1919. When asked in 1919 if he expected to fly the Atlantic again some day, Albert C. Read replied "Yes, I expect to do so inside of a few years and I will take my wife and baby with me."[21] As for the NC flight, Read was certain that its great expense was warranted, and he was aware that every step in material progress has been afflicted by the incantations of "economy-minded" Cassandras: "The few who still doubt that the expense was justified are those who always believe that the more tangible things that can be turned to present use are to be preferred to research work for future benefit."[22] As far as that future was concerned, to Read the horizons were unlimited:

> ... anyone in the present age of new and startling inventions who says positively that we will never attain an altitude of 60,000 feet, will never fly at 500 miles an hour, or will never be able to cross to Europe in the forenoon and return in the afternoon is a most courageous person, with a courage similar to that of those doubters in the olden days who proclaimed that iron or steel ships would never be successful.[23]

Before Albert C. Read died on 10 October 1967, he had lived to see his visions of 1919 reduced to very modest proportions. By 1967 jetliners had been flying the Atlantic for almost a decade, the British and

198

French were building a supersonic airliner and the Americans were talking about one; more than four million persons were shuttling back and forth across the Atlantic annually, and men were preparing to jump off for the moon.

What Read and his contemporaries probably never appreciated was that their flight, and the other intercontinental flights of 1919, represented one more of those portentous "great leaps for mankind" in the realm of transportation that has had a peculiar way of occurring every fifty years. Through aeons of time man had done his work by means of crude machines that depended upon man power or animal power until 1769, when James Watt harnessed steam for the purpose of pumping out coal mines. Fifty years later, in 1819, the sailing ship *Savannah* crossed the Atlantic with the assistance of a steam auxiliary engine, and fifty years after that in 1869 a golden spike was driven at Promontory Point, Utah, that joined two ends of a continent with steel rails. In 1919 men began flying between continents—and fifty years after that, in 1969, they were walking on the moon.[24]

There was at least one man in 1919 who grasped the ultimate meaning of the flight of the *NC-4* and the other intercontinental flights made before the end of the year. He was Dr. George Bothezat, an aeronautical engineer of the National Advisory Committee for Aeronautics. He wrote with knowledgeable prescience:

The crossing of the ocean by the airplane makes aircraft the first universal means of transportation and by this fact alone opens a new era of civilization, with such an increased rate of progress that it is almost impossible for the human mind of today to appreciate its whole significance.[25]

So it was—and so it would be. Some years before that, however, there was a man who sensed the ultimate promise of aeronautics, and well before the dramatic demonstrations of 1919. His name was Rudyard Kipling. In 1908, a year before Louis Bleriot sputtered across the English Channel, Kipling wrote a story called *With The Night Mail,* which he subtitled *A Story of A.D. 2000.*[26] The narrative is less interesting for its fanciful and now pathetically quaint descriptions of operations across the North Atlantic airway than it is for Kipling's provocative assertion that *"Transportation is Civilisation."* The world is still a quarter of a century distant from the year 2000 so there is yet time for men to prove Kipling's shrewd estimate correct. Meanwhile, the science of aeronautics has not only surpassed but has completely transcended Kipling's baroque vision—except for the hope that transportation may yet prove to be synonymous with civilization.

199

If and when that day arrives, the flight of the *NC-4* deserves full recognition as one of the first significant steps toward its realization. Not just because it made the first flight across the Atlantic, but because it showed *how* the Atlantic had to be flown, in 1919 and perhaps for all times, if that hazardous stretch of air space is going to be flown with regularity. A half century after the *NC-4*, every Douglas DC-8, Vickers VC-10, Ilyushin Il.62, and Boeing 747, not to mention all the military aircraft operating through the North Atlantic's busy air corridors, were flying under what may well be called an *"NC-4* system"—good radio communications, adequate weather intelligence from the North Atlantic's rimland supported by ocean station vessels, and an air-sea rescue network to provide assistance in the now rare event of a ditching. *This is the legacy of the NC-4.*

The difficulties of the NC Transatlantic Expedition were best appreciated by the Navy, and the most significant lesson learned in 1919 was that no European aggressor was going to be able to launch an air force across the Atlantic against the United States without providing plenty of notice. What is more, flight operations from Europe to the United States would be far more difficult than the *NC-4's* flight to Europe because westward-bound aircraft would have to fly against the prevailing wind.

During the seven years between 1919 and 1926, Brigadier General Billy Mitchell was forever whipping up terrifying visions of great clouds of enemy bombers hurdling the Atlantic to rain bombs on New York and Washington—even as far west as Detroit and Chicago. The much maligned "Battleship admirals" of the 1920s knew that this was absolutely impossible, and Mitchell's noisy persistence eventually convinced them that he was no "prophet of airpower" but a charlatan with illusions of grandeur. In the forseeable future the Navy would remain the "First Line of Defense"—but it had to be a Navy with its own naval aviation; it could not execute its missions with a clutter of airplanes borrowed from an alien air force that was operated by an ideologue like Billy Mitchell.

The *NC-4* was the first in 1919 and for all times; but her place in history and the significance of her flight have long been smudged by the mass mind's love of heroics. Americans have been the worst on this count, and this was demonstrated by the United States Congress. It was not President Wilson who decorated the NC fliers; nor was it President Harding, nor even President Coolidge. All of a decade slipped by without Congress appropriating the paltry funds necessary for the striking of the special NC medals. Meanwhile, the NC fliers had scattered to other

200

duties, some had retired from the Navy, others had returned to civil life; and Louis Barrin, copilot of the *NC-1,* had been killed in an airplane accident.

Finally, on Friday 23 May 1930, a small handful of the NC fliers met at the White House where President Herbert Hoover awarded the decorations won eleven years before.

Today the interested person may go out to Lester's Field, now a residential suburb of St. John's, and he will find a modest bronze plaque that commemorates the takeoff of Alcock and Brown. Near Clifden, Ireland, there is a handsome stone monument; while outside of the Transatlantic Terminal at London Airport, Heathrow, there is a magnificent statue of the immortal pair; and their *Vimy* aircraft is proudly displayed in the Science Museum in South Kensington.

In the 1920s the historically conscious British dedicated a plaque on Plymouth's Barbican to commemorate the arrival of the *NC-4* in England; and in 1949 the Portuguese dedicated a similar historical marker in Lisbon. There is an *NC-4* plaque even in Trepassey, which was only a stop along the way. In the United States, however, all of a half century passed before a historical marker was placed at Rockaway, New York, and it is owed solely to the citizens of that community.

The American aircraft builders whose airplanes have dominated the Atlantic's air corridors since 1945, and the American airlines that have reaped nothing but profits from their operations over the North Atlantic airway, have never seen fit to erect even the most inadequate memorial to the NC Transatlantic Expedition in the International Arrivals Building of New York City's John F. Kennedy International Airport. Yet every transatlantic flight that takes off from JFK's runway 25L barely has its gear and flaps up when it is overflying the site of the long-gone and long-forgotten Rockaway air station. As for the *NC-4,* she is in the custody of the Smithsonian Institution's National Air and Space Museum; and for more than a half century she has been hidden away from public view, gathering dust in a warehouse under the watchful eyes of the museum's curators. In spite of efforts to the contrary, even the fiftieth anniversary of the *NC-4's* flight passed as a rather muddled affair, regarded as a nuisance by too many persons and institutions who should have been concerned with its observance.[27]

In the summer of 1919 the American composer Frederick E. Bigelow was moved to write a lively marching tune called *The NC-4 March.*[28] From that day to this it has been a very popular and widely played piece of marching music, and millions of Americans have tapped their soles to its beat. But very few persons associate the music with its name; and if they do, they probably wonder at the cryptic title. Few if

201

any persons associate the music's inspiration with the great flight of 1919.

Sic transit gloria aeronautica Americana.

The *NC-4*'s flight, its timeless lessons and legacy remain largely forgotten or ignored. The American who is asked today about the first transatlantic flight will very likely insist that it was made by Charles A. Lindbergh. Instead of being eight years off the mark, an Englishman will be wrong by only nineteen days, because he will very likely say that it was flown by Alcock and Brown. If the *NC-4* is recalled at all, her flight will be discounted as a simple and unsportsmanlike operation, cluttered with battleships and destroyers, a flight that took an incredibly long time and which really proved nothing. And no one will remember the names of the men who flew her across. They were:

> Lieutenant Commander Albert C. Read, U.S. Navy
> Lieutenant Elmer F. Stone, U.S. Coast Guard
> Lieutenant Walter Hinton, U.S. Naval Reserve Force
> Lieutenant James L. Breese, U.S. Naval Reserve Force
> Ensign Herbert C. Rodd, U.S. Naval Reserve Force
> Chief Machinist's Mate Eugene S. Rhoads, U.S. Navy

And the flight was conceived, organized, planned, and led by Commander John H. Towers, U.S. Navy.

They deserve a better remembrance than they have received.

202

John T. McCutcheon Cartoon
The Chicago Daily Tribune, 28 May 1919

Afterword

These pages had their origins in 1960, when I was researching data that concerned rigid airships. I became impressed, if not to say absolutely fascinated, by the Zeppelin-type airship's phenomenal transoceanic capabilities as compared to the airplane's short-leggedness and its pathetic payloads, not only in 1919, but also during the twenty years thereafter. And I began gathering comparative data on transoceanic flights. The *NC-4*'s flight was of especial interest; not because it was an American flight, nor because it was the first—but *because it took so long*. There had to be some good reasons for such a lengthy passage. I like to believe that they have been adequately explained in the preceding pages.

The casual reader may complain that some of my treatments are tediously detailed and that others become repetitive; but the reality was even more tedious to the men of 1919 and their experiences were every bit as repetitious. Air transportation has come so far so fast—really too fast for the historian to as yet get a firm grip on its consequences—that it can be very difficult for a person today to truly grasp how vastly different the world was only fifty years ago. Without making clear the details that afflicted the flight from hour to hour and from day to day, a reader could be led to the assumption that the men of 1919 were hopping over their route in an aircraft that was *almost* as good as a modern airplane and that they enjoyed en route facilities that were *almost* as good as today's. Their problems could be dismissed in terms of "Well, things were a lot tougher then." They were indeed tougher in 1919, but precisely *because* the day's hardware was so primitive and men were so relatively ignorant of the environment that they sought to penetrate. It is a safe guess that, viewed from the year 2019, the flight of *Apollo 11* will appear similarly primitive.

Within the NC Flight Operation, I discovered the reason why the *NC-4* made it to the Azores and the other two aircraft did not. In

205

discussing this in the early 1960s with Lee Pearson, historian of what was then the Navy's Bureau of Aeronautics (now Naval Air Systems Command), I found him convinced that it was due to the *NC-4*'s more resourceful use of radio. I had been inclined to believe that it was because of the *NC-4*'s somewhat greater speed, which allowed her to outrun the fog that overtook the others. Subsequent research proved that Lee was far more correct than I.

If there was a "hero" aboard the *NC-4* he most certainly was Herbert C. Rodd, which is one reason why his report has been included as an appendix to this book. Also, Rodd could write an official report with a sense of humor, (which may be a lost art); and no other document generated by the flight provides a better idea of what it was like from hour to hour. There is nevertheless much to be said for Albert C. Read's vigorous use of his radio officer and his willingness to act upon Rodd's information. Indeed, Read's resourceful use of "all systems" is the outstanding command lesson of the flight.

The research relating to the flight itself was quite simple as compared to that required to put the operation into a framework corresponding to its correct technological context. In these researches I found myself wandering around in areas of potential historical endeavor in which few persons have even dabbled. One such area is the development of modern aerology as a science, and especially how it developed so rapidly as a result of the active interface between it and the everyday requirements of aviation. Prior to the airplane, a weather bureau's primary function was to tell farmers when they might safely plow, plant or harvest. Compared to the static nature of agriculture, the 100-mile-an-hour airplane applied all kinds of urgent pressures upon aerology. It deserves note that the Navy was a leader in this area within the United States. The Navy was using the Norwegian system of air mass analysis almost a decade before other agencies; and the man chiefly responsible for this was F. W. Reichelderfer.

Another area is that of aircraft radio, both as a means of communication and as a navigation aid. Ultimately, this led to radar; but that is another story. One need only consider how the airlines *might* function today (or even thirty years ago) without radio. The degree of chaos staggers the imagination. Or how would they operate if their radio was no better than Herbert Rodd's? Such harsh transpositions of mind are necessary to appreciate the vital importance of the development of radio. Radio has long since become such a fixture of everyday life that it is absolutely taken for granted. Most persons cannot imagine life without it; and more than a few unconsciously assume that the world has enjoyed its use always.

Yet a further area is the development of aircraft instruments, which also tends to be taken for granted. Historians probably ignore the subject because they have not done the spadework which establishes a relationship among the several consitituents along the all-important time-line; or perhaps they simply regard it as dull stuff. Yet all of these elements—aerology, radio, and instruments—are the *sine qua non* of aeronautical progress as it developed after 1919 to the air transportation we enjoy today. It may be said in a general way that after men learned how to build and operate successful "flying machines" between 1903 and 1919, at least half of the aeronautical progress realized thereafter must be related in terms of aerology, radio, and instruments. But that is *not* the way aeronautical history has been presented thus far.

The aviation historian's obsession with airframes *per se* (with scant regard even to engine development; as if an airplane would go very far without an engine) has unfortunately served almost to preclude investigations in these areas. At the other end of the spectrum, the academic historian's love of re-inventing the wheel many times over in terms of aviation "policy" or "strategy" and other stuff of the "big picture" that lends itself to easy generalizations and results in books that are inevitably subtitled *A Study of—,* has served equally to leave these important areas quite untouched. These three areas are nevertheless legitimate fields of historical endeavor. Any graduate student will find his labors in these virgin territories extremely fascinating and quite rewarding.

The final fact that this work illuminated is the curious and deplorable degree to which the NC Flight Operation has consistently been put at a discount over the past half century. It is doubtful if the Russians or any Western European people would be so disdainful of a heritage in which they could take justifiable pride. I have always been fascinated by the game of one-upmanship that the British invariably play on this point. At any mention of the *NC-4,* the Britisher is quick to say, "Oh, but the first nonstop flight was made by Alcock and Brown!"

The United States of America will never be regarded as a Greece, noted for its philosophy, art, and culture. American philosophy, such as it might be, is best described as a universal *ad hocism.* And the ephemeral stuff of American art and culture, pasted together as it is by a few effete tastemakers enjoying an opportunist's hour, will never be judged more than a hodge-podge of sociological curiosities having the historical durability of Kleenex.

The United States *will* be recalled as a Rome, not only because of its economic, military and political imperiums, but because it has been and remains a nation of great engineers and organizers.

207

The Romans were great highway builders; the Americans have been great airway builders—across the continental United States in the 1920s, over the length of Latin America and transpacific in the 1930s, and transatlantic in the 1940s. Since the 1930s the American airways have been a model to the world. Perhaps the reason this has received so little attention is that it has less to do with airplanes *per se* than with the development of frightfully unromantic ground facilities—the logistics system. It tends to be a tale of wretched terrain, mud, bulldozers, cement mixers, brick and mortar, which inevitably results in the creation of the radioroom and the Met' office. Although it may seem a contradiction in terms, the gritty fact is that an airway is built on the surface of the earth.

The building of the North Atlantic airway is largely owed to American efforts; and the historical precedent occurred with the NC flight's how-to-do-it demonstration of 1919. When you fly the Atlantic today you are still flying by the "*NC-4* System."

Appendixes

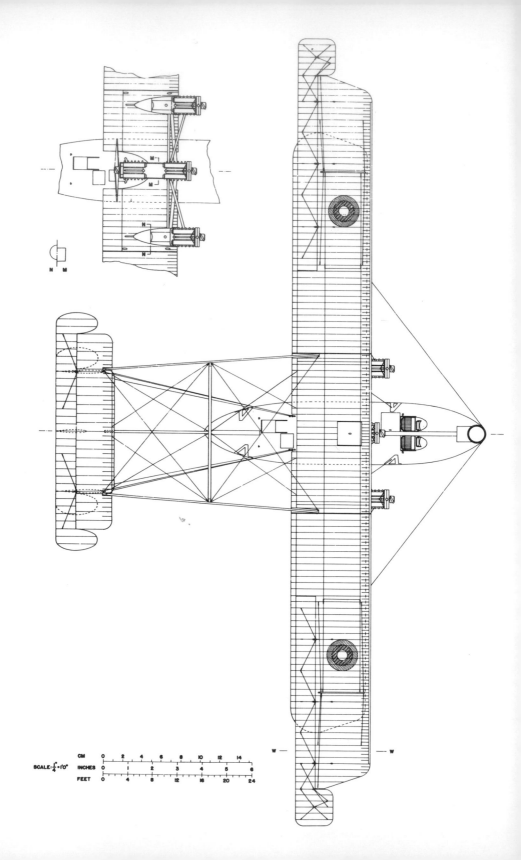

SCALE: $\frac{1}{4}$" = 1'0"

CM   0 2 4 6 8 10 12 14
INCHES 0   1   2   3   4   5   6
FEET   0   4   8   12   16   20   24

Specifications:
NC-4 Flying Boat

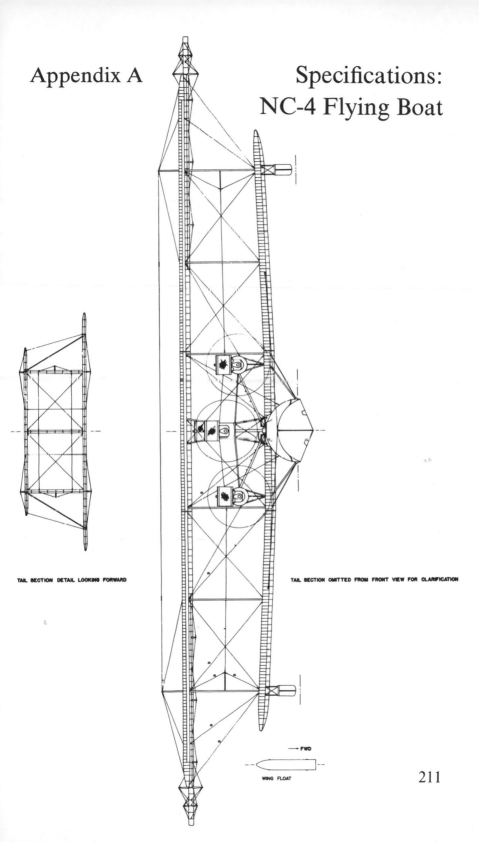

TAIL SECTION DETAIL LOOKING FORWARD

TAIL SECTION OMITTED FROM FRONT VIEW FOR CLARIFICATION

→ FWD

WING FLOAT

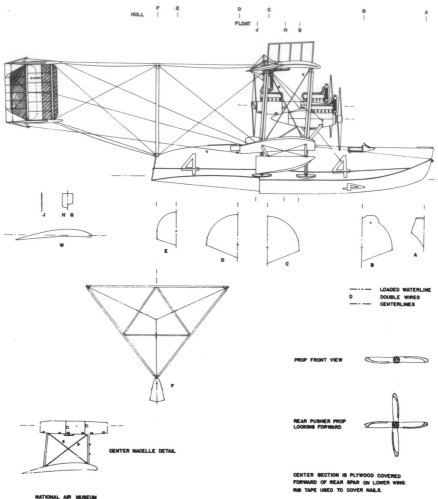

HULL | F | E | D | C | B | A
FLOAT | | | J | H G | |

```
----- LOADED WATERLINE
  D    DOUBLE WIRES
-·-·- CENTERLINES
```

PROP FRONT VIEW

REAR PUSHER PROP
LOOKING FORWARD

CENTER SECTION IS PLYWOOD COVERED
FORWARD OF REAR SPAR ON LOWER WING.
RIB TAPE USED TO COVER NAILS.

CENTER NACELLE DETAIL

NATIONAL AIR MUSEUM
DIVISION OF FLIGHTCRAFT
SMITHSONIAN INSTITUTION

COLOR SCHEME

HARBOR GRAY ENAMEL – (MEDIUM GRAY WITH SLIGHT BLUISH TINT) – USED ON HULL, FLOATS, TAIL BOOMS, STRUTS, & PLYWOOD COVERED LOWER CENTER SECTION.

NATURAL ALUMINUM – ENGINE NACELLES (UNPAINTED), ENGINE BLOCKS, & NACELLE FACEPLATES.

PAINTED ALUMINUM – RADIATORS

BROWNISH YELLOW – ALL FABRIC COVERED SURFACES NOT PAINTED SOME COLOR. (BROWNISH YELLOW CAST CAUSED BY AGING OF NATURAL VARNISH WHICH CONTAINED AN ORGANIC HANSA YELLOW PIGMENT.

BLACK – TAIL NUMBERS, CYLINDER BANKS, LEATHER PADDING AROUND COCKPITS

VARNISHED WOOD – PROPS (WITH BRASS LEADING EDGES) & COCKPIT SEAT SLATS

COPPER – TUBING & WATERLINES

WHITE – NO. 4 ON HULL SIDES & BOTTOM

RED, WHITE, & BLUE – WING ROUNDELS & TAIL STRIPES
ROUNDELS – RED OUTSIDE RING, BLUE MIDDLE RING, & WHITE CENTER
VERTICAL STABILIZER TAIL STRIPES (OUTSIDE SURFACES ONLY) – BLUE, WHITE, & RED FROM FRONT TO BACK IN 3 EQUAL SPACES. RUDDER WAS ALL RED.

Span, upper wing: 126′
Span, lower wing: 94′
Length: 68′5$\frac{1}{2}$″
Height: 24′5$\frac{1}{8}$″
Wing chord: 12′
Gap between biplanes: 13$\frac{1}{2}$′ to 12′
Airfoil: R.A.F. No. 6*
Angle of wings to hull: 3°
Angle of engines to hull: 0°
Angle of Stabilizer to hull.   2°
Upper wing dihedral: 0°
Lower wing dihedral: 3°
Wing area, including ailerons: 2,380 sq.ft.
Aileron area: 268 sq.ft.
Rudder area: 69 sq.ft.
Elevator area: 240 sq.ft.
Fin area: 79 sq.ft.
Weight, empty: 15,874 lbs.
Weight, loaded: 28,000 lbs.
Useful load: 12,126 lbs.
Gravity fuel tank, capacity: 91 gal.
Main fuel tanks, number of: 9
Capacity, each fuel tank: 200 gal.
Total capacity, main tanks: 1,800 gal.
Total fuel capacity: 1,891 gal.
Total fuel capacity: 11,346 lbs.
Oil tanks, capacity: 160 gal.

Type engines: Liberty V-12
Horsepower, each engine: 400
Number of engines: 4
Total horsepower: 1,600

* R.A.F. is the abbreviation for Royal Aircraft Factory—not Royal Air Force.

Weight, one engine unit:

One engine, bare and dry	820 lbs.
Water in engine	45
Water in radiator	50
Radiator	105
Propeller	60
Bijur electric starter	35
Lubricating oil	200
Total	1,315 lbs.

Performance:

Max. spd. at 28,000 lbs.:	74 knots
Min. spd. at 28,000 lbs.:	58 knots
Max. spd. at 24,000 lbs.:	84 knots
Min. spd. at 24,000 lbs.:	55 knots

Weight Distribution:	lbs.	%	%
Tail surfaces & outriggers	1,019	6	3.6
Wings, struts, wires, fairings	4,042	25	14.4
All tanks, piping, & fittings	892	6	3.2
Four power plants, complete	4,799	30	17.2
Installation & foundations	742	5	2.7
Hull, wing floats, controls, and misc. fixed equipment; (bare wgt. of hull, 2,800 lb.)	3,740	24	13.4
Weight empty	15,874	100 %	
Useful load	12,126		43.2
Gross weight	28,000		100.0 %

Appendix B

Chronological Development of the NC Flying Boat

1917

6	April	United States declares war on Germany.
30	May	Design of the Liberty engine begun.
25	August	Liberty engine passes 50-hour test and Admiral D. W. Taylor prepares his proposal for a transatlantic flying boat.
10	September	Navy conference with Glenn Curtiss.
24	November	Design contract let to Curtiss.
7	December	Admirals Taylor and Griffin propose the NC Project to the Secretary of the Navy.
21	December	Secretary of the Navy Daniels approves the procurement of four NC flying boats.

1918

8	January	Production Contract No. 34141 is let to the Curtiss Engineering Co. for four NC boats.
4	October	First flight of the *NC-1;* gross weight 18,970 lbs.
31	October	John H. Towers proposes a transatlantic flight operation using the NC boats.
7-9	November	*NC-1* flies from Rockaway to Washington, D.C., Hampton Roads, and return.
11	November	The Armistice is signed ending World War I.
27	November	*NC-1* makes record flight with 51 persons on board; gross weight 22,028 lbs.
9	December	*NC-1* takes off at a gross weight of 22,141 lbs. and makes a 3-hour, 45-minute flight to Montauk and return.

1919

10	January	*NC-2* fully assembled at Rockaway.
11	January	*NC-2's* engines tested; fire in the port engine.

215

16 January	C. J. McCarthy determines that with four Kirkham engines an NC boat should be able to get off the water at a gross weight of 30,000 lbs.
17 January	*NC-1* makes her last flight with low compression engines and is removed from flight status for modification with high compression engines.
1 February	Report of the Navy's Transatlantic Planning Board.
3 February	*NC-2* makes her first flight, the first of four this day totaling 7 hours, 40 minutes, in her original trimotor configuration, center engine a pusher.
4 February	Secretary of the Navy approves the report of the Transatlantic Planning Board.
6 February	John H. Towers is assigned command of the NC Transatlantic Flight Operation.
7 February	*NC-2* makes her last flight as a trimotor; is removed from flight status for modification with four engines in tandem units.
13 February	Decision taken to modify *NC-1* into a 4-engine aircraft with a center tandem unit; *NC-2* into a 4-engine aircraft with twin tandem units; *NC-3* the same as *NC-2* but with Kirkham K-12 engines; and *NC-4* to the same configuration as the *NC-1* (center tandem), with geared high compression Liberty engines.
14 February	John Towers formally establishes his Transatlantic Section in Room 3403, Main Navy Building.
18 February	Modification of the *NC-2* is begun.
6 March	It is determined that the geared-down models of the Liberty engine will not be available in time for the flight.
18 March	Modified with high compression engines the *NC-1* demonstrated her ability to get off the water at a gross weight of 24,780 lbs., but is unable to get off at 25,200 lbs. At this time the *NC-1* was still a trimotor.
27 March	Hugo Sunstedt's *Sunrise* crashes at Bayonne, N.J.
28 March	The *NC-1* is damaged by a storm at her moorings; her port wing a total loss.
29 March	It is calculated that with four high compression Liberty engines an NC boat should be able to

	get off the water with a 28,000 lb. gross weight.
1 April	NC-2 makes her first flight as a 4-engine aircraft and hereafter is called the NC-2T, "twin tandem."
4 April	A decision is made to cannibalize the NC-2T to restore the NC-1 to flight status as a 4-engine aircraft with a centerline tandem unit.
15 April	Albert C. Read arrives in New York.
18 April	Assistant Secretary of the Navy Franklin D. Roosevelt is taken for a flight in the NC-2T at Rockaway; the British Daily Mail fliers Wood and Wylie ditch their Short "Shirl" in the Irish Sea.
23 April	The NC-3 makes her first flight, the first of the NC boats to fly as a 4-engine aircraft with the centerline tandem unit. John Towers arrives at Rockaway, and the NC-2T is stripped of her port wings to make the NC-1 flyable.
1 May	NC-4 makes her first flight.
3 May	NC Seaplane Division One is formally placed in commission.
4 May	NC-1 maker her first flight as a 4-engine aircraft.
5 May	Fire in the NC Hangar; the NC-1's starboard wings are destroyed, the NC-4's tail singed. The NC-2T is cannibalized of her starboard wings to restore the NC-1 to flight status.
6 May	Bad weather cancels takeoff of the NC boats for Halifax; NC-1's flares start a fire in a paint locker.
7 May	NC Flight remains grounded by bad weather; Chief Machinist's Mate Edward H. Howard of the NC-4 loses hand in the airplane's after propeller.
8 May	The NC Flight takes off from Rockaway; the NC-3 at 1000, the NC-4 at 1002, and the NC-1 at 1009.

Appendix C

The Flights of the NCs: May 1919

	NC-1		NC-3		NC-4		Local
	Day	Hr.	Day	Hr.*	Day	Hr.*	Time
Lv. NAS Rockaway	8	1409	8	1400	8	1402	(1002)
Forced landing at sea off Cape Cod					"	1853	(1453)
Ar. NAS Chatham, Mass.					9	0925	(0525)
Secured at Chatham					"	1125	(0725)
Lv. Chatham					14	1307	(0907)
Ar. Halifax, N.S.	8	2308	8	2300	14	1710	(1310)
Lv. Halifax, N.S.	10	1145	10	1307	15	1253	(0853)
Forced landing off Egg Island, N.S.			"	1410			
Return to Halifax			"	1500			
Lv. Halifax			"	1659			
Forced landing off Storey Head, near Musquodbolt Harbour					15	1323	(0923)
Takeoff, Storey Head					"	1545	(1145)
Ar. Trepassey, Nfld.	10	1841	10	2231	15	2159	(1759)
	NC-1		NC-3		NC-4		
Lv. Trepassey, Nfld.	16	2210	16	2200	16	2205	(1805)
NC-4 sights Flores					17	1127	(0927)
NC-1 lands at sea, 40–45N, 34–40W	17	1310					

* These times are in GMT. New York is ordinarily five hours behind GMT, but in May 1919 it was on Daylight Saving Time, making its local time the same as Atlantic Time, which is that used in the Canadian Maritime Provinces and Newfoundland.

219

	NC-1		NC-3		NC-4		Local
	Day	Hr.	Day	Hr.*	Day	Hr.*	Time
NC-4 lands by mistake							
at Pta. Ribeirinha					17	1315	(1115)
NC-4 arrives Horta					17	1323	(1123)
NC-3 lands at sea,							
37–58N, 30–05W			17	1330			
NC-1 crew rescued by							
Greek ship IONIA	17	2020					
NC-3 arrives at Ponta							
Delgada (on surface)			19	1830			
NC-4 leaves Horta					20	1239	(1039)
NC-4 ar. Ponta Delgada					"	1424	(1224)
Derelict NC-1 sinks,							
49–00N, 29–25W	20	1940					
Lv. Ponta Delgada					27	1018	(0818)
Sight Cape Roca, Portugal					"	1939	(1939)
Ar. Lisbon					"	2001	
Lv. Lisbon					30	0529	
Forced landing,							
Mondego River, Port.					"	0721	
Takeoff					"	1338	
Ar. El Ferrol, Spain					"	1647	
Lv. El Ferrol					31	0627	
Overflies Brest, France					"	1105	
Sights coast of England					"	1312	
Ar. Plymouth					"	1327	

Appendix D

The Radio Log of Herbert C. Rodd

From: Ensign H. C. Rodd, USNRF
To: Commanding Officer, Seaplane NC-4
Subject: Radio Report, Trans-Atlantic Flight.

1. The following report, compiled entirely from the radio log, is submitted in detail.

2. A notation was not made of the wave length of each communication copied, but it may be generally understood that 1500 meters was used by the destroyers, except when requested to use 1200, 952 or 756, by the plane, in order to eliminate interference; 425 meters was the wave length used by the plane.

3. All distances are given in nautical miles, and the time used is Greenwich mean time.

4. The times given for our passing the destroyers are those given in their broadcasts on 756 meters immediately after we flew over them. This information was then broadcasted on 425 meters by the plane.

5. Radio report, NC-4:

The radio installation on the NC-4 was the last to be completed at Rockaway, the finishing touches being applied about 3:30 A.M. of May 6, the day on which we were called at 4:30 A.M. to make ready for the start. Due to an unfavorable weather report the flight was delayed and consequently I was able to spend most of the day sitting in the plane, selecting vacuum tubes for both the amplifier and continuous wave transmitter, taking bearings on Norfolk during this afternoon schedule, to make sure that the fixed condensers in the radio compass control panel were adjusted to 1500 meters. This had been done with a wavemeter but no test had been made with a station.

No flights had been made to test the radio apparatus and it looked as though we would leave without knowing whether things functioned in the air, or not. The weather cleared, however, the afternoon of May 7th, and about 5 o'clock we were ready to make a test flight. Just as we were about to slip down the runway the Engineer Officer put his foot through the radio propeller, breaking both blades. The center tractor motor had been turning over and this caused the radio generator to run fast enough so as not to be seen. I told the Navigator that it would probably take fifteen minutes to change, so we left without effecting repairs, as it was growing dark.

221

I had an opportunity to test the continuous wave transmitter with Rockaway Station and it worked quite satisfactorily. The skid fin antenna was used and the buzzer signals were very readable in the air, although the telephone did not work entirely satisfactorily, except when on the water with the motors stopped. I let out the antenna several times and reeled it in just to see how the metal reel worked, as I had never used one. I was surprised at the ease of operation, especially as there was a sharp turn in the wire.

We stayed up until about 7:30 and a sufficient number of distant stations was heard with the amplifier to warrant no further worry on that score.

We left Rockaway at 2:00 P.M. GMT, or 10 A.M. local time, May 8, getting off just after NC-3 and just before NC-1.

I nearly jumped out of the cockpit with joy when upon throwing in the field switch and touching the key, a beautiful clear spark note greeted my ears through the telephones, indicating that everything was hooked up properly. I was afraid that in our rush, and through working outside the hangars at night with a poor light, we might have mixed up our power leads. After adjusting the variometer my radiation showed three amperes on the skid fin antenna, and the NC-1 came back immediately saying my spark was good. Rockaway then sent a good luck message to me signed Wise, Jones, Parks and the rest—all men who had worked hard to get us in shape. By 2:27 all three planes had adjusted things and were in communication with each other.

New York and Boston broadcasted at 2:40 that the NC boats had started the trip to Halifax. I then let out my trailing wire.

At 2:43 we received a congratulatory and good luck message from Admiral Coffman.

At 2:50 came a long message via Rockaway, emanating from Admiral Knapp in London, telling us that the British Air Ministry had made arrangements to extend every facility and convenience to NC flying boats at Plymouth after Trans-Atlantic flight, and offering us the Air Station in the Scilly Islands as a temporary repair or refueling point.

At 3:10 Fire Island called and wished us good luck.

At 3:25 I told Rockaway "Everything O.K. 200 feet altitude." This is the last communication I had with Rockaway, as the interference around New York was bad. Norfolk, on 952, 400 miles distant, came in with the s/s (KBEA) calling Boston. My deep cupped helmet was becoming uncomfortable by this time so I changed to one employing ordinary bath sponges—a helmet made at Hampton Roads by Lieutenant Commander Taylor, and which I had used several hundred hours in the air with great comfort and good success.

At 3:50 as we were passing Montauk I got a bearing on Philadelphia on 1500 meters, which checked up roughly. His signals were loud on the radio compass and this was an early indication that the apparatus was O.K.

NC-3 then started working destroyers 1 and 2. Each sent a weather report. Both 2 and 3 were loud at 4:40 when they transmitted their compass signals, it being noticed that 3 was on 1200 meters instead of 1500.

At 4:30 New York asked us to listen for his telephone on 1200 meters, but it was not audible.

Siasconset then asked if we had anything for him and NC-3 asked him who he was.

Destroyer 1 sent a message to us from Secretary Roosevelt at 4:51, which I think he had just received from Boston.

At 5 o'clock (or 1:00 P.M. New York time) I got the time tick from Arlington, switching it to the Navigator's phones so he could check his chronometers.

Immediately afterward Chatham Air Station sent a request for our position, followed by a relay from the BALTIMORE at Halifax, giving weather conditions at that point. One thing in the report which alarmed me was a wind velocity of 37 miles per hour from the northwest at 4 P.M. This I immediately passed forward to the Navigator, as we had not yet become accustomed to the intercommunicating phones. Chatham had evidently not heard us acknowledge the messages from Admiral Knapp and the Acting Secretary, as he repeated them for which I was obliged to gently rebuke him as it was causing undue interference.

At 6 P.M. NC-3 sent a message to Siasconset to the effect that the NC Division had passed Chatham Light at 5:47.

At 6:30 the Navigator had me send a message to the Flagplane that we had passed over Destroyer 1 at 6:18, and that we were running on three motors.

At 6:45 we landed, after having shut down both center motors. I tried to send during the glide, but could not get a spark, consequently could not tell the destroyers that we were landing. It was afterward determined that the radio generator turned up only when the center tractor was running, showing that the air speed of the plane did not influence the speed of the generator. From the pilots I learned that this had been a very flat glide. Other reasons will be discussed later as to why the generator should be located clear of the propeller slipstream.

After we landed, the Navigator passed me a message to send, in the event that I could raise one of the stations. It was to the effect that we were in Lat. 42-21, Long. 68-21 and would probably not require assistance.

I called Destroyer 1 and 2 and Chatham, but with no results. They were all busy on higher wave lengths. It might be well to state here that all continuous wave transmitters tune very sharply at the receiving end, especially on the shorter wave lengths so that I was not surprised that we were not heard; still I thought that within an hour or two somebody would happen on our tune. That was not to be, for all night, whenever I noticed an opening, I would send S.O.S. signals, not because we were in any danger, but because I figured it might attract attention where an ordinary call would not. I sent always on buzzer modulated with radiation varying from .5 to .8 amperes, according to filament input.

While on the water, Bar Harbor and Cape Sable were heard working the other planes, and ships 300 miles at sea were heard working New York and Boston. Until 2 A.M. the destroyers kept up almost a continuous run of conversation, inquiring whether anyone had seen NC-4 and telling each other what course they were patrolling. Their signals were loud enough to be heard by the Navigator in the front cockpit, nearly 50 feet away. He suggested taking bearings on them to determine which one we were nearest, but even though on the skid-fin antenna they were as loud as just stated, on the compass coils they were inaudible, because they were using 756 and 952 meters. It may be stated here that the range of wave length of the compass panel was only about 200 meters above and below 1500 meters the radio compass wave length.

At 5 A.M. we sighted a ship and signalled it with the Aldis lamp, but received no answer. At one time we were within sight of a destroyer, and I signalled long and loud at him but he could not have been listening on short

223

wave lengths. Siasconset's signals seemed very, very loud, and I hailed him continuously between 6 and 7 A.M., then called Chatham Air Station. We were off Nanset Light at 6:20. At 9:10 we were off the entrance of the channel at Chatham, and just at this time I heard Chatham Station tell the destroyers that we had been sighted by Coast Guard Station No. 40.

The destroyers on this leg had rather poor operators and it required 45 minutes for them to acknowledge this message.

A boat came out to meet us and we reached the dock at Chatham at 11:35 GMT, 7:35 A.M. local time. Two planes had been dispatched to search for us, but they were not carrying radio operators.

During the five days' stay at Chatham, charging the storage battery was the only attention required by the apparatus. The battery had run the six valve amplifier continuously for 22 hours, and the continuous wave set for 2 hours, approximately a discharge of 80 ampere hours, with no signs of deterioration.

The radio helmet was most comfortable during the entire 20 hours it had been worn, never being taken off. The plane was visited every day to be sure that everything was all right. Everything was kept well covered with balloon fabric to protect it from rain which fell the entire time we were there, and which leaked through the deck in places. Norfolk was just audible on the direction finder at Chatham, while on the water. Chatham Station was called each day on the continuous wave set and reported signals fine, both on buzzer and telephone. The W.E. [Western Electric] transmitter showed up better than the Magnavox in these tests.

We left Chatham at 12:10 of May 14, but landed at 12:18 to inspect propellers and clear an oil line. I worked Chatham on the skid fin antenna during this short period in the air.

We got off again at 1:07, or 9:07 local time. At 1:22 Boston was broadcasting on 600 and 952 that we had started flight.

At 1:35 I heard Fire Island calling the [airship] C-5.

At 1:55 Fire Island broadcasted our starting time. One minute later we flew over Destroyer 1. At 2:21 Destroyer 2 was bearing 8° to the right.

At 2:40 Chatham inquired as to how much gas we had taken and informed us that the C-5 had passed over Chatham at 2:10.

At 2:48 Bar Harbor called and told me to stand by for a rush message from Washington, D.C., to be answered immediately for relaying to all parts of the world. He then sent a long weather report on 600, after which he shifted to 1400 meters.

At 3:19 the following message was received: WHAT IS YOUR POSITION? ALL KEENLY INTERESTED IN YOUR PROGRESS. GOOD LUCK, ROOSEVELT.

At 3:21 we sent the following: ROOSEVELT, WASHINGTON, THANK YOU FOR GOOD WISHES. NC-FOUR IS 20 MILES SOUTHWEST OF SEAL ISLAND, MAKING 85 MILES PER HOUR. READ.

Then a message was received from Chatham, stating that Commander Whiting [in Washington, D.C.] wished our total loading, amount of gasoline, etc.

At 3:30 Bar Harbor sent a service message: TOOK THREE MINUTES FOR ROOSEVELT TO SEND DISPATCH TO NC-FOUR AND RECEIVE YOUR REPLY. THIS BEATS ALL KNOWN RECORDS.

Then Cape Sable sent a weather report. We passed over him at 3:54.

At 4:15 I started working the BALTIMORE at Halifax, and told him that we would land there for a few minutes, as at this time we thought we would keep on to Trepassey.

At 4:44 we flew over Destroyer 4 and he told me his station was 10 miles 137° true from Cross Island.

At 5:09 we landed at Halifax. Five minutes previously, while in very rough air, I worked Bar Harbor, and told him we would land soon. He had requested that I give him a call from Halifax. Operator "DN" at Bar Harbor certainly was a good man and it was a pleasure to work fast with him.

The run from Chatham had been accomplished in four hours, so that the storage battery still read high, with a hydrometer which we carried, but was charged in the engine room of the BALTIMORE nevertheless.

The start for Trepassey was made at 12:52 GMT on the following day, May 14, but a landing was made at 1:23 because of no oil pressure on the center tractor motor. Without any changes in adjustment whatsoever, the small battery set which had failed to reach anybody at Chatham, worked the BALTIMORE and Camperdown Station very well, the distance being 18 miles, according to the Navigator. I told them that we had landed off Story Head and would leave soon.

I tried the continuous wave telegraph with Camperdown, but he could not hear it, probably because he had a non-oscillating circuit receiver. The motors were running during these communications.

At 12:51 the BALTIMORE inquired when we expected to start, to which we replied that we would complete repairs in an hour. Camperdown relayed this message for me, as the BALTIMORE complained of interference. Just before leaving the water a message from Washington, signed Bowie, was copied from Bar Harbor as he sent it to the BALTIMORE, saying that the weather over the eastern part of the big course [to the Azores] was unfavorable for a start, which certainly encouraged us.

We left the water at Story Head at 3:47 P.M. The BALTIMORE had the air until 5 P.M., exchanging traffic with Bar Harbor. The BALTIMORE still complained of interference, although Bar Harbor was loud and easily copied aboard the plane.

At 5:15 the BALTIMORE requested our position. Told him: PASSED CAPE CANSO AT 5:15. By this time we were using the interphones successfully. Canadian stations were sending out broadcasts, requesting ships to restrict the use of their radio.

At 5:40 Destroyers 1, 2, 3 and 4 were all audible, sending their compass signals.

At 6:05 the following was sent to Destroyer 1: REQUEST CHANGE IN PROCE-DURE AS FOLLOWS: AS SOON AS SEAPLANE IS SIGHTED, STEAM ON COURSE AT FULL SPEED AND CONTINUE COURSE UNTIL NEXT DESTROYER OR STATION REPORTS PLANE PASSING.

This procedure would have solved our difficulties at Chatham, for we had landed just between two ships back there.

At 6:13 a weather report was requested of Destroyer 3 and reply received in six minutes.

At 6:34 sent above message to Destroyer 2 and requested weather. Received reply in six minutes. He added that he was making smoke.

Worked BALTIMORE at 6:50, at which time we flew over Destroyer 1.

Captain Simpson and Captain Lee both sent messages to our captain, who answered, telling them he hoped he hadn't kept them waiting too long.

225

We passed Destroyer 2 at 7:25 and 3 at 7:45. We were getting near icebergs at this time and a note in the radio log, "Temperature getting low," expressed it fully.

At 8:46 the following message was copied: NAVY DIRIGIBLE C-5 BROKE ADRIFT FROM MOORING AT PLEASANTVILLE PERIOD RIP CORD BROKE PERIOD NO ONE ON BOARD NO CASUALTIES EDWARD PROCEEDING IN A NORTHEASTERLY DIRECTION WITH INSTRUCTIONS TO ATTEMPT BRING DOWN WITH ANTIAIRCRAFT FIRE.

About that time the pilots sighted her, but the fact was not communicated to the operator, so no report was sent.

At 9:00 P.M. we passed Destroyer 4 and a few minutes later Destroyer 3 on the Azores leg was heard to tell No. 8 that she could not arrive on station until 1:00 A.M., that she was taking No. 3 position. This was our first suspicion that the other planes were going to attempt a start.

At 9:10 sent message to Commander Towers, requesting that arrangements be made to change forward center motor.

The AROOSTOOK told us to look for NC-1 and NC-3 as we came in.

A landing was made in Trepassey Bay at 9:39. With the center motor running it was possible to send during the glide on the skid fin antenna.

The battery was charged aboard the AROOSTOOK and a number of spare parts left with Lieutenant Mirick, as everything had functioned well that far, and many parts were not considered necessary. The following articles were carried during the remainder of the flight to Plymouth:

1 coil antenna wire
1 lead fish
1 electrode insulator
1 spare generator propeller
6 Moorehead tubes
2 power tubes for CG-1104A
4 Magnavox transmitters
1 box assorted screws, carbon brushes, springs, etc.

The CQ-1300 transmitter was inspected again and new brushes with stiffer springs put in. The rubber gaskets under the cover had pulled out and rubber tape was substituted. The linen on the propeller tips showed some signs of wear, but went through the flight O.K. The skid fin antenna was taut and there was nothing to do except wipe up the apparatus with Three-in-One oil.

The following day at 21:36 GMT (about 6 P.M. local time), we left the water at Trepassey; landing [again] at 21:54 to wait for NC-3, and rising again at 22:02.

The AROOSTOOK was immediately heard broadcasting the time of our departure and requesting that it be passed down the line to all destroyers.

Considerable water had been shipped in the take-off, and the lead out to the skid fin antenna leaked slightly at first when transmitting on the skid fin antenna.

Immediately started working NC-1 and at 22:47 put out trailing wire, which was not to be reeled until Station 19 the following day.

At 22:50 NC-3 was heard testing, and communication with her was established at 23:00. She asked if we were just astern of her, to which we asked her to turn on her running lights. We were over Station 1 at this time. We passed 2 at 23:35, working Cape Race between ourselves.

NC-1 asked NC-3 what course he was steering and he replied "150 magnetic." NC-3 told Station 3 at 23:59 to cease firing star shells as they had sighted her. The next set of compass signals were heard all the way to Station 10, then over 350 miles distant.

It was not until NC-3 was nearly to Station 4 that she was able to let out her trailing wire.

At 12:33 the following was copied from the MAUMEE on 756 meters: MAUMEE WILL NOT BE ABLE TO MOVE FOR THREE DAYS COMMA THAT HEAVY- - -. It was afterward learned that she was in the vicinity of the Azores at this time. All three planes passed Station 4 at 00:43. At this point Cape Race said signals good and Boston, then 1,000 miles distant, was heard calling the ACUSHNET.

At 01:20 I told the destroyers that we were going to use the Aldis lamp to inspect the motors.

At 01:22, in shifting from 1500 meters down to 425, signals were heard on 1200 meters. The station was calling "FFK" (Brest) and signing "NEC". The following message was then copied:

"S/S GEORGE WASHINGTON, COMFRAN, POSITION EIGHT PM GMT MAY SIXTEENTH LAT 47-05, LONG 23-00. EXPECT ARRIVE BREST SEVEN PM GMT SUNDAY MAY EIGHTEENTH PERIOD PLEASE FURNISH FIVE HUNDRED TONS FRESH WATER COMMA EIGHT HUNDRED TONS COAL AND STEVEDORES UPON ARRIVAL PERIOD CARRYING CAPACITY THREE HUNDRED FIRST CLASS PASSENGERS SIX THOUSAND THREE HUNDRED THIRTY FIVE TROOPS AND ONE HUNDRED FORTY STRETCHER CASES SUBJECT TO MATERIAL REDUCTION IF PRESIDENT [Wilson] AND PARTY- - -SWEDISH MINISTER TO UNITED STATES ON BOARD PERIOD PLEASE RESERVE PARIS TRAIN ACCOMMODATIONS (interference here from UBZ calling CQ) AFTERNOON PERIOD MAJOR GENERAL SQUIERS AND AIDE ON BOARD PERIOD PLEASE RESERVE PARIS TRAIN ACCOMMODATIONS FOR- - -EIGHTY SACKS NAVY MAIL (broadcast from Destroyer 5, who we were directly over at 01:31 interfered with remainder of message).

The distance of the GEORGE WASHINGTON was 1,175 nautical miles or 1,325 statute miles at this time, and her signals were very good. She was heard throughout the night working on 1200 meters.

At 02:00 Cape Race asked for a short story of the flight, distance and anything of interest, also asking if I could get a report of NC-3. I was not authorized to do this, so merely told him that everything was going O.K.

We passed Destroyer 6 at 02:03 and the S/S ABERCORN asked if she could help us in any way. Said her position was Latitude 43-30, Longitude 45-50.

At this time Destroyer 7 was bearing 7° to the right. We passed her at 02:43. Her compass signals were audible 30 miles as nearly as I could compute.

Reported passing of each destroyer to Cape Race, and he seemed to hear us well for he answered promptly each time.

At 03:25 the S/S ADWAY was heard asking Bar Harbor if he had two messages for Wauconda.

We flew over Destroyer 8 at 03:29 and at 03:50 I sent a 22-word message to my mother in Cleveland, Ohio, through Cape Race.

Cape Race marveled at our being able to hear signals through the noise of four Liberty motors when I told him that his signals were still good, the distance being 425 miles at this time.

Requested a weather report from Destroyer 9 at 04:06 and received reply at 04:10.

At 04:47 a station who said she was the S/S HERCULES tried to communi-

227

cate with Destroyer 9, telling 9 that seaplanes had just passed over her. A weather report was then sent to NC-1 by Destroyer 10.

At 05:30 Cape Race asked what time we passed Destroyer 10. I had missed 10's broadcast so did not know. Cape Race replied with a lengthy message, asking to be kept advised as to our position. He said: SIGNALS GREAT.

Compass readings were taken on Destroyer 10, which were dying out at 05:40, indicating that we had passed her.

At 06:00 Destroyers 12, 13, 14, 15, 16 and 17 were heard on their compass schedule. Number 16 (HOPEWELL) was noted to be very loud, 200 miles distant.

We passed Destroyer 13 at 06:25. I reported this to Cape Race. He then asked what power and radiation we used, telling me he used 5 KW. I then heard him call the AROOSTOOK and sent a 14-word message, telling her how he was getting great signals from us. Cape Race used 600 meters during all communications.

The NC-1 then inquired whether I had heard the NC-3. I listened and found her working Destroyer 13. Shortly afterward NC-3 asked Destroyer 16 for a weather report.

Just before we passed Destroyer 14 at 07:06 I heard NAND and SIERRA calling Bar Harbor. Bar Harbor was heard faintly. At 07:18 and 07:30 I sent our position to Cape Race, but did not hear him answer. The distance at the last time I had worked him was 650 nautical miles. We crossed the steamer lane at this time and there was considerable interference on 600 meters. The s/s INVERTON was working Ponta Delgada. We passed Destroyer 17 at 07:45. NC-3 was calling 17 but seemed a good distance ahead according to his signal strength. NC-1 was loud at this time, being just one station behind.

At 08:03 the s/s IMPEROYAL wished us good luck and sent his position as Lat. 41-00, Long. 37-00, New York to Spain with gasoline.

At 08:10 NAMG called Cape Race with a message, and at 08:15 NESV told some station that he had met two planes and had a good time working with them.

At this time it was possible to hear two destroyers at once with the amplifier entirely disconnected from the receiver antenna and counterpoise.

At 08:38 the NC-1 asked Destroyer 16 for a weather report and received a reply in one minute.

At 09:31 Destroyer 17 advised that NC-3 had just called with a rush message, but that she could barely hear her. This was the last heard of NC-3 as at 09:45 we struck heavy fog, and from then on I stayed up on 1500 meters to get all the compass bearings possible. Although I did not hear No. 18 broadcast our passing time, No. 19 said we were reported by 18 at 09:45.

At 10:30 I asked Destroyer 19 if he had heard our motors, telling him that we were flying between the fog and clouds. She replied that they had not seen us, but the operator somehow thought that we were off her port bow. I was just about to ask for compass signals when the Navigator came aft and asked me to inquire about fog close to the water at Destroyers 19 and 20. No. 19 immediately answered that it was very thick near the water, and No. 20 said it was misty. The wind direction was 83° true at No. 19 and 250° No. 20. No. 20 inquired whether we were flying high or low. I told him: HIGH, BUT WE WANT TO COME DOWN IF IT'S CLEAR AT SURFACE.

At 11:13 requested weather conditions at Destroyer 21, to which she replied at 11:14: VISIBILITY AT SURFACE TEN MILES, WIND 220 [degrees], FORCE 20 MILES [per hour]. No. 21 bore 25° to left [on the radio direction finder] at 11:15.

At 11:30 we sighted Flores and came down near the surface so that I had to reel in and use the skid fin antenna. I asked Destroyer 22 for compass signals but he did not hear me, probably due to a slight change in our tune.

At 12:35 I asked Destroyer 23 whether he had heard the other planes, to which he replied that NC-1 passed No. 18 at 10:14 and that he had intercepted a message that NC-3 was off the course between 17 and 18. He added that he had just heard NC-1 asking for bearings. I then asked No. 23 for a weather report and he answered: WIND 240 TRUE, FORCE 15 KNOTS, OVERCAST, NO FOG, VISIBILITY FAIR.

At 13:05 we picked up land again, which I told Destroyer 24 I thought was Pico. At 13:10 No. 24 sent a weather report which corresponded to the one No. 23 had sent 15 minutes previously.

At 13:14 we started to land and I worked the COLUMBIA as we were coming down.

There was nothing to do to the apparatus at Horta except charge the storage battery. The high voltage batteries still read 69 volts. The same voltage as they had at Rockaway.

The CQ-1300 transmitter was in fine condition, the sparking disc and stationary electrode insulator being only slightly coated with oxide. This was cleaned off with an oily cloth.

Left Horta at 12:35 GMT on May 20. The skid fin antenna insulator leaked because we shipped a little water in getting off, so that I could not send until I could let out the trailing wire at 13:00 and sent a broadcast.

At 13:06 Destroyer 24 informed us that she was making heavy black smoke. The COLUMBIA then advised that weather conditions at No. 24 and 25 were improving.

Worked the MELVILLE at Ponta Delgada at 13:17. We flew over No. 24 at 13:22 and two minutes later took a radio compass bearing of 351° on Destroyer 25 (distance 50 miles).

At 13:37 I worked Destroyer 4 on the Lisbon leg (WILKES), and he said our signals were fine as soon as we left Horta.

We passed Station 25 at 13:45. The MELVILLE then inquired what time we expected to arrive and the Navigator answered: ABOUT 14:20. We were off the harbor at 14:20 and landed at 14:24.

We were not quartered on board the MELVILLE, consequently I could not supervise charging of battery, but sent a message from shore requesting that it be removed from the plane, charged and returned.

The following morning, May 21, when we went aboard the plane at 5:00 A.M. I found a new battery which when read by hydrometer only showed a specific gravity of 1100. A boat was immediately despatched for a new one which read 1250. We did not get off this morning so I was able to get the old battery back the following day, and it showed 1290.

We left Ponta Delgada at 10:17 GMT of May 27. For about a half hour I burned the amplifier tubes on 12 volts by mistake and fully expected that I had injured them, but upon plugging in 6 volts, destroyers five stations away were heard loudly, so I rested more easily. I relayed some traffic to Destroyer 4 for the MELVILLE. At 11:09 a message was sent to Admiral Jackson back at Ponta

Delgada thanking him for his hospitality and stating that we seemed to be on our way.

At 11:10 I requested wheather reports and received replies all the way down the line. The reports were all favorable and they all wished us good luck.

We passed over Destroyer 1 at 11:12 and 10 miles to the southward of No. 2 at 11:38, sending No. 2 a message to that effect as she did not see us. At this time Destroyer 6 (GAMBLE) seemed exceptionally loud, considering his being 200 miles distant. At the same time No. 7, 250 miles distant, advised us that our signals were strong.

We missed Station 3, who incidentally did not seem to radiate very well on 1500 meters, so I requested several series of compass signals from Destroyer 4. At 12:20 he was bearing slightly to the left, at 12:30 20° to the left, at 12:35 45° to left. We then changed course and passed over No. 4 at 12:50. At the rate we were flying it appears that radio compass signals had been audible 50 miles, the best distance a destroyer was heard throughout the trip.

I had a conversation with No. 4 (WILKES) as she was the ship which had been assigned to Hampton Roads for Trans-Atlantic Flight tests, and had given us very excellent cooperation there in all radio experiments. She said she was making 32 knots for us, and asked us to see how far we could hear her on the regular antenna.

At 13:10 Destroyer 7 advised that he had heard us as soon as we left Ponta Delgada, a distance of 350 miles. At 13:40 the bearing of No. 6 was 15° to the left. We passed her at 14:05.

Destroyer 11 was a very good station, for he was loud at 300 miles.

First heard Destroyer 7 weak on radio compass at 14:15. At 14:31 he bore 8° to the right, and we passed him at 14:40.

Requested weather reports from No. 8 and No. 9 at this time and received prompt answers. At 15:00 exchanged a message between our captain and Captain Simpson of No. 7.

Worked No. 4 for a test as we passed No. 8 at 15:16.

At 15:30 a weather report was secured from No. 11 in 5 minutes, and at 15:45 a report from No. 12 in 7 minutes. We passed No. 9 at 16:18.

There was no Destroyer 10 for some reason. No. 9 had been moved 17 miles to the eastward and No. 11 17 miles to the westward.

At 16:46 received a weather report from No. 14 and worked No. 4. Both said signals strong.

Called the SHAWMUT at Lisbon at 17:00 but she did not answer.

We passed No. 11 at 17:05. She had been audible for 25 minutes on the radio compass, approximately 40 miles.

At 17:20 another test communication with No. 4 was carried out. She advised that she had left her station for Ponta Delgada at 14:00. Her signals were still good on 756, but weak on 1500.

The ROCHESTER at Lisbon then called us and said that Admiral Plunkett was on board. The Admiral then sent a message saying: FINE WORK. COME ALONG. At 17:50 I exchanged signals with the SHAWMUT at Lisbon and at 18:05 we passed No. 12.

I then worked No. 4 again. Wiseman [the *Wilkes'* radio operator] said he was only using 4 KW and that they would arrive Ponta Delgada about 10 P.M. This indicated that she was about at Station 2, making the distance something like 520 miles. I promised him to call him at 18:30 but was busy with the

230

ROCHESTER for about a half hour and forgot about the WILKES. The ROCHESTER inquired when we expected to arrive, to which our Navigator replied: EXPECT TO ARRIVE ABOUT EIGHT O'CLOCK GMT. PLEASE HAVE SEARCHLIGHT ON WATER TRAINED INTO WIND. SHALL I LAND TO NORTH OR SOUTH OF SHAWMUT? After a reply had been received I called the WILKES at 18:47, but didn't hear her reply.

We had passed Destroyer 13 at 18:35. At 19:00 No. 14 bore 28° or 32° to the left and we passed to the right of him at 19:16. No. 14 then passed this information along the line for the MELVILLE. Many Portuguese stations were heard working. Cadiz (EBY) near Gibraltar was very loud and clear.

At 19:47, just as the sun was getting low, we entered the Tagus River, landing at Lisbon at 20:01. I sent to the ROCHESTER and the SHAWMUT on the skid fin antenna as we were landing.

No repairs were necessary at Lisbon. We left there at 05:29 of May 30, circling back over the harbor and finally clearing the main land at 05:55, at which time I let out the trailing wire. The SHAWMUT was busy broadcasting until 06:12, when we sent the following to her: FOR AMERICAN MINISTER. REQUEST YOU EXPRESS TO ALL HEARTFELT APPRECIATION OF COMMANDING OFFICER AND CREW OF NC-FOUR FOR WONDERFUL WELCOME. READ.

Although originally it was not planned to have destroyers between Lisbon and Cape Finisterre, five were sent out, the CONNER, RATHBURNE, WOOLSEY, YARNALL and TARBELL, Using A, B, C, D and E, respectively, for call letters.

At 06:25 CTV (Monsanto), sent the following broadcast: TRANSATLANTIC SEAPLANE FLIGHT NOW IN PROGRESS. SHIPS ARE REQUESTED TO RESTRICT USE OF RADIO APPARATUS TO AVOID INTERFERENCE WITH SEAPLANES. This message did not have much effect, for considerable interference was experienced on this leg from Spanish and Portuguese ships, which called each other with QRW signals.

Weather reports from A, B and C were secured between 06:35 and 07:00, but with some difficulty. At 06:48 a message was dispatched to the SHAWMUT asking her to request destroyers to listen on 425 meters. We passed Station A at 06:33.

At 07:10 I told B: WE MAY HAVE TO LAND. STICK CLOSE ON 425 METERS FOR MY BUZZER MODULATED SET IF I SEND THE WORD "LANDING".

At 07:12 I sent: WE HAVE GAS LEAK ON PORT MOTOR AND MAY LAND SOON. B acknowledged promptly for these messages.

At 07:15 I reeled in my antenna and sent: LANDING, LANDING, SENDING ON EMERGENCY ANTENNA. We landed at 07:21. I had not looked out of the hatch, consequently did not know we were landing in a river, else I should have added that information.

At 07:23 the Navigator told me that we were in the Mondego River at Figueira.

At 07:50 we went aground on a sand bar and I called B with the battery set. Hearing no reply, I shifted to 756 meters and copied the following, although I missed the call letters: NC-FOUR PASSED STATION A, BUT RATHBURNE (B) HAS NOT SIGHTED YET. SEA SMOOTH.

At 08:30 the SHAWMUT on 756 sent the following: TO NC-FOUR, WHAT IS YOUR SITUATION? WHERE ARE YOU? ANSWER VIA DESTROYERS, SHAWMUT. Then the following: DESTROYERS PLEASE LISTEN ON 425 METERS FOR MESSAGE FROM NC-FOUR.

I then called B, but upon listening found her sending the following to the SHAWMUT at 08:34: NC-FOUR NOT SIGHTED. AM SEARCHING TO SOUTHWARD OF POSITION. SEA SMOOTH, VISIBILITY VERY GOOD.

At 08:43, the first opening I noticed, I called B again, only to hear some destroyer on 756 reply: PROCEEDING TO ASSISTANCE OF NC-FOUR.

At 08:45 Ensign Dowd, an aircraft radio officer, divining our situation, sent the following from the SHAWMUT: DESTROYERS PLEASE LISTEN ON 425 METERS FOR MESSAGES FROM NC-FOUR. Destroyer C acknowledged for this message, but instead of heeding it, the operator called ISW about two minutes, then sent the SHAWMUT's message, repeating each word and sending very slowly. His intentions were good but we might have sunk several times during the five minutes which he occupied in so doing.

When he finally finished, B called me at 08:51 and asked: HAVE YOU LANDED? I answered very quickly, telling our position; but when I listened, A and C were working. A said: NC-FOUR LAST SEEN FULL SPEED. B's signals were audible over 100 feet away.

He then sent the following to the SHAWMUT at 09:04: NC-FOUR REPORTED LEAK IN GAS TANK. WOULD PROBABLY LAND. AM SEARCHING TO SOUTHWARD OF POSITION NOW. LAST SIGNAL TRANSMITTED BY NC-FOUR WAS ON EMERGENCY RADIO SET.

This showed that B must have heard me say we were landing.

The SHAWMUT did not get all of the above message the first time, and it was 09:15 before they finished communicating.

At 09:18, when things finally quieted down, I called B again on the battery set, and he answered. After telling him to listen in the future, instead of sending, I sent the following message: IN MONDEGO RIVER. MUST WAIT HIGH TIDE AT TWO GMT. SEAPLANE O.K. CANNOT MAKE PLYMOUTH TONIGHT. REQUEST DESTROYERS KEEP STATIONS. WHAT IS BEST PORT TO NORTH TO LAND WITHIN THREE HUNDRED MILES. REQUEST REPORT SITUATION COMFRAN AND PLYMOUTH. READ.

B advised that our signals were faint, but readable. The distance at this time was between 20 and 25 miles.

At 09:50 the following was received: WE HAVE FORWARDED AND BROAD-CASTED YOUR MESSAGE. WILL LAND UP IN THE RIVER WITHIN AN HOUR. SYMINGTON.

I then went on deck for a breath of air, telling B I would see him at 10:30.

At 10:30 I talked to him on the radio telephone, and at 10:45 Lieutenant Commander Geer phoned that Commander Symington [Commanding Officer of the *Rathburne*] was on his way in a boat.

Captain Read then went ashore. At 13:05 B sent us the following by radiophone: BEST PORT IS VIGO BAY. WILL YOU NEED GASOLINE? PLEASE INFORM SHAWMUT OF PROBABLE MOVEMENTS (signed) SHAWMUT.

At 13:14 the following was sent from B to C, having been semaphored to the RATHBURNE by Captain Read: TO CONFRAN BREST AND SIMSADMUS LONDON FROM NC-FOUR, REQUEST DESTROYER OF COAST DIVISION NEAREST FERROL HARBOR PROCEED THERE IMMEDIATELY ANCHOR IN POSITION WHEN SEAPLANE CAN SECURE ASTERN AND ACT AS TENDER FOR THE NC-FOUR. EXPECT LEAVE FIGUEIRA ONE THIRTY GMT AND STAY FERROL TONIGHT, LEAVING FOR PLYMOUTH TOMORROW MORNING AT EIGHT WEATHER PERMITTING. READ.

We left the water at Figueira at 13:18. At 13:50 the following was sent to the SHAWMUT: LEFT FIGUEIRA 1:38 GMT FOR FERROL, REQUIRE NO GAS.

I called Destroyer C at 14:20 and A also called her, but she was working with Destroyer 1 and ignored our signals until we were right over her. She broadcasted that he had passed Oporto at 14:40.

At 14:51 Station E sent us the following: TARBELL WILL ARRIVE FERROL BAY

4:30 P.M. And at 14:53 Station D: BEST PLACE NORTH MONDEGO RIVER IS FERROL AND SECOND VIGO. This had been relayed from VIF and was somewhat delayed.

I asked D at 14:56 if she was in position, to which she replied she was. We passed her at 15:10.

At 16:08 we told the TARBELL we would arrive Ferrol at 5 o'clock. The interphone world the nearest to perfectly at this time.

Greetings were exchanged with the stations at Oporto and Cape Finisterre at this time. At 16:15 Station No. 1 sent the following: HARDING WILL ACT AS MOORING SHIP AT FERROL WITH ANCHOR IN INNER HARBOR ON ARRIVAL UNLESS YOU WISH ME TO MEET YOU OUTSIDE.

At 16:20 we replied: DO NOT DESIRE YOU TO MEET US OUTSIDE.

At 16:21 No. 1 replied that she would arrived entrance Ferrol at 4:45 GMT.

The operator then added that he had heard us 450 miles.

At 16:28 Station E sent: WILL BE OUTSIDE MAKING BIG SMOKE.

At 16:37 the station at Ferrol inquired in Spanish if we were "Hydroero plane North Americans," to which I replied that we were.

I reeled in at 16:45 and we spiraled down to a landing at 16:47.

The HARDING came in from sea about 15 minutes later. I did not charge the battery at this point, even though it had been used considerably at Figueira.

We left Ferrol at 06:27 the following morning (May 31), climbing rapidly, so that I was working on the trailing wire at 06:33.

The HARDING was sending our time of departure to Station 2 for relaying to ComFran, Brest, and Admiral Plunkett at Plymouth.

At 06:37 Destroyer 4 was heard to send the message to the ROCHESTER.

At 06:45 I requested reports from Nos. 2, 3 and 4.

No. 2 replied at 06:51, No. 3 at 07:04, and No. 4 at 07:11 with full reports. The visibility was very good at No. 2, good at No. 3, and fair at No. 4.

No. 5 (BIDDLE) was very loud on his compass schedule but two minutes ahead of time, so I called him and corrected his time.

Requested compass signals from No. 2 at 07:30. His bearing was 5° to the right. We passed No. 2 at 07:43.

At 07:51 I asked No. 3 for compass signals. He started but broke down, then started again at 07:58, at which time his bearing was 30° to the left. It had begun to get foggy, and the Navigator requested further readings. At 08:06 his bearing was 35° to the left, and at 08:23, 40° to the right.

No. 5 then sent a weather report saying the visibility was 15 miles.

At 08:30 No. 3 was 45° to the right, getting fainter and at the same time No. 4 was 20° to the left, changing at 08:48 to 40° to the left. This proved that we were too far inside for the bearing or No. 3 was a stern bearing.

I phoned this to the Navigator and at 90:01 he said No. 4 was in sight.

I had been informed that there would be a No. 6 destroyer (STOCKTON) near Plymouth, but had not heard her. At 09:19 I inquired of the No. 5. He wasn't sure, but the No. 4 volunteered the information that she was, although No. 6 did not answer when I called.

At 09:31 I was surprised at the signal intensity of the ROCHESTER at Plymouth. She was calling with a message and I told her to "shoot it" as her signals were loud. The following message was received: DESIRABLE NC-FOUR LAND INSIDE BREAKWATER NEAR ROCHESTER THEN TAXI TO MOORING IN CATTEWATER WEST OF

233

MOUNT BATTEN. BRITISH PLANE WILL PROBABLY LEAD YOU TO MOORING. AROOSTOOK BOAT AT MOORING.

I requested a weather report from the ROCHESTER as I told her I couldn't get No. 6. No. 6 evidently heard this, for at 09:50 she sent a full report saying visibility was seven miles on surface and hazy overhead.

At 09:56 the ROCHESTER sent the following: WEATHER IN PLYMOUTH FINE, LIGHT NORTHEASTERLY BREEZES, CLEAR OVERHEAD BUT SLIGHTLY HAZY AROUND HORIZON. APPARENTLY SPLENDID FLYING WEATHER. STOCKTON IS IN POSITION.

I had neglected to get bearings from No. 5 and at 10:01 she was between 45° and 50° to the right. As we had been to the eastward of the line I assumed that we must have passed her and that the bearing was a reciprocal, so advised her that we had passed her.

At 10:21 No. 6 sent a weather report saying conditions were improving (they were anything but that where we were), and inquiring what time we would arrive at his station. I replied that we had passed No. 5 about 10 A.M. and that I thought we were going to fly over Brest.

I then happened to think about getting a time tick from the Eiffel Tower, but upon inquiring from No. 5, I learned that I had just missed his schedule. I learned that Nauen, Germany, sent at noon, but 4000 meters was beyond the range of my receiver.

At 10:50 the GEORGE WASHINGTON at Brest called and informed us that she would handle any messages for ComFran.

We were flying low at this time and I was using the skid fin antenna.

At 11:10 Brest Station called and said: BON VOYAGE, BON JOUR. Not knowing much French, I could only answer: MERCI.

Between 11:20 and 11:45 the GEORGE WASHINGTON tried to talk with their powerful radiophone on 1800 meters, but either this modulation was poor or else we were too near, for although the carrier wave was extremely loud and the tune remained steady, I could not understand the voice very well. All I got was the word "congratulations."

At 11:15 I had sent the following: TO COMFRAN BREST, GREETINGS FROM NC-FOUR. I AM SORRY WE CANNOT STOP. READ. To which the following reply was received at 11:43: TO NC-FOUR, CONGRATULATIONS ON YOUR MAGNIFICENT FEATS. SORRY YOU CANNOT STOP AND LET US ENTERTAIN YOU. GOOD LUCK. HALSTEAD.

Leaving Brest we flew very low and not until we had sighted Plymouth were we high enough at any time to let out the trailing wire. The GEORGE WASHINGTON had difficulty in hearing our signals after we left and communication was maintained through the U.S.S. HANNIBAL at anchor in Brest.

At 12:00 and 12:07 No. 6 sent weather information, saying visibility was seven miles, and the sun shining. I told her we were flying very low in fog and only using small antenna. She replied that our signals were faint but getting louder.

At 12:25 No. 6 informed us that she was making heavy black smoke and that our signals were good.

At 12:30 her bearing was 50° to the right and three minutes later it was 55° to the right (or reciprocal).

I then asked if our signals were louder. The reply was YOU SEEM ABOUT THE SAME.

At 12:41 No. 6 said that the visibility was eight miles and that our signals were weaker.

At 12:41 I told No. 6 that I thought we had passed to the eastward of her.

At 12:51 upon looking out of the hatch I saw a merchant vessel. I could not distinguish what flag she was flying but I hoped she could tell us her position and thus we could know ours, so I sent the International Abbreviations for "What ship is that?" and "What is your position?"

The operator was probably on deck watching us, for no answer was received on 600.

At 12:57 No. 6 sent the following: THERE ARE TWO SAILING VESSELS ABOUT FOUR MILES APART, BEARING 150° TRUE EIGHT MILES FROM STOCKTON.

We had not seen them, and I had visions of missing Plymouth, so asked the Navigator if it would be possible to climb to 400 feet so that I could call Plymouth station and request compass signals. It has always been so much easier to take bearings on a shore station that I thought I would be able to get accurate bearings and help find the harbor. We started to climb but had to come down again.

The ROCHESTER then called at 13:10 and said our signals were getting louder.

Her signals were good but not as good on the skid fin antenna as they were on the trailing wire four hours previously when we were only half way across the Bay of Biscay, consequently it seemed to me that Plymouth was much further distant than it really was.

At 13:12 the AROOSTOOK called with best wishes.

At 13:15 I was able to put out the trailing wire as we had sighted land and found ourselves headed right for the harbor.

At 13:19 No. 6 called and said that the visibility was 10 miles, and the sky clear. I told her that we had sighted land and were all right.

At 13:25 we spiraled down and landed inside the cattewater at Plym outh, ending the flight.

I was afterward told that two British planes which had started out to meet us were equipped with 1600 meter continuous wave transmitters, but I did not know it, consequently did not tune for them.

The radiation on the skid fin antenna changed slightly during the flight across the Channel, but could be kept to 3 amperes by adjusting the variometer from time to time. This was no doubt caused by the varying amount of moisture in the air at different times or at different altitudes.

The radiation on the trailing wire averaged 3.3 amperes throught the flight and nothing but praise can be said of the CQ-1300 transmitter. It was not oiled throughout the flight of 54 hours or 4,100 nautical miles. The frequency of the generator was never quite up to 500 cycles, as near as could be judged by the ear, due to being mounted too near the deck and not getting the proper rush of air, except when the center tractor engine was running. The generator should be mounted on an upper wing out of the slipstream of the propellers so that in a glide with the motors out it would be possible to send signals. Another reason is that the generator propeller is apt to become broken, being in the path of all traffic over the hull when on the water. Similarly, in the air, if anything such as a pair of goggles were blown off, they would break the propeller turning 5,000 r.p.m.

The oil field switch, sending key and antenna switch functioned properly, requiring no adjustments or repairs of any kind.

The 6-valve amplifier worked perfectly also during the entire flight. Four

235

extra tubes were carried but were never tried out, nor was it ever necessary to transpose tubes for a better combination after they had been selected at Rockaway, even after 12 volts had been applied to the filaments for about a half hour by mistake.

The only tendency for the amplifier to oscillate was slightly above 1500 meters.

The plate battery gave a reading of 68.5 volts at Plymouth after approximately 100 hours of usage, only falling off 1/2 volt. A voltmeter was carried on the flight so that the readings were taken with the same meter. The value of immersing the cells in parafin is very evident, as much rain and fog was encountered during the period of three weeks which the flight covered, and ordinary batteries would not have stood up.

The cut-down SE-950 receiver gave no trouble of any kind. Interference was seldom experienced, therefore tight coupling was generally used. It was noticed especially on this flight that maximum inductance and minimum capacity gave the sharpest tuning possible, also the best audibilities.

It might be stated here that the amount of amplification necessary to overcome the mechanical noises of the engines has been reached with the above mentioned amplifier, and there was never any necessity to press the telephones close to the ears, i.e. with the amount of induction experienced from the ignition system, although the signal audibility is increased by increasing the pressure of the phones, no better readability is obtained.

The induction when using the compass coils was much worse than on the antenna. This coupled with the fact that the signal intenisity without any induction interference is so much less than on an antenna, explains why the ratio of audibility on the same destroyer was about 1-to-8.

Many readings were taken on the "A" coil only, because of the enormous increase in induction experienced when the "B" coil was thrown in. It is possible to read within 5 to 10 degrees with the single coil, using maximum method and taking the mean of the points when signals faded out, after rotating the coil either away from the maximum point.

In this method a peculiar condition was always noted, i.e. that no matter what direction a destroyer bore from the plane, readings could only be taken one way with the "A" coil. When rotated 180° from a bearing just taken, the induction noises would be too severe to hear anything on the reciprocal bearing. No mechanical difficulty was experienced with the compass coils or controls.

The entire flight was made without losing a trailing wire or fish, and the tension on the skid fin antenna was the same at Plymouth as it had been at Rockaway, no sag having developed. All insulators held up except the lead-in from the skid fin antenna. After being rubber taped at Ponta Delgada, covering all exposed surfaces, no further leakage was experienced when using the power transmitter.

The desirability of having the operator where he could see out, or else near the Navigator, was very evident.

H. C. Rodd
Ensign, USNRF

Appendix E   Engineering Report of
Lieutenant James L. Breese

From: Engineering Officer, NC-4
To: Commanding Officer, NC 1
Subject: Report on S. E. [Steam Engineering] items in connection with the trans-Atlantic flight with the NC-4.

Enclosure: (a) Tabulated results.

1. During the trans-Atlantic flight from Rockaway to Plymouth the following troubles were experienced and are given as nearly as possible in chronological order.

(a) At Rockaway it was found necessary to replace the semi-rotary auxiliary gasoline pump by one of the old type. These semi-rotary pumps are not suitable as now constructed to handle a large load of gasoline, as the valves leak and the construction is weak.

(b) Between Rockaway and Halifax, owing to the high consumption of the two center engines, the oil became too low, the oil thickened and would not flow through the strainers. The forward engine bearings were burned out in consequence and a connecting rod broken. At Chatham the strainers were removed and more oil used; no further trouble from this cause ensued. A low compression engine was installed in place of the forward high compression engine.

(c) At Chatham, Halifax, and Ponta Delgada at least one carburetor jet became clogged with bits of rubber. This was directly traceable to poorly designed and poorly constructed rubber gasoline joints.

(d) At Chatham a starter was broken. This was the fault of the inexperienced local mechanics who installed it and not that of the starter.

(e) At Halifax a second starter was broken. In this case also it was due to carelessness. The turn-off valve to the primer having been left open a cylinder filled with gasoline and when the engine was cranked over the piston came up against a full cylinder of gasoline, thus causing a tooth on the starter gear to give away.

(f) Between Chatham and Halifax, Halifax and Trepassey, and Trepassey and Horta, the forward center tachometer shaft failed; between Ponta Delgada and Lisbon the rear center shaft also failed. In each case these failures were due principally to poor installation.

(g) Between Trepassey and Horta the center oil tank, which is flat sided,

237

began to open along the baffle plate seams. This leak around the rivets increased continually until the end of the trip. This is a common occurrence with flat-sided riveted tanks and therefore was not peculiar to the NC-4.

(h) At Trepassey the metal tipping of the three tractor Olmsted propellers cracked at a point about one fourth the distance from the tip to the hub on compression side and had to be removed. At Halifax the pusher Olmstead had been replaced for the same reason. The crack was due to the localization of a continuous vibration. The oak Paragons and the Lang pusher, which replaced these propellers, were in good condition at the end of the trip and proved very conclusively that oak was an ideal wood when working in spray or rain.

(i) Between Trepassey and Horta the semi-rotary hand pump for the auxiliary water was removed and replaced by a standard type bilge pump. The trouble with this type pump has already been touched on.

(j) Between Halifax and Trepassey, and again between Ponta Delgada and Lisbon, the aluminum feed pipe for the gasoline pump to the gravity tank split. This was due partly to vibration and partly due to excessive pressure by the one-cylinder pump.

(k) Between Lisbon and the Mondego River a leak started in one of the cylinder water jackets. This was repaired by pumping in a can of radiator anti-leak into the water system.

None of the rotary gasoline gauges worked well enough at any time to be used, and all readings were made from the gauge glass.

The gasoline feed pipes to the port and starboard engines were air-bound after every overnight stop. This was due to the position of the strainer between the cylinders making an in inverted syphon in the line. Vents had been specified but they were never installed.

In conclusion it can be stated that no major trouble developed during the entire trip except in the case of the oil failure at Chatham which was really the result of a minor trouble. The NC-4 had never been flown sufficiently to find out such things as are peculiar to each individual machine, so these had to be found out during the trip, together with making all the small adjustments which are necessary to all machines and cannot rightly be classed under the head of "troubles." When the NC-4 landed in Plymouth it was probably better fit for a fifteen hour run than when it left from Trepassey, and except for a slight reduction in power would have made the trip as well as it did the first time.

2. The following recommendations are made as a result of the experience given above:

(a) In view of the fact that most of the delays in starting were due to dirt stopping the carburetory jets, it is recommended that only metal-to-metal unions be used in the gasoline; joints may be protected by rubber, but no rubber slip joints should be used. In this connection the carburetors should be placed on the outside of the motor instead of the rather inexcessive [sic] position which they now hold between the cylinders. This can be done by changing the camshafts and making suitable manifolds.

(b) As the starting battery is now used also for ignition it would simplify the charging and ignition circuit if both circuits were twelve volts, the present ignition circuit being eight volts.

(c) Do away with the differential type throttle and use a separate control for each engine, first, because the present device gives considerable trouble after being exposed to the weather, and second, because the separate method is preferred by the pilots.

238

(d) Place the gauge glass in the center of gravity of the fuel tanks so that the level will be a true reading of the amount in the tanks and will not be influenced by the angle of the boat.

(e) Have separate oil tanks for each engine so that in case of a leak only one engine is affected.

(f) The engineer should have on his instrument board: airspeed meter, altimeter, air thermometer, water thermometer, tachometer, oil pressure gauge, and the necessary ameters, switches and fuses to control all the circuits on the boat. The pilots' board should contain, besides the airspeed meter and altimeter, only tachometers. In this connection a pneumatic chronometric tachometer should be used so that two or more heads can be installed and long flexible shafts done away with.

(g) Develop geared engines in order to obtain higher propeller efficiencies than are now possible with the straight drive engine.

J. L. Breese
Lieutenant, USNFR

	Elapsed Time in Air		Distance Miles		Average Speed	
	Hr.	Min.	Naut.	Stat.	Grnd.	Air
Rockaway to off Cape Cod	4	51	284	328	59	68
Chatham to Halifax	4	03	335	409	88	68
Halifax to Trepassey	6	23	474	545	75	69
Trepassey to Horta	15	13	1206	1389	79	68
Horta to Ponta Delgada	1	45	153	176	88	70
Ponta Delgada to Lisbon	9	43	786	905	80	65
Lisbon to Mondego River	1	52	134	154	74	
Mondego River to Ferrol	3	09	237	273	75	65
Ferrol to Plymouth	6	59	487	561	70	
TOTAL	53	58	4796	4740	76	68

Gasoline:			Engine Oil:		
Gal. Con-sumed	Per Hr.	Av. Per Naut. Mile	Gal. Con-sumed	Av. per Hour	Takeoff Weight
420	84	1.22	40	8	25,298
450	100	1.46	31.5	7	25,113
572	88	1.28	40	6.6	24,810
1340	86	1.28	110	6.4	28,249
135	84	1.20	10.5	6.0	20,896
860	86	1.42	55	5.5	26,216
					26,026
1020	85	1.40	72	6.0	
4797	85.5	1.32	359	6.6	

NOTES

The Atlantic Air Barrier

1. Wise's efforts are set out in his book *Through The Air* (1873), *passim*.

2. *The Complete Stories and Poems of Edgar Allan Poe* (Garden City: Doubleday, 1966), 496-505; also Martin Cole, "With a Balloon the Atlantic Cross," *American Aviation Historical Society Journal*, Vol. 14, No. 4 (Winter 1969), 229-231.

3. The best available summary of these efforts is in L. T. C. Rolt, *The Aeronauts* (N.Y.: Walker & Co., 1966), 137-158.

4. Walter Wellman, *The Aerial Age* (N.Y.: A.R. Keller & Co., 1911), 270-383.

5. "The New Daily Mail Prizes," *Flight*, Vol. 14 (5 April 1913), 375-376.

6. "$50,000 for Trans-Atlantic Hydro Flight," *Aero and Hydro*, Vol. 6 (5 April 1913), 1-2.

7. "The Wanamaker Cross-Atlantic Project," *Flying*, Vol. 3 (April 1914), 86-88; and (May 1914), 107.

8. "The America Proves Ability on Initial Trails," *Aero and Hydro*, Vol. 8 (27 June 1914), 153-154. However, the best summary of information relating to the Curtiss-Wanamaker effort is to be found in Albert F. Zahm (Ed.), *Aeronautical Papers, 1885-1945, of Albert F. Zahm* (South Bend: University of Notre Dame Press, 1950), Vol. I, which includes nine articles that he wrote about the *America* and preparations for the flight. Also Chapter 20, "Atlantic Fantasy" in C.R. Roseberry, *Glenn Curtiss: Pioneer of Flight* (N.Y.: Doubleday, 1972).

9. John Cyril Porte, "Ready to Start for the Cross-Atlantic Flight," *Flying*, Vol. 3 (July 1914), 165-166; and "Lieutenant Porte's New Route," *Flight*, Vol. 27 (26 June 1914), 689-690; and Henry Woodhouse, "Important Developments in the Trans-Atlantic Flight Project," *Flying*, Vol. 3 (August 1914), 203-204, 221.

10. William S. Brancker, "Flight Across the Atlantic Should be Made as Soon as Possible," *Flying*, Vol. 7 (July 1918), 509–513. The author is the same Sir W. Sefton Brancker who, as director of England's Civil aviation, died in the crash of the airship *R.101*, 4 October 1930.

11. "$50,000 Transatlantic Prize Renewed," *Flying*, Vol. 7 (August 1918), 628.

12. Alfred E. Poor, "A Flight Across the Atlantic Made July 28–29, 1918..." *Flying*, Vol. 7 (August 1918), 618–622. The hoax is subsequently explained in the magazine's September number, p. 729.

13. "A Flight Across the Atlantic," U.S. Naval Institute, *Proceedings*, Vol. 44, No. 187 (September 1918), 2150–2157, which reproduces the *Flying* article in full; the correction is under "Aeronautics," No. 188 (October 1918), 2418–2419.

14. Giovanni Caproni, "To Deliver General Pershing's Reports to President Wilson by Air in 48 Hours," *Flying*, Vol. 6 (December 1917), 937–938.

15. The original rules are set out in "The Daily Mail Atlantic Prize," *Flight*, Vol. 36 (21 November 1918), 1316; the revisions are in *Flight*, Vol. 37 (6 February 1919), 150.

16. Evan J. David, "Christening of the First American Made Handley Page," *Flying*, Vol. 7 (August 1918), 611–614; and "Plans for Transatlantic Flight Taking Concrete Form," *Flying*, Vol. 7 (July 1918), 534–535; *New York Times*, 2 July 1918 (5:4); 3 July 1918 (9:1); 5 July 1918 (20:5); 7 July 1918 (8:1); 16 July 1918 (6:6); and 18 July 1918 (5:5); also, memo from W.J.H., Inventions Section of General Staff to Lt. Col. A.A. Maybach of Invention Section, War Plans Division, Army War College, 17 July 1918, in RG-72, BuAer Correspondence 1917–25, Op-Air file 068-A, Box 72, National Archives. The memo discusses flaws and hazards in the Handley Page ferry scheme and tends to view it as a publicity effort by the manufacturer.

17. Sunstedt's *Sunrise* is well described in *Jane's All The World's Aircraft, 1919*, 488a–499.

Admiral Taylor Creates a Requirement

1. On Thursday 20 June 1940 the Bureau of Construction and Repair, which was responsible for hull design and construction (among many other related things), was merged with the Bureau of Engineering (formerly Bureau of Steam Engineering), which was responsible for propulsion plants (among other things), to form the Bureau of Ships.

2. Biographical information re D.W. Taylor is taken from Dr. William Hovgaard's "Biographical Memoir of David Watson Taylor, 1864–

1940, *National Academy of Science Biographical Memoirs,* Vol. 22, No. 7 (1941), 135-153.

3. Jesse G. Vincent, "The Liberty Engine," Society of Automotive Engineers, *Transactions,* Vol. 14, Part I (1919), 385-432; and for a more broad survey, Philip S. Dickey, *The Liberty Engine, 1918-1942,* The Smithsonian Annuals of Flight, Vol. 1, No. 3 (National Air and Space Museum, 1968).

4. Quoted in Navy Press Release, 19 May 1919; Record Group 45, Box 117, National Archives.

5. Biographical information re Hunsaker is taken from Maurice Holland, *Architects of Aviation* (N.Y.: Duel, Sloan & Pearce, 1951), 7-25.

6. G. C. Westervelt, H. C. Richardson, and A. C. Read, *The Triumph of the NC's* (N.Y.: Doubleday, 1920), 4. Most of the information relating to the design and construction of the NC boats is taken from Westervelt's section of this book, pp. 3-167; or from his "Design and Construction of the NC Flying Boats," U.S. Naval Institute, *Proceedings,* Vol. 45, No. 9 (September 1919), 1529-1581. Jerome C. Hunsaker's "Progress in Naval Aircraft," Society of Automotive Engineers *Journal,* Vol. 5, No. 1 (July 1919), 31-44, and the same title, but more detailed in the S.A.E.'s *Transactions,* Vol. 14, Part II (1919), 236-252 provide further data.

7. Louis S. Casey, "Curtiss Flying Lifeboat," *American Aviation Historical Society Journal,* Vol. 10, No. 2 (Summer 1965), 102-104.

8. Memo, R. E. Basler to LCdr. Garland Fulton, 21 January 1919, f/c-34141(A), RG-72, BuAer Correspondence 1917-25, OpAir files, file 068-A, Box 72, National Archives.

9. A copy of this item of correspondence was found among the NC boats' work books and flight test logs which are in the office of Lee M. Pearson, historian, Naval Air Systems Command; copies of these documents are now in the "NC files" of the National Air and Space Museum, Washington, D.C., and the Naval Aviation Museum, Pensacola, Florida.

10. An excellent contemporary account of the N.A.F.'s wartime activities is F. G. Coburn, "Problems of the Naval Aircraft Factory During the War," Society of Automotive Engineers, *Transactions,* Vol. 14, Part I (1919), 304-332.

11. Information re the Rockaway air station (and other air stations), is taken from Charles R. Mathews, "Patrolling and Patrol Stations on the Western Atlantic," RG-45, Naval Records Collection, ZGU file, Box 788, National Archives.

12. *The* (Washington, D. C.) *Evening Star,* 9 November 1918 (18:3).

13. G. H. Scragg, "How Forty-One of Us Flew over London," *Flying,* Vol. 7 (January 1919), 1131-1132.

14. "Navy's World's Biggest Seaplane Carriers 50 Passengers in Test Flight," *Flying*, Vol. 7 (January 1919), 1130-1131.

John Towers' Epoch-Making Event

1. Cdr. John H. Towers, Memo to CNO, OpAir S-63-1, 31 October 1918, file 068-A RG-72 BuAer Correspondence 1917-25, Box 72, National Archives.

2. Towers was Naval Aviator No. 3; but in 1918 Cdr. Theodore G. Ellyson (Naval Aviator No. 1), was in England, assigned to shipboard anti-submarine duties; and Cdr. John Rodgers (Naval Aviator No. 2), was commanding Submarine Division 10. This should not be regarded as deplorable, much less unusual; prior to the mid-1920s it is noteworthy how many aviation officers were also qualified in submarines. What Towers meant in this memo was that he was the senior aviator currently on aviation duty.

3. *New York Times* 2 July 1918 (5:4); 3 July 1918 (9:1); 5 July 1918 (20:5); and 7 July 1918 (8:1).

4. *Ibid.,* 16 July 1918 (6:6).

5. Memo from Major W.J.H. to Lt. Col. A. A. Maybach, Army War Plans Div., 17 July 1918, copy in OpAir file 068-A, BuAer Correspondence, 1917-25, RG-72, Box 72, National Archives. The memo discusses flaws and hazards in the Handley Page ferry scheme and tends to view it as a publicity effort by the manufacturer. However, it remarks in passing that a Col. Arnold (probably Henry H. "Hap" Arnold) had informed them that the Army Air Service was working on a plan of its own to ferry bombers directly across the Atlantic to the Western Front.

6. Information on these plans for ferrying F-5Ls to Europe via Newfoundland, the Azores and Portugal is very vague; only sketchy references were found to it in the Navy files. However, it appears that the planning was becoming substantial by the summer of 1918, and there seems little doubt that if the war had continued for another year, the Navy would have been ferrying F-5Ls to Europe before the end of 1919.

7. *New York Times,* 9 February 1919 (1:4); 1 March 1919 (4:2); 9 March 1919 II (3:4); and 16 March 1919 (1:2).

8. W. E. Knowles Middleton, *Invention of the Meteorological Instruments* (Baltimore: Johns Hopkins Press, 1969), *passim*.

9. As far as could be determined, there is no such thing as a written history of the development of aerology as a science, much less one that shows its applications and how the requirements of aeronautics accelerated and broadened its development. The closest approximations are Donald R. Witnah, *A History of the United States Weather Bureau*

(Urbana: University of Illinois Press, 1965), which is essentially an administrative and political history; and Patrick Hughes, *A Century of Weather Service, 1870-1970* (N.Y.: Gordon & Breach, Science Publishers, 1970), which is a rather superficial survey, however well written.

10. Willis Ray Gregg, "The First Transatlantic Flight," *Monthly Weather Review*, Vol. 47, No. 5 (May 1919), 279–283; and his "Transatlantic Flight and Meteorology," *Aviation*, Vol. 6, (1 May 1919), 370–372, and (15 May 1919), 422–425.

11. *Ibid.*

12. Harry E. Wimperis, *A Primer of Air Navigation* (London: Constable, 1920).

13. Only vague, general references to the Byrd bubble sextant were found; strangely, Byrd published nothing of his own about it. However, correspondence makes it rather clear that it was the U. S. Naval Observatory's staff who actually made the instruments used on the flight. A slim historical survey of aerial navigation and its instruments is Arthur J. Hughes, *History of Air Navigation* (London: George Allen & Unwin, 1946). It is deplorable that after more than a half-century of transoceanic flight that this appears to be the only history of the subject.

14. George H. Littlehales, "The chart as a means of finding geographical position by observations of celestial bodies in aerial and marine navigation," U.S. Naval Institute, *Proceedings* Vol. 44, No. 181 (March 1918), 567–584.

15. From conversations with Captain Robert A. Lavender during the spring of 1969.

16. Linwood S. Howeth, *History of Communications-Electronics in the United States Navy* (Washington: Government Printing Office, 1963), 278.

17. *Ibid.*

18. Robert A. Lavender, "Radio Equipment on *NC* Seaplanes," U. S. Naval Institute, *Proceedings*, Vol. 46, No. 10 (October 1920), 1601–1607. Also informative is Edgar H. Felix, "Aircraft Radio Direction Finding Equipment Developed by the Navy Department," *Aerial Age Weekly*, Vol. 9 (14 July 1919), 852–853; and "Aircraft Transmitting Equipment, Type SE-1310," *Aviation*, Vol. 6 (1 June 1919), 476–477.

Final Preparations

1. On 13 May 1942 the Bureau of Navigation was reorganized as the Bureau of Naval Personnel, which it remains today.

2. P.N.L. Bellinger to CNO (Aviation), f/068-A-354, 1 April 1919, RG-72, BuAer Correspondence 1917–25, Box 73, National Archives.

3. Transcription of telephone conversation between J. H. Towers and A. C. Read, 15 April 1919, file 068-A (OpAir), RG-72, BuAer Correspondence 1919–25, National Archives. Towers had a practice of putting a stenographer on an extension to transcribe important phone conversations in that day before the dictaphone became available, not to mention the tape recorder, with very happy results for the historian. This practice is far superior than a tape recorder. Because most tapes are never transcribed onto paper, they cannot be skimmed but must be listened to in "real time", and the conversations are subsequently lost when the tapes are re-used.

4. Descriptions of the various and several changes to the NC design are provided by Westervelt and Hunsaker; see Footnote 6, Chapter 2, above.

5. H. C. Richardson, *Triumph of the NC's*, 246.

6. Transcript of Richardson-Towers telephone conversation, 18 April 1919, file 068-A, RG-72, BuAer Correspondence 1917–25, Box 73, National Archives.

7. Week-to-week accounts of the *Daily Mail* competition and its contestants are to be found in the British aviation weeklies, *The Aeroplane* and *Flight*, with the former usually providing the best coverage.

Getting There

1. Board of Investigation, NC Hangar Fire, 5 May 1919, file 068-A-513 (OpAir), RG-72, BuAer Correspondence 1917–25, Box 73, National Archives.

2. Dispatch, AsstSecNav to J. H. Towers, 6 May 1919, file 068-A, (OpAir), RG-72, BuAer Correspondence 1917–25, Box 72, National Archives.

3. *New York Times*, 9 May 1919 (2:1).

4. *Ibid.* (2:2).

5. *Ibid.*

6. *Ibid.* (1:6).

7. The NCs' fuel system is described in James L. Breese, "Precautions That Spelled Success," *The Scientific American*, Vol. 121 (19 July 1919), 55, 74.

8. Ed Snow, "Former Chatham Residents Assisted in First Transatlantic Flight 50 Years Ago," *Lower Cape Cod Chronicle*, 8 May 1969, p. 2.

9. J. D. F. Kealy and E. C. Russell, *A History of Canadian Naval Aviation, 1918–1962* (Ottawa: The Naval Historical Section, Canadian Forces Headquarters, 1965), 7–9.

10. Graham Wallace, *The Flight of Alcock & Brown* (London: Putnam, 1955), 172.
11. "Propellers for NC Planes Were Two-Day Rush Job," *Aerial Age Weekly,* Vol. 9 (16 June 1919), 692.
12. *New York Times,* 14 May 1919 (1:1).
13. Quoted in Graham Wallace, *The Flight of Alcock & Brown, Op.Cit.,* 148.

The Lame Duck and the Rubber Cloud

1. St. Johns, Newfoundland, *Evening Telegram,* 13 May 1919 (4:1); 15 May 1919 (6:3).
2. A good general description of the C-ship can be found in J. C. Hunsaker, "Naval Airships," Society of Automotive Engineers, *Transactions,* Vol. 14, Part I (1919), 578–589; but more detailed is "U.S. Navy Class 'C' Dirigible," *Aerial Age Weekly,* Vol. 9 (25 August 1919), 1095–1098, including a 3-view drawing.
3. *New York Times,* 12 January 1919 (3:5); 13 January 1919 (4:5); and 16 January 1919 (16:7).
4. *Ibid.,* 19 February 1919 (11:4).
5. Materials found relating to the proposed *C-3* and *C-5* flights in the Navy files consulted were sketchy in that no detailed plans for the Newfoundland-to-Europe flight were found: bits and pieces were scattered throughout the OpAir 068-A files, RG-72, BuAer Correspondence 1917–25, Boxes 72, 73, and 74; and in RG-45, Naval Records Collection, 1911–27, Boxes 117, 118 and 119, National Archives.
6. *New York Tribune* 15 May 1919 (2:2).
7. Transcript of telephone conversation between K. Whiting and A. C. Read, 9 May 1919, file 068-A (OpAir), RG-72 BuAer Correspondence 1917–25, Box 73, National Archives.
8. Conversation with RAdm. Karl Lange, U. S. Navy (Ret.), at Akron, Ohio, 10 October 1970. There were two airships at Chatham, the B-19 (A-5467) and the B-18 (A-5465), which was delivered as recently as 12 April. The F-5L that delivered the starter was No. A-3336; unfortunately, its pilot's name goes unrecorded. It took off from Montauk at 2315 on the 13th and alighted at Chatham 0050 on the 14th.
9. Misc. communications from airship *C-5,* RG-45, Naval Records Collection, 1911–27, Box 118, National Archives.
10. St. John's, Newfoundland, *Evening Telegram,* 16 May 1919 (8:1); "Record of a Court of Inquiry Convened On Board the USS CHICAGO ... to Inquire Into the Loss of U.S. Navy Dirigible C-5"; SecNav file

26283-2529 (Aero file 068-273), 16–19 May 1919, from the files of the historian, Naval Air Systems Command.

"Let's Go!"

1. Kerr's own account of his abortive effort at a transatlantic flight is given in his book *Land Sea and Air; Reminiscenses of Mark Kerr* (N.Y.: Longmans, Green & Co., 1927), 298–338.

2. These are the times given in the NCs' official reports; however, aboard the *Aroostook* their lift-offs were observed at 2206, 2207 and 2209, respectively, and these figures seem more reliable. Richardson himself chose to use them in his section of *Triumph of the NC's.*

Read, Rodd, Radio—and Horta

There are no footnotes for Chapter 8; data herein is taken wholly from the official reports and logs of the flight and the aircrews' published accounts thereafter.

The Saga of the *NC-3*

1. The *Fairfax's* chase after the derelict *NC-1* makes for interesting reading; one can get the impression that Cdr. W. W. Smith, commanding officer of the ship, his officers and crew, made something of a game out of it, and in spite of the heavy seas running had some fun out of the chase; his report of 23 May 1919 is in RG-45, Naval Records Collection, 1911–27, Box 118, National Archives.

2. The basic source for information of the *NC-1's* difficulties was Bellinger's own official report, subsequently published along with the other NC reports as Appendix G to U.S., Department of the Navy, *Annual Reports of the Navy Department, 1919,* 216–232; and this was supplemented by newspaper accounts.

3. The basic sources for the saga of the *NC-3* were Towers' own official report in the SecNav *Annual Report* (see note 2 above), his magazine article, "The Great Hop," *Everybody's Magazine,* Vol. 41 (November 1919), 9–15, 74–76; Richardson's section in *Triumph of the NC's;* conversations with Capt. Robert A. Lavender during the spring of 1969; and various contemporary newspaper accounts.

4. *New York Times,* 20 May 1919 (1:1).

Beat the Yanks!

1. *The Washington* (D.C.) *Times* 18 May 1919 (2:3). Wilson's chilly intellectual response to the NC flight forms an interesting contrast to the gracious enthusiasm of subsequent Presidents to later history-making transoceanic flights, 1924-38, not to mention the receptions accorded American astronauts since 1961.

2. *The Chicago Tribune* 18 May 1919 (2:5).

3. *The New New York Herald* 18 May 1919 (3:2).

4. "The Trans-Atlantic Flight," *The Yale Graphic,* Vol. 1, No. 5 (7 May 1919), 185-186. There is no by-line on the article, but according to Mathew Josephson in his *The Empire of the Air; Juan Trippe and the Struggle for World Airways* (N.Y.: Harcourt Brace, 1943), 24, Trippe is its author. Trippe joined the Navy 5 April 1918, was sent to the aviation school at M.I.T., then to NAS Bay Shore, Long Island (where Albert C. Read was commanding officer at that time), and finally to Pensacola, where he won his wings as Naval Aviator No. 1806 and was commissioned an ensign, 7 December 1918.

5. *The Chicago Tribune* 18 May 1919 (2:3)

6. *The Brooklyn Eagle* 17 May 1919 (6:1).

7. *The New York Tribune* 23 May 1919 (12:4).

8. *The New York Times* 3 May 1919 (6:3).

9. *Ibid.* 8 May 1919 (16:4).

10. The best account of the preparations of the *Daily Mail* contestants' in Newfoundland is Graham Wallace's *The Flight of Alcock & Brown, Op. cit.,* which is an excellent job.

11. A. C. Read, *The Triumph of the NC's,* 214.

12. Relative to the attempt of Hawker and Grieve, the editorial "On the Trans-Atlantic Attempt and Some Criticism," *The Aeroplane,* Vol. 16 (28 May 1919), 2102-2103, is very interesting, especially as the source is British.

13. This situation—if not to say tangled dilemma—is best described in the report of Admiral C. P. Plunkett, ComDesFor, to CinC, file 216-4115, 24 June 1919, in RG-45, Naval Records Collection, 1911-27, Box 118, National Archives. The Plunkett report is a six-page letter covering eleven enclosures all relative to the flight; among many other things, Admiral Plunkett notes:

"The Force Commander expected Towers to proceed from Azores in NC-4, since in accord with the Operating Order for the planes, *approved in the Department [sic]* he had authority to shift from one plane to another if his was disabled. It was therefore surprising when a message was received from the Department forbidding him to take passage in NC-4, and especially it was surprising as it was not under-stood how a contingency already provided for should have been again referred to the Department. It developed later that unknown to Towers, to me, or to anyone in my force, that ComUSNavForces, Azores, had on his own initiative, asked the Department's permission for Towers to go on in the NC-4. It appears too that this action on his part later led to controversy at home of which Towers was made the victim, and of which he knew nothing until the flight was entirely over. In this case, through the action of an officer, not connected with the flight and ignorant of the Operating Orders for it, undertaking to handle matter not under his jurisdiction or cognizance, Towers has become victim of popular prejudice and placed in the light of trying to take from one of his subordinates the glory of accomplishing the flight.

"As matter of fact, Towers attitude was one of simple devotion to duty and carrying out of his orders and there would have been no question as to its correctness had the approved Operations Orders been carried out without being interfered with by an officer not familiar with them. Furthermore, the wonderful exhibition of grit, skill, seamanship, navigation, and devotion to his mission shown by Towers in successfully taking the NC-3 to Ponta Delgada stands out as the greatest accomplishment of the flight and clearly demonstrates the officer's exceptional ability under the most trying circumstances." Josephus Daniels never saw fit to make this letter available to the press, nor to Congress, nor to include Admiral Plunkett's report with the others relating to the NC flight that were put together for the SecNav's annual report to the President; indeed, it was filed away for a half century.

14. Remarked during converstions with Capt. R. A. Lavender in the spring of 1969; with Mrs. John H. Towers, conversations in 1967 and 1969; and with Eugene S. Rhoads, 1 May 1969.

15. *The New York Times* 22 May 1913 (1:3).

16. U.S. Congress, House, Committee on Naval Affairs, *Hearings on Estimates Submitted by the Secretary of the Navy, 1919* [No. 1], "Statement of the Hon. Josephus Daniels," 66th Cong., 1st Sess., 1919, 21–36.

17. Josephus Daniels, *The Wilson Era; Years of War and After, 1917–1923* (Chapel Hill: University of North Carolina Press, 1946), 567–570.

18. Dispatch (Double Priority) 19329, OpNav to USS *Melville* (For Commander Towers), 20 May 1919, OpAir 068-A-545, RG-72, BuAer Correspondence 1917–25, Box 73, National Archives.

19. Dispatch 822 (priority), Knapp, London, to OpNav, 20 May 1919, OpAir 068-A-545, *Ibid.*

20. Dispatch 3668, OpNav to SimsAdmUS., London, 20 May 1919, OpAir 068-A-545, *Ibid.*

21. *The New York Times* 30 May 1919 (1:2). Orteig was proprieter of the LaFayette and Brevoort hotels in New York City; eight years later during 20-21 May 1927 it was Charles A. Lindbergh who won the Orteig Prize with his flight from New York to Paris in 33 hours and 30 minutes. Lindbergh subsequently wrote of the NC flight, "When I stop to think about it logically, I know that I've got a better chance of reaching Europe in the *Spirit of St. Louis* than the NC boats had of reaching the Azores. I have a more reliable type of engine, improved instruments, and a continent instead of an island for my target"; in his *The Spirit of St. Louis* (N.Y.: Charles Scribner's Sons, 1953), 295. In passing, it deserves note that Lindbergh's flight was the eighth made across the Atlantic; before him there was not only the *NC-4*'s, Alcock and Browns' and the *R.34*'s round-trip of 1919, but in 1924 the two Douglas DWC World Cruisers remaining in the U. S. Army Air Service's around-the-world flight, the *New Orleans* and *Chicago*, hippety-hopped across the North Atlantic from Scotland via the Orkney Islands, Iceland, Greenland and Labrador; and during 12-15 October 1924 the German Zeppelin *LZ-126*, under the command of Dr. Hugo Eckener, flew from Friedrichshafen, Germany, to Lakehurst, N.J., where the airship was turned over to the U.S. Navy and subsequently commissioned as the USS *Los Angeles*. Of further note is that with the flight of the *LZ-126* a total of seventy-eight persons had flown the North Atlantic; Charles Lindbergh became the seventy ninth.

22. Hawker and Grieve subsequently wrote a book about their experiences, *Our Atlantic Attempt* (London: Methuen & Co., 1919). Only two years later, 12 July 1921, Hawker was killed in an air crash. His widow wrote a biography which further illuminates his career, Muriel Hawker, *H. G. Hawker: His Life and Work* (London: Hutchinson & Co., 1922).

The *NC*... First!

1. Herbert Rodd, "Radio Report, Trans-Atlantic Flight," 30 June 1919, RG-45, Naval Records Collection, 1911-27, Box 118, National Archives. See Appendix D, pp. 221-236.

2. U.S. Congress, House, Committee on Naval Affairs, *Hrgs on Estimates*, etc. [No. 1] "... Josephus Daniels" *Op. cit.*, 21; and U. S. Congress, *The Congressional Record*, Vol. 58, No. 8 (27 May 1919), 66th Cong., 1st Sess., 286 and 289.

3. *Ibid.*

4. Herbert Rodd, "Radio Report," *Op. cit.*

5. *Ibid.*

6. A. C. Read, *The Triumph of the N.C's*, 220.

7. *The New York Times* 1 June 1919 (1:1).

8. *Ibid.*

9. *Ibid.*

10. Logbook of the USS *Rochester,* 27 May 1919, Record Group 24, National Archives. An outstanding example of what a poor source of information the log of a Navy ship can be! Yet they are preserved while the Quartermaster's Notebooks are subsequently destroyed.

11. *The New York Times* 1 June 1919 (1:1).

12. Dispatch, Read to Wortman, 27 May 1919, file 068-A-600, RG-72, BuAer Correspondence 1917–25, Box 74, National Archives.

13. *The* (Washington, D. C.) *Evening Star* 29 May 1919 (5:3).

14. *The New York Times* 28 May 1919 (2:3).

15. *Ibid.*

16. *The Rocky Mountain News* 29 May 1919 (6:1).

17. *The New York Times* 18 May 1919, II (1:1).

18. *Ibid.* 28 May 1919 (14:2).

19 *The New York Herald* 30 May 1919 (10:3).

20. *The* (Washington, D. C.) *Evening Star* 28 May 1919 (6:1).

21. *The Chicago Tribune* 29 May 1919 (8:1).

22. *The New York Times,* 29 May 1919 (1:2).

23. *The New York Herald Tribune,* 29 May 1919 (1:3); and *The New York Times* 31 May 1919 (2:4).

24. C. G. Grey, "On the Defeat of the Atlantic," *The Aeroplane,* Vol. 16, No. 22 (4 June 1919), 2197–2202. Ironically, many Britons in recent years have come to adjudge Grey (now deceased), as "anti-American"; yet all he was doing from 1919 to 1939 was warning England that if it failed to get a grip on its air policy and rationalize its aircraft industry, the Americans would surely run away with the world airplane market— as they indeed did.

25. *Ibid.* For lack of an airliner with adequate transatlantic range and payload, the British Foreign Office consistently obstructed Pan American Airways' efforts to inaugurate service across the North Atlantic from 1933 until 1939, when PanAm made a successful end-run on the problem by gaining access to Lisbon and Marseilles, and being able to overfly Bermuda en route. Although British Imperial Airways (predecessor organization to BOAC), flew eight scheduled round-trips between England and the United States, using the Short S.30 flying boats *Cabot* and *Caribou* between 5 August and 30 September 1939, the aircraft were stripped down to carry mail only and had to be flight refuelled by Handley Page HP.54 Harrow tankers over Foynes, Ireland, westbound, and similarly refuelled over Hatties Camp (Gander), Newfoundland, eastbound. It was something such as this that C. G. Grey foresaw over

the preceding twenty years, although through a glass, darkly. Curiously, the problem of an adequate transatlantic airliner bedeviled British aviation for more than a quarter of a century (1933–57); it was not until December 1957 that the Bristol 310 Britannia turboprop appeared on the North Atlantic airway, the first British-built airliner with a viable transatlantic capability.

To Plymouth by Seaplane . . .

1. *The New York Times* 29 May 1919 (1:1).
2. *The* (London) *Times,* 2 June 1919 (6:1).
3. *The New York Times,* 1 June 1919 (1:8).
4. "Hendon Welcomes Atlantic Fliers," *Flight,* Vol. 37 (5 June 1919), 728–733.
5. *The Washington* (D. C.) *Times,* 4 June 1919 (1:6).
6. "John Porte, 1884–1919," *The Aeroplane,* Vol. 17 (29 October 1919), 1502–1504, 1506.
7. *The* (London) *Times,* 6 June 1919 (7:1).
8. *Ibid.,* 10 June 1919 (12:4).

. . . And Home by *Zeppelin*

1. Arthur Whitten Brown, *Flying The Atlantic In Sixteen Hours* (N.Y.: Frederick A. Stokes Co., 1920); however, Graham Wallace's *The Flight of Alcock and Brown, Op cit.,* provides the grand overview, although it suffers badly as a reference for want of an index. On 21 June 1919, before the NC fliers arrived in the United States, both British airmen were knighted for their flight. The British wasted no time in recognizing unusual merit. However, Sir John Alcock was killed in an air crash in France, 18 December 1919, six months after his transatlantic victory. He was only 27 years old. Sir Arthur Whitten Brown was so stricken by Alcock's death that he retired from aviation to a quiet career in engineering. Over the years the attendants in the Science Museum came to look for his spare, limping figure on a cane (he was crippled as a result of an air crash in the World War and inadequate medical attention in a German prison camp thereafter) around the middle of June, when he would quietly look at their *Vimy,* perhaps trying to recapture a few moments of those wild sixteen hours he spent in that airplane with Alcock. He lived to see thousands of American bombers with wholly inexperienced flight crews span the Atlantic between the United States and the United Kingdom during 1942–45, and DC-6s, Constellations and Stratocruisers moving across the Atlantic daily with thousands of

passengers in any week thereafter. And he knew that the DeHavilland had its DH.106 Comet, the first jetliner in the world and the first such to fly the Atlantic, ready to fly before he died at Swansea on 4 October 1948. He was 62 years old.

2. *The New York Times,* 17 June 1919 (5:4).

3. U.S. Congress, *The Congressional Record,* Vol. 58, No. 25, 66th Cong., 1st Sess. (16 June 1919), 1248. On pp. 1263 and 2334-35 Hicks proposed H.J. 118 relative to recognizing the flight of the *NC-4;* also on p. 1263 is LaGuardia's measure, H.J. 119 relating to Alcock and Brown.

4. Data on the USS *Zeppelin* is from RG-45, Naval Records Collection Subject file, 1911-17, OS-Series, Box 398. Further data is in N. R. P. Bonsor's encyclopedic *North Atlantic Seaway* (Prescot, England: T. Stephenson & Sons, Ltd., 1955), 177, 179, 191.) The *Zeppelin* was laid down for the Norddeutscher Lloyd, but launched only after the war had begun and never saw passenger service until she flew the Stars and Stripes. She was in commission as a ship of the U.S. Navy from 29 March to 1 October 1919, when she served to return several thousand soldiers to the United States. After decommissioning, she passed into the hands of the U. S. Shipping Board, which turned her back to Germany in 1920. Renamed *Ormuz,* the *Zeppelin* ended her career on the rocks of the Norwegian coast, 20 June 1934, where she ran aground and sank. The USS *Zeppelin* played a further role in American aviation history in that during August 1919 she carried the controversial "Crowell Commission" to Europe; with the exception of Captain Henry Mustin, U.S. Navy (its one dissenting member), this was a group determined to create an empire of "airpower" a-la-Billy Mitchell, and destroy naval aviation in the process.

5. *The New York Herald,* 28 June 1919 (1:4).

6. *Ibid.;* also *The New York Tribune,* 28 June 1919 (1:1); and *The New York Times,* 28 June 1919 (4:2).

7. *The New York Herald,* 29 June 1919 (7:3).

8. *Ibid.*

9. *The New York Times,* 28 June 1919 (4:2).

10. Arthur Whitten Brown, *Flying the Atlantic in Sixteen Hours* (N.Y.: Frederick A. Stokes Co. 1920), 109.

11. The best account of this flight is E. M. Maitland, *The Log of H.M.A. R.34; Journey to America and Back* (London: Hodder & Stoughton, 1920). Of note is that aboard the *R.34* as official American observer for the westward flight was LCdr. Zachary Lansdowne, U. S. Navy (Naval Aviator No. 105), who thereby became the first American to fly the Atlantic nonstop. Six years later, Lansdowne was killed in the wreck of U. S. Navy rigid airship *Shenandoah,* of which he was com-

manding officer, when the airship broke up in a thunderstorm over Ohio, 3 September 1925. The *R.34*'s westward crossing, 2–6 July, against the prevailing wind, took 108 hours, 12 minutes; her eastward return flight, to Pulham, England, 10–13 July, took 75 hours and 3 minutes. On her return flight the American observer on board was Lt. Col. William N. Hensley, U. S. Army Air Service.

12. *The New York Herald,* 29 June 1919 (7:3).

13. *Ibid;* and *The New York Times,* 29 June 1919 II (2:1).

14. *The Washington Times,* 30 June 1919 (7:2).

15. *The* (London) *Times,* 2 June 1919 (6:2).

16. *The* (London) *Observer,* 2 June 1919 (5:2).

17. The only counterpart to the *NC-4*'s flight in 1919—and even more remarkable in some of its aspects—was that of the Australian brothers Keith and Ross Smith from Hounslow, England, to Darwin, Australia, 11,060 miles, 12 November to 10 December 1919 (and on to Melbourne and Adelaide later), using a Vickers Vimy similar to Alcock and Browns'. It, too, demonstrated all the shortcomings of aeronautics as of 1919, which are well described in Ross Smith, *14,000 Miles Through The Air* (N.Y.: The Macmillan Co., 1922).

18. Three examples of such optimism are, "Lunch in America—Breakfast in Europe," *The Scientific American,* Vol. 120 (28 June 1919), 680; William Dinwiddie, "Let's Drop in on England," *Century Magazine,* Vol. 97 (April 1919), 836–844; and Kaempffert Waldemar, "Going to Europe in 1925," *The Ladies Home Journal,* Vol. 36 (October 1919), 47, 100, 102, in which he predicts passenger fares at $5 per pound, a 20 lb. baggage limit and an average one-way fare of $825. The airplane would have a speed of 200 mph (which no transatlantic airliner had until the Douglas DC-4 of 1942); automatic tapes would record engine performance, but in fog a wire would be trailed from the airplane for an altimeter!

19. Contrary to widespread misconception, the *Hindenburg* did not simply fly to the United States and "blow up." Between 6 May and 10 October 1936 the *Hindenburg* made ten very successful return flights between Rhein-Main and Lakehurst, N. J., on which she carried a total of 1,021 passengers, and between these North American operations she made six return flights between Germany and Brazil. It was not until 6 May 1937 that the *Hindenburg* was destroyed by fire at N.A.S. Lakehurst.

20. The *Yankee Clipper*'s flight was limited to mail only; passenger service over this route did not begin until 28 June 1939, when the *Dixie Clipper* took off from Port Washington for Lisbon, via the Azores, with

22 passengers on board. Neither Albert C. Read nor any of the other NC fliers were invited to make either of these inaugural flights.

21. A. C. Read, *Triumph of the N.C's*, 231.

22. *Ibid.,* 229–230.

23. *Ibid.,* 231.

24. No pretentious "theory" is claimed for this peculiar pattern of chronology, and I am very much aware that all kinds of other developments occurred in the years between (such as the Wrights violating the "rhythm" by thoughtlessly flying in 1903); but it nevertheless makes for an interesting pattern and leads one to wonder what men will be doing in the year 2019.

25. George DeBothezat, "The Meaning for Humanity of the Aerial Crossing of the Ocean," *Scientific Monthly,* Vol. 9 (November 1919), 433–442.

26. Rudyard Kipling, "With The Night Mail," in the collection *Actions and Reactions* (London: Macmillan, 1951), 113–169. Kipling expanded upon this story in his "As Easy as A.B.C." of 1912, collected in *A Diversity of Creatures* (London: Macmillan, 1966), 1–42; and in 1929 he wrote a poem called "The Hymn of the Triumphant Airman, Flying East-to-West at Over 1,000 M.P.H.", which is probably the first (and perhaps only) poem written on the phenomenon of supersonic flight. In spite of his far-ranging interests the intellectual community still loves to stereotype Kipling in terms of the "white man's burden", etc.

27. In the early 1920s the *NC-4* was turned over to the Smithsonian Institution. In 1923 the airplane was briefly put on exhibit with a collection of other historic aircraft around the Washington Monument and it was exhibited again at the sesquicentennial of the American Revolution observed in Philadelphia in 1926. The *NC-4* was not fully assembled again until 1969. Because the airplane is so large, it could not be easily erected inside any of the Smithsonian buildings, so only the boat hull was placed on exhibit; this was in the tin shed on Independence Avenue (a "temporary" building left over from World War I), which still serves as the United States' National Air and Space Museum. However, looking at the *NC-4's* hull alone was like trying to appreciate the reality of a dinosaur by viewing only one-half of the animal's rib cage.

In 1958, over the protests of the museum's curators, even the *NC-4's* hull was removed to storage when the Smithsonian's exhibits specialists decided to "clean up" the aeronautical exhibits to meet their own peculiar tastes. From that day until very recently, the counsel of the professional curatorial staff has been at a discount; historical significance too often being sacrificed for prettiness, or the noisy and gaudy stuff of Disneyland.

258

In 1962 Paul Garber, the museum's veteran curator and historian, who had been keeping a close watch on the *NC-4* since 1919, set in motion the effort to prepare the *NC-4* for the flight's 50th anniversary in 1969. Although the museum had the *NC-4*'s hull it did not have the wings and tailgroup, or all of the engines, which were still being stored by the Navy. Over the years Garber had kept track of their storage by the Navy in their movement from the old Naval Aircraft Factory in Philadelphia to a depot in Alexandria, Virginia, to yet another warehouse in Norfolk. Since last exhibited in 1926, most of the fabric of the wings and tailgroup had split or rotted away, some dry rot had developed in their wood frameworks, and it was obvious that a complete restoration would be necessary. Well aware that the Air Museum was at the bottom of the list of the Smithsonian's priorities and that nothing on behalf of airplanes could ever be done quickly, Garber started early and very shrewdly enlisted the aid of the Navy Department.

If it can be said that the Navy's enthusiastic cooperation is owed to any one man it is Vice Admiral Thomas F. Connolly, U.S. Navy (Ret.), who at that time was Deputy Chief of Naval Operations (Air). He gave the project his every possible assistance. The expensive and painstaking labors of restoring the *NC-4* are well described in Ted Wilbur's "Paint, Pluck—and the NC-4" in the U.S. Naval Institute *Proceedings,* (May 1969), 146-149.

With the assistance of the Navy and several members of the aircraft industry, S. Paul Johnston, who was then the museum's director, planned a handsome building of geodesic design that would house the *NC-4* alone, to be erected on what was then (and is yet) a parking lot at Seventh Street and Jefferson Drive, east of the Smithsonian building on the Capitol Mall. The building was a prefab structure easily erected and dismantled, and it was anticipated that it and the *NC-4* and her supporting exhibits would be dismantled and returned to storage after the summer of 1970. This would allow visitors at least two summers to see the airplane whose storage they had been paying for through taxes over the past half century. The Capitol Fine Arts Commission, however, ruled that the building would not "harmonize" with the new Hirschorn art gallery to be built across the street. The fact that a geodesis is spherical and that the new gallery would be round, much less that the *NC-4* and its building would be gone before the art gallery's foundation could even be excavated, made no difference whatsoever.

With abstract aesthetics ruling the day, the *NC-4* was finally staked down out of doors on the Capitol Mall during the month of May 1969 only. Even permission for this was obtained with difficulty.

In June the *NC-4* was dismantled and returned to the museum's storage facility in Silver Hill, Maryland. Her components are still there today, all carefully draped with polyethelene coverings, waiting for 4 July 1976 when she will hopefully be placed on permanent exhibit in the new National Air and Space Museum building, which is currently under construction.

28. Frederick E. Bigelow, *The NC-4 March* (N.Y.: Walter Jacobs, Inc., 1919). The copyright on this piece of music was renewed in 1947, to finally expire in 1975. Its Library of Congress catalogue number is M-1978/.A4B.

Sources

The materials used in putting this book together were taken from three principal sources, all in the National Archives, mainly from Record Group 72, Bureau of Aeronautics Correspondence 1919-1925, which tended to have its materials conveniently concentrated in the OpAir 068-A file. There were various related files within Record Group 45, The Naval Records and Library Collection. The logs of the several ships employed in the NC Flight Operation are in Record Group 24, Bureau of Naval Personnel Records.

The research in these areas was done twice, once during 1964-67 on note cards for my own use; and again in 1968 at the instance of Louis S. Casey, curator of aircraft in the National Air and Space Museum, to put all possible documentation relating to the NC flying boat and the NC flight on microfilm for the museum. These films, plus xerox copyflow reproductions that are filed in a more rational order than found in the Archives, are presently in Lew Casey's custody in the Air Museum.

In working on this book I incurred obligations to many persons, but most of all to Lee M. Pearson, historian of the Naval Air Systems Command, who offered many comments and criticisms, and with whom I enjoyed many an argument over various aspects of the NC flight. Harry Schwartz, archivist in the Modern Military Records Branch of the National Archives, cheerfully assisted me with his long acquaintanceship with the Navy's records. And my former colleagues at the National Air and Space Museum were of constant encouragement and assistance. Paul Garber provided many insights and little known items of information; Lew Casey made available his vast files and knowledge of Curtiss aircraft; Rob Meyer was always available when I had a problem with engines or propellers; Bob Wood cheerfully unearthed various obscure items from the library that only he fathoms so well; while Lou Purnell and Dusty Doster were always ready to have their ears bent on any

261

problem I had with the NC flight. Claudia Oakes, the museum library's girl-of-all-work chased down several small but important items that are never discovered to be missing until the eleventh hour.

Most of the NC fliers and those persons associated with the airplane's development and the organization of the flight are now deceased. However, I had the pleasure of some long talks with Captain Robert A. Lavender, U.S. Navy (Ret.) who illuminated many aspects of the flight, especially with regard to radio. At the *NC-4*'s fiftieth anniversary I met Eugene Rhoads, who added some personal details to the story. And it was a unique experience to be able to call upon Dr. F. W. Reichelderfer, as I did many times, whenever I had a problem with the weather.

Mrs. John H. Towers, who is working on a biography of her late husband that will hopefully be completed soon, provided her gracious assistance. Dr. Louis Gebhard of the Naval Research Laboratory, who was well acquainted with Herbert Rodd, provided very useful background information on Rodd and the problems of radio in 1919. And on at least two occasions Vice Admiral T. G. W. Settle, U.S. Navy (Ret.) submitted to being my consultant on the NCs' navigation problems.

I also owe thanks to the Embassy of Portugal in Washington, D.C.; the U.S. Naval Attaché in Lisbon; the U.S. Consul in the Azores; the office of the Royal Canadian Navy in the U.S. Navy Department; and to the mayor's office in Plymouth, England, for their gracious assistance in a project that was quite marginal to their daily concerns.

The staff at the St. John's Public Library, the people at the *Evening Telegram,* and Miss Bobbie Johnson of the Newfoundland Historical Society helped in rooting out primary materials on aviation in Newfoundland during 1919. Also, Henriette L'Massón was of inestimable assistance.

I am also grateful to Dr. E. Raymond Lewis and Norman Polmar, the American editor of *Jane's Fighting Ships;* and for the assistance of David Rosenberg. Commander Ted Wilbur of *Naval Aviation News* supplied illustration material.

The book's conclusions, however, are quite naturally my own.

In the small bibliography which follows, the names of primary sources are of significance, and their publications are listed in the conventional way. However, because science and technology invariably develop along a time-line, it seemed to me to make more sense to list those items relating to meteorology and radio in chronological order of publication. The secondary sources take no particular form, while those relating to the *Daily Mail* competition and the *R.34* follow the conventional form.

262

If this varying approach to the bibliography results in making the further researches of some interested reader a trifle easier it will have served its purpose.

Primary Sources

Coburn, F. G. "Problems of the Naval Aircraft Factory During the War." Society of Automotive Engineers, *Transactions*, Vol. 14, Part I (1919), 304-332. Illus. Coburn had been the manager of NAF.

Byrd, Richard Evelyn. *Skyward*. N.Y.: Putnam, 1928. 359 pp. Chapters 4 and 5 treat with his part in the NC operation.

Breese, James L. "Precautions that Spelled Success; Some Engineering Features of the First Flight Across the Ocean." *The Scientific American*, Vol. 121, No. 3 (19 July 1919), 55, 74. Drgs.

Hunsaker, Jerome C. "Progress in Naval Aircraft." Society of Automotive Engineers, *Transactions*, Vol. 14, Part II (1919), 236-252. Illus.

———. "How American Ingenuity Designed the NC Boats." *Automotive Industries*, Vol. 41 (10 July 1919), 68-72; (17 July 1919), 120-123; and (24 July 1919), 172-176. Illus., tab. data.

Lavender, Robert A. "Radio Equipment on NC Seaplanes." U.S. Naval Institute, *Proceedings*, Vol. 46, No. 10 (October 1920), 1601-1607. Illus.

Richardson, Holden C. "Airplane and Seaplane Engineering." Society of Automotive Engineers, *Transactions*, Vol. 14, Part I (1919), 333-372. Illus. Condensed in *Aviation* Vol. 7, No. 1 (1 August 1919), 36-38. Illus.

———. "Some Lessons of the Transatlantic Flight." *Aviation*, Vol. 9, No. 1 (1 July 1919), 445-446.

Rodd, Herbert C. "Across the Ocean in the NC-4." *The Wireless Age*, Vol. 6, No. 11 (August 1919), 13-17; No. 12 (September 1919), 25-28; and Vol. 7, No. 1 (October 1919), 13-19. Illus.

Roosevelt, Franklin D. "Why Naval Aviation Won." *U.S. Air Services*, Vol. 1, No. 6 (July 1919), 7-9.

Sperry, Elmer A. "Aerial Navigation Over Water." Society of Automotive Engineers, *Transactions*, Vol. 12, Part I (1917), 153-165. Illus., diagrs.

Towers, John H. "Operations of Naval Aircraft." Society of Automotive Engineers, *Transactions*, Vol. 14, Part I (1919), 373-385. Illus.

———. "The Great Hop." *Everybody's Magazine*, Vol. 41 (November 1919), 9-15, 74-76. Illus. Very good; many little details not found elsewhere.

U.S., Department of the Navy. *Annual Reports of the Navy Depart-*

ment, 1919. Appendix G, "Trans-Atlantic Flight," these reports, pages 216–232, include verbatim reproductions of the reports of Towers, Read and Bellinger (although not the subsidiary reports of their flight crews) on the NC Flight Operation.

U.S. Congress, House, Committee on Naval Affairs. *Hearings on Sundry Legislation Affecting the Naval Establishment, 1920–1921*. [No. 4] "Legislation Proposed by the Secretary of the Navy and Discussion of Naval Policy and Building Program." 66th Cong., 3rd Sess., 1920. Pp. 71–142. On pp. 121–122 is discussion of preserving the *NC-4* as an historical relic.

———— . *Hearings on Sundry Legislation Affecting the Naval Establishment, 1921–1923*. [No. 71] "Transfer of Naval Seaplane NC-4 to Smithsonian Institution." 67th Cong., 1st Sess., 1921. 357.

Vincent, J. G. "The Liberty Aircraft Engine." Society of Automotive Engineers, *Transactions,* Vol. 14, Part I (1919), 385–432. Illus.; includes a large fold-out drg. of the engine. All-in-all, a very informative item.

Westervelt, George C. "The Flight of the NC Boats." *World's Work* Vol. 38 (August 1919), 424–438. Illus.

———— . "Design and Construction of the NC Flying Boats." U.S. Naval Institute, *Proceedings,* Vol. 45, No. (September 1919), 1529–1581. Illus., drgs. An outstanding source of technical information.

———— . Richardson, Holden C., and Read, Albert C. *The Triumph of the NC's.* N.Y.: Doubleday, Page & Co., 1920. 308 pp. Illus. Written in three parts; Westervelt treats with design and construction, pp. 3–170; Read, the flight of the *NC-4,* 171–234; and Richardson provides some historical background and an account of the *NC-3's* experiences, 235–308.

The Flight of the *C-5*.

"Naval Airship C-5 Makes 1100-Mile Flight." *Aviation,* Vol. 6, No. 9 (1 June 1919), 475–476. Illus.

"Official Story of C-5 Dirigible's Record Flight to Newfoundland." *Aerial Age Weekly,* Vol. 9, No. 14 (16 June 1919), 683, 702.

"U. S. Navy Class 'C' Dirigible." *Aerial Age Weekly,* Vol. 9, No. 24 (25 August 1919), 1095–1908. Illus., 3-view drg.

Allen, Hugh. "C-5 and the Transatlantic Race." Wingfoot Lighter-Than-Air Society, *Bulletin,* Vol. 11, No. 11 (October 1964), 6–7.

264

Meteorology and the North Atlantic

Marvin, Charles F., and Blair, William R. "Meteorology and Aeronautics." National Advisory Committee for Aeronautics, *Third Annual Report* (1917). Report No. 13, 35-82. Diagrs., charts and tab. data.

Bowie, Edward F. "Special Forecasts and Warnings." *Monthly Weather Review,* Vol. 47, No. 5 (May 1919), 347. Relates to the NC Operation.

"Effect of Winds and Other Weather Conditions on the Flight of Airplanes." *Monthly Weather Review,* Vol. 47, No. 8 (August 1919), 523-532.

Gregg, Willis R. "The First Trans-Atlantic Flight." *Monthly Weather Review,* Vol. 47, No. 5 (May 1919), 279-283. Illus. Also in *The Scientific American Supplement,* Vol. 87 (3 May 1919), 274-275; and (10 May 1919), 300-302.

————. "Transatlantic Flight and Meteorology." *Aviation,* Vol. 6, No. 7 (1 May 1919), 370-372; and No. 8 (15 May 1919), 422-425. Includes a bibliography of 28 items.

Bjierknes, Jakob, and Solberg, H. *Life Cycle of Cyclones and the Polar Front Theory of Atmospheric Circulation.* Kristiana, Norway: Geofysike Publicationer, 1922. 18 pp. Abstracted in the American *Monthly Weather Review,* Vol. 50 (September 1922), 468-474.

Gregg, Willis R. *Aeronautical Meteorology.* N. Y.: The Ronald Press, 1925. 144 pp. Illus. His Chapter 12, "Flying Over the North Atlantic and in the Polar Regions," pp. 112-119, probably digests just about all there was known on the subject as of 1925.

McAdie, Alexander. *War Weather Vignettes.* N. Y.: Macmillan, 1925. 62 pp. Illus. Five interpretative essays on the influence of weather on World War I.

————. "The Flier's Aspects of Aerography; The Various Instruments and Methods Used by Pilots and Their relative Value in Weather Forecasting." *Aviation,* Vol. 22, No. 20 (16 May 1927), 1043-1044. Illus.

Gregg, Willis R. "Meteorology of the North Atlantic and Trans-Atlantic Flight." *Aviation,* Vol. 23, No. 5 (1 August 1927), 242-245, 262, 264, 266. Illus. To be compared with his similar papers of 1919.

Reichelderfer, Francis W. "Post Graduate Courses in Aerology and Meteorology for Naval Officers." *Bulletin of the American Meteorological Society,* Vol. 9 (August-September 1928), 149-151.

————. *Norwegian Methods of Weather Analysis.* Washington, D. C.: U. S. Navy Department, 1932. 45 pp.

————. "Aerological Data as used for Map Analysis in Germany and

Norway." *Bulletin of the American Meteorological Society,* Vol. 13 (November 1932), 208-209.

Nelson, Frederick J. "The History of Aerology in the Navy." U. S. Naval Institute, *Proceedings,* Vol. 60, No. 4 (April 1934), 522-528.

Krick, Irving B. "A Comparison of American and European Meteorological Services." *Journal of the Aeronautical Sciences,* Vol. 2, No. 1 (January 1935), 16-21.

O'Brien, T. J. "The Navy's Part in Modern Aerological Development." U. S. Naval Institute, *Proceedings,* Vol. 61, No. 3 (March 1935), 385-399. Illus.

Entwhistle, F. "Atlantic Flight and its Bearing on Meteorology." *Journal of the Royal Meteorological Society,* Vol. 64, No. 276 (July 1938), 355-389. Illus.

———. "The Meteorological Problem of the North Atlantic." *Journal of the Royal Aeronautical Society,* Vol. 43, No. 1 (January 1939), 69-104. Illus.

Reichelderfer, Francis W. "Meteorological Research in Connection With Growth of Trans-Ocean Flying." American Geophysical Union, *Transactions,* Vol. 20, Part III (1939), 341-352.

Whitnah, Donald R. *A History of the United States Weather Bureau.* Urbana: University of Illinois Press, 1961. 267 pp. Illus.

Middleton, W. E. Knowles. *Invention of the Meteorological Instruments.* Baltimore: The Johns Hopkins Press, 1969. 362 pp. Illus. Up to and including the radiosonde of the 1930s.

Radio Communications

Marconi, Guglielmo. Speech, 13 January 1902. American Institute of Electrical Engineers, *Transactions,* Vol. 14 (1902), 98-102.

Bullard, William H. G. "The Naval Radio Service; Its Development, Public Services and Commercial Work." Institute of Radio Engineers, *Proceedings,* Vol. 10, No. 4 (1915), 7-27.

———. "Arlington Radio Station and Its Activities in the General Scheme of Naval Communications." Institute of Radio Engineers, *Proceedings,* Vol. 4, No. 5 (1916), 421-448. Illus.

Marriotte, Robert H. "United States Radio Development." Institute of Radio Engineers, *Proceedings,* Vol. 5, No. 3 (June 1917), 179-198.

U.S. Navy Department, Operations-Aviation. *Radio for Aircraft, Training Manual* (September 1918) Compiled by the Bureau of Steam Engineering. Washington, D.C.: Government Printing Office, 1918. 46 pp., Illus., drgs., diagrs. This booklet describes all of the Navy's aircraft radio hardware as of World War I and how it worked.

Felix, Edgar H. "Aircraft Radio Direction Finding Equipment Developed by the Navy Department." *Aerial Age Weekly,* Vol. 9, No. 18 (14 July 1919), 852-853. Illus.

"The Radio Compass and the NC Flight." *The Wireless Age,* Vol. 6, No. 11 (August 1919), 19. A long interview with Towers in which he attributes loss of *NC-3* and *NC-1* to inadequate use of radio.

"NSS—The Annapolis Radio Station." *The Wireless Age,* Vol. 5, No. 3 (December 1919), 10-14. Illus. An important anchor in the weather network re the NC Operation.

Lavender, Robert A., See Primary Sources.

Rodd, Herbert C., See Primary Sources.

"A History of the Development of Aircraft Wireless." *The Aeroplane,* Vol. 19 (1 September 1920), 443-444, 446; (8 September 1920), 480-482, 484; (15 September 1920), 515-516, 518; and (22 September 1920), 549-550, 552. Illus. An excellent survey as far as it goes.

Johnson, Theodore. "Naval Aircraft Radio." Institute of Radio Engineers, *Proceedings,* Vol. 8, No. 1 (February 1920), 3-58; and No. 2 (April 1920), 87-141. Illus., diagrs., graph data. Excellent.

———. "Naval Radio Tube Transmitters." Institute of Radio Engineers, *Proceedings,* Vol. 9, No. 5 (October 1921), 381-433. Illus.

Marconi, Guglielmo. "Radio Telegraphy." Institute of Radio Engineers, *Proceedings,* Vol. 10, No. 4 (August 1922), 215-238.

Jolliffe, C. M., and Zandonni, Elizabeth M. "Bibliography of Aircraft Radio." Institute of Radio Engineers, *Proceedings,* Vol. 16, No. 7 (July 1928), 985-999. Subdivided into topical categories, the lists include 257 items.

Howeth, Linwood S. *History of Communications-Electronics in the United States Navy.* Washington, D. C.: Government Printing Office, 1963. 657 pp. Illus., diagrs., appendicies. Chapter 23, pp. 267-282, surveys early aircraft radio, with 278-281 devoted to the transatlantic flight of the NCs.

Secondary Sources

Arthur, Reginald Wright (Editor). *Contact! Careers of U.S. Naval Aviators Assigned Numbers 1 to 2000.* Washington, D.C.: The Naval Aviator Register, 1967. 612 pp., very well illustrated. This is a book about the size of a metropolitan telephone directory that provides excellent career summaries of the first 2000 naval aviators. It is a labor of love and was Volume One of a series. Unfortunately, the author (Naval Aviator No. 1501), died shortly after its publication, and it would seem that there will be no Volume Two, which is a pity.

It is strange that no similar book has been compiled re aviators of the Army Air Corps.

Pearson, Lee M., and Van Fleet, Clarke (Editors). *United States Naval Aviation, 1910-1970* (2nd Ed.) Washington, D.C.: Government Printing Office, 1970. 440 pp. Very well illustrated. This is a highly detailed chronology and an extraordinarily useful book. It is no less than amazing that the Air Force has produced nothing comparable, and it is a disservice that after all these years they have not.

Steirman, Hy, and Kittler, Glenn D. *Triumph; The Incredible Saga of the First Transatlantic Flight.* N. Y.: Harper, 1961. 199 pp. Illus., maps. A journalistic account of the flight; however, they had the advantage of interviewing several NC fliers, including Read, while they were still alive.

"Naval Transatlantic Flight Expedition." *Aviation,* Vol. 6, No. 8 (15 May 1919), 420-422. Illus.

"Development of the NC Seaplanes; The History of the Inception and Development ... With Additional Information on Some of Their Hitherto Unknown Constructional Features and Equipment ..." *Aviation,* Vol. 6, No. 9 (1 June 1919), 468-474. Illus., drgs. Very informative.

Wardrop, G. Douglas. "The Transatlantic Flight," *Aerial Age Weekly,* Vol. 9, No. 10 (19 May 1919), 486-488; No. 11 (26 May 1919), 534-535; No. 12 (2 June 1919), 578-581; No. 13 (9 June 1919), 630-635, 650; and No. 17 (7 July 1919), 807, 825, Illus., maps, 3-view drgs.

Kaempffert, Waldemar. "The Transatlantic Flight—A Magnificent Scientific Experiment." *U. S. Air Services,* Vol. 1, No. 6 (July 1919), 10-14.

Casey, Louis S. "Curtiss Flying Lifeboat." American Aviation Historical Society, *Journal,* Vol. 10, No. 2 (Summer 1965), 102-104. Illus., foldout 3-view drg. The aircraft which probably inspired the NCs' peculiar hull configuration.

"The Bijur Airplane Electric Starter." *Aviation,* Vol. 6, NO. 1 (1 February 1919), 33-34. Illus.

"Propellers for NC Planes were Two-Day Rush Job." *Aerial Age Weekly,* Vol. 9, No. 14 (16 June 1919), 692.

Glenn H. Curtiss on the Trans-Atlantic Flight." *Aerial Age Weekly* Vol. 9, No. 10 (19 May 1919), 485, 510.

"Glen Hammond Curtuss: A Biography." *Aviation,* Vol. 6, No. 12 (27 June 1921), 803-806. Illus.

"On a Pioneer of Aviation." *The Aeroplane,* Vol. 34 (30 July 1930), 273-274, 276, 278, 279-280. An obituary; Curtiss died 23 July 1930, age

52. Ironically, The British showed a greater appreciation of his career than any American aviation journal.

Roseberry, C. R. *Glenn Curtiss: Pioneer of Flight.* N.Y.: Doubleday, 1972. 514 pp. Illus. Of the three other available biographies of Curtiss, this latest one is unquestionably the best, although its account of the NC boats is somewhat muddled.

The Daily Mail Competitors and the *R.34*

Brown, Arthur Whitten. *Flying the Atlantic In Sixteen* Hours. N. Y.: Frederick A. Stokes, 1920. 178 pp. Illus.

Brackley, Frida H. *Brackles: Memoirs of a Pioneer of Civil Aviation.* Chatham, England: W & J Mackay & Co., 1952. 695 pp. Illus. H. G. Brackley was the pilot of Mark Kerr's Handley Page.

Hawker, Harry G., and Grieve, Kenneth MacKenzie. *Our Atlantic Attempt.* London: Methuen & Co., 1919. 128 pp. Illus.

"The Late Harry Hawker." *The Aeroplane,* Vol. 21 (20 July 1921), 64.

Hawker, Muriel. *H. G. Hawker, Airman: His Life and Work.* London: Hutchinson & Co., 1922. 319 pp. Illus.

Kerr, Mark. *Land, Sea and Air: Reminiscences of Mark Kerr.* N. Y.: Longmans, Green & Co., 1927. 406 pp. Illus. Pages 298–338 treat with his abortive transatlantic attempt.

"John Porte, 1884–1919." *The Aeroplane,* Vol. 17 (29 October 1919), 1502–1504, 1506.

Lansdowne, Zachary. "The Hold of an Aerial Liner." *U.S. Air Services,* Vol. 2, No. 1 (August 1919), 7–9. His observations while American observer on the westward flight of the *R.34.*

Maitland, E. M. *The Log of H.M.A. R.34; Journey to America and Back.* London: Hodder & Stoughton, 1920. 168 pp. Illus., track chart, and six informative appendicies.

Wallace, Graham. *The Flight of Alcock & Brown, 14–15 June 1919.* London: Putnam, 1955. 312 pp. Illus. An excellent overall survey of the *Daily Mail* competition.

"The Trans-Atlantic Competition." *The Aeroplane,* Vol. 16 (26 March 1919), 1300–1302; (2 April 1919), 1334; (9 April 1919), 14388A–1438B; (16 April 1919), 1602; (23 April 1919), 1694; (30 April 1919), 1789; (7 May 1919), 1884; (21 May 1919), 2016. Well illustrated, including 3-view drgs. of the aircraft.

Transatlantic Vickers Vimy at South Kensington." *Flight,* Vol. 11 (18 December 1919), 1628. Illus.

"The Death of Captain Sir John Alcock, KBE, DSC." *The Aeroplane,* Vol. 17 (31 December 1919), 2144.

"Sir Arthur Whitten Brown," *The Aeroplane,* Vol. 75 (8 October 1948), 464; and (15 October 1948), 495. Death notice and an appreciative obituary.

NC-4 Fiftieth Anniversary

Johnston, James. "The NC4 Preserved." U.S. Naval Institute, *Proceedings,* Vol. 95, No. 795 (May 1969), 94-105. A pictorial.

Robb, Izetta W., and Johnston, James. "A Time for Reminiscing." *Naval Aviation News* (July 1969), 12-17, Illus. Excellent coverage of the Air Museum's formal opening of the *NC-4* exhibit and the old timers present for it.

Wilbur, Ted. "The First Flight Across the Atlantic." *Naval Aviation News* (May 1969), 7-36. Profusely illustrated, the issue is devoted to the NC flight. The NC pages were concurrently published as a separate booklet.

_____ . "Paint and Pluck—And the NC-4." U.S. Naval Institute, *Proceedings,* Vol. 95, No. 795 (May 1969), 146-149.

Index

271

Composed CRT ten point Times Roman with two points of leading by the
George Banta Company, Menasha, Wisconsin.

Printed offset on sixty-pound Hi-bulk Danforth and bound in Columbia Fictionette
FNV 3265 by The Maple Press, York, Pennsylvania.

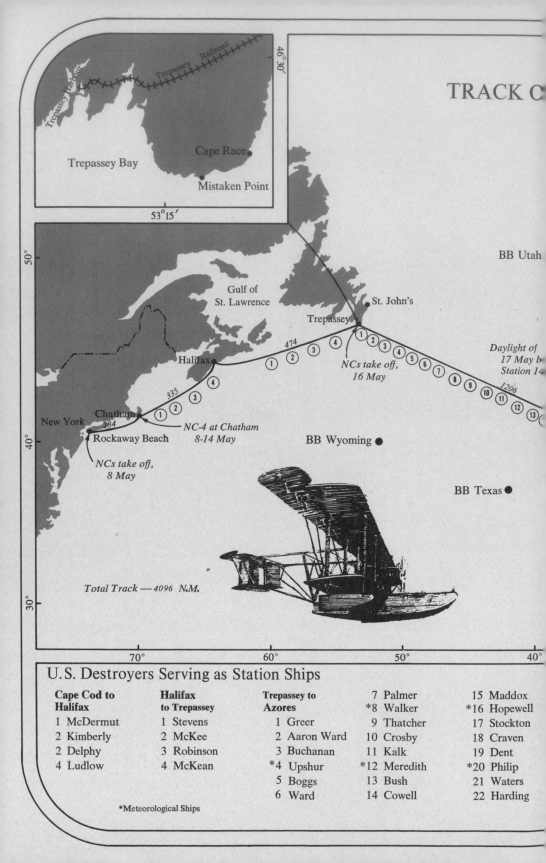

TRACK C

Inset map (top left)
Trepassey Railroad
Trepassey Harbour
Trepassey Bay
Cape Race
Mistaken Point

46° 30′
53° 15′

Main map
50°
Gulf of St. Lawrence
BB Utah
St. John's
Trepassey
Halifax
474
NCs take off, 16 May

Daylight of 17 May b Station 14

335
Chatham
New York
284
Rockaway Beach
NC-4 at Chatham 8-14 May
NCs take off, 8 May

40°
BB Wyoming

1206

BB Texas

30°
Total Track — 4096 N.M.

70°   60°   50°   40°

U.S. Destroyers Serving as Station Ships

Cape Cod to Halifax	Halifax to Trepassey	Trepassey to Azores		
1 McDermut	1 Stevens	1 Greer	7 Palmer	15 Maddox
2 Kimberly	2 McKee	2 Aaron Ward	*8 Walker	*16 Hopewell
2 Delphy	3 Robinson	3 Buchanan	9 Thatcher	17 Stockton
4 Ludlow	4 McKean	*4 Upshur	10 Crosby	18 Craven
		5 Boggs	11 Kalk	19 Dent
		6 Ward	*12 Meredith	*20 Philip
			13 Bush	21 Waters
			14 Cowell	22 Harding

*Meteorological Ships